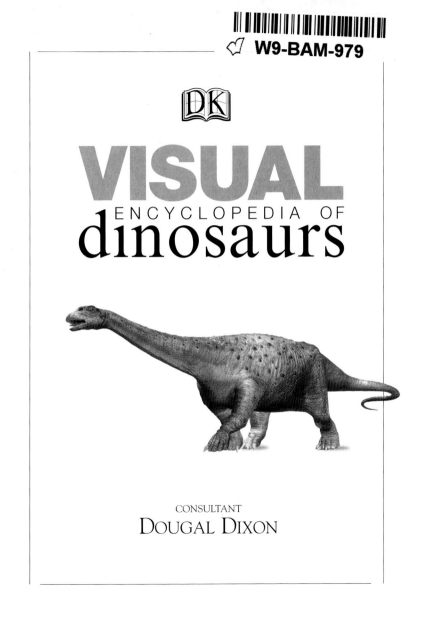

VISUAL
ENCYCLOPEDIA OF
dinosaurs

CONSULTANT
DOUGAL DIXON

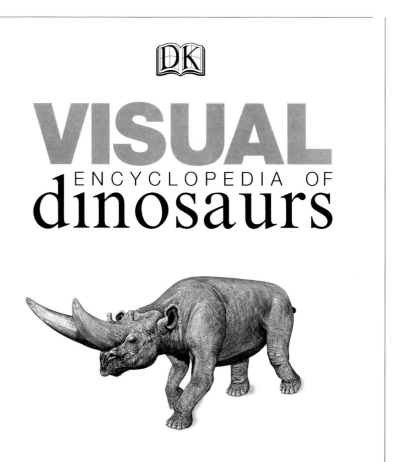

VISUAL

ENCYCLOPEDIA OF

dinosaurs

CONSULTANT

DOUGAL DIXON

CONTENTS

DK

**LONDON, NEW YORK, MELBOURNE,
MUNICH & DELHI**

DK London
Project Editor Rosie O'Neill
Senior Editor David John
Editor Sarah Phillips
Managing Editor Andrew Macintyre
Managing Art Editor Jane Thomas
DTP Designers Natasha Lu, Siu Yin Ho
Production Controller Rochelle Talary
Picture Researcher Rob Nunn
Picture Librarian Sarah Mills

With thanks to the original teams

DK Delhi
Project Editor Sheema Mookherjee
Editor Chumki Sen
Designers Mugdha Sethi, Kavita Dutta
DTP Designer Balwant Singh
Manager Aparna Sharma

Consultant Dougal Dixon

First American Edition, 2005

Published in the United States by
DK Publishing, Inc., 375 Hudson Street,
New York, New York 10014

05 06 07 08 09   10 9 8 7 6 5 4 3 2 1

Material in this edition has appeared previously
in the following books:
Encyclopedia of Dinosaurs and Prehistoric Life
© 2001 Dorling Kindersley Limited
Dinosaurs and Prehistoric Life
© 2003 Dorling Kindersley Limited
Backpack Books – 1,001 Facts about Dinosaurs
© 2002 Dorling Kindersley Limited

A Cataloging-in-Publication record for this book
is available from the Library of Congress.

ISBN 0-7566-0858-9

Reproduced by Colourscan, Singapore
Printed and bound in Singapore by Star Standard

Discover more at
www.dk.com

CONTENTS

HOW TO USE THIS BOOK

THIS BOOK STARTS with the evolution of life, followed by four sections on fishes and invertebrates, amphibians and reptiles, dinosaurs and birds, and mammals. A final section tells you about the study of dinosaurs, and the people who studied them.

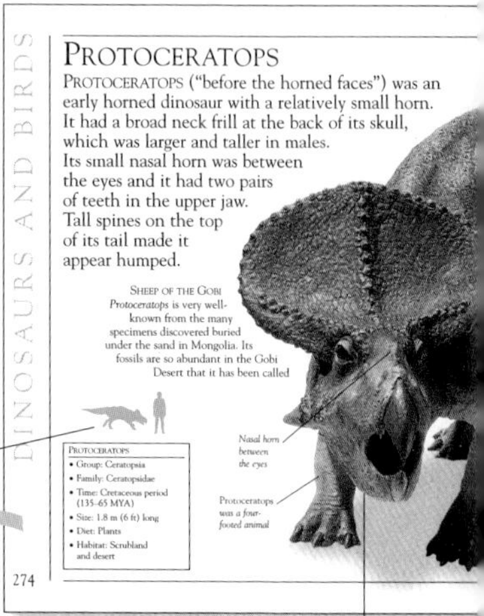

DINOSAURS AND BIRDS

PROTOCERATOPS

PROTOCERATOPS ("before the horned faces") was an early horned dinosaur with a relatively small horn. It had a broad neck frill at the back of its skull, which was larger and taller in males. Its small nasal horn was between the eyes and it had two pairs of teeth in the upper jaw. Tall spines on the top of its tail made it appear humped.

SHEEP OF THE GOBI
Protoceratops is very well-known from the many specimens discovered buried under the sand in Mongolia. Its fossils are so abundant in the Gobi Desert that it has been called

Nasal horn between the eyes

PROTOCERATOPS
• Group: Ceratopsia
• Family: Ceratopsidae
• Time: Cretaceous period (135–65 MYA)
• Size: 1.8 m (6 ft) long
• Diet: Plants
• Habitat: Scrubland and desert

Protoceratops was a four-footed animal

274

Animal size compared with that of an adult man

THEMED PAGES
These pages expand on general themes related to prehistoric animals and dinosaurs, such as feeding habits, shown below. They also describe main groups, such as theropods or ankylosaurids.

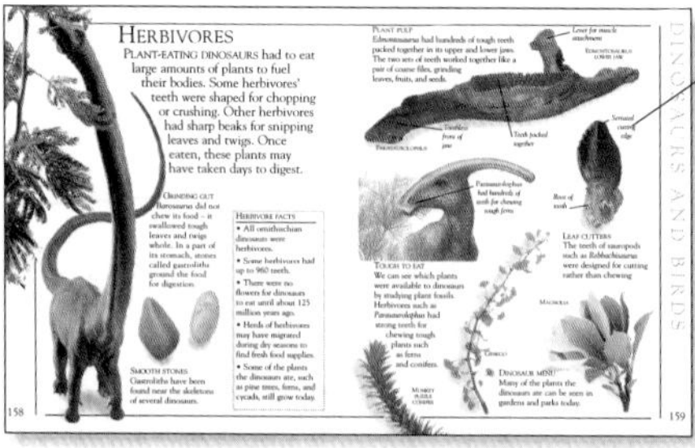

PROTOCERATOPS
• Group: Ceratopsia
• Family: Ceratopsidae
• Time: Cretaceous period (135–65 MYA)
• Size: 6 ft (1.8 m) long
• Diet: Plants
• Habitat: Scrublands and deserts

The main picture recreates the animal's looks based on fossil evidence

FACT BOX
Quick reference facts provide data on the animal's group, family, time period, size, diet, and habitat.

Annotations highlight characteristic features about the animal

HERBIVORES
PLANT-EATING DINOSAURS had to eat large amounts of plants to fuel their bodies. Some herbivores' teeth were shaped for chopping or crushing. Other herbivores had sharp beaks for snipping leaves and twigs. Once eaten, these plants may have taken days to digest.

ABBREVIATIONS USED IN THE BOOK		
MYA million years ago		
U.S. CUSTOMARY	METRIC	
ft	feet	m	meters
in	inches	cm	centimeters

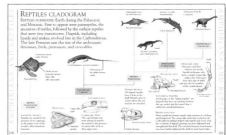

Red dots on the map show the main fossil finds

Hump in tail for display or for fat storage

The Velociraptor's arm is gripped by the Protoceratops' beak

Protoceratops

Velociraptor

Large eyes

FOSSILIZED BATTLE SCENE
This famous fossil was discovered in the Gobi Desert in 1971. It preserves a *Protoceratops* locked in battle with a *Velociraptor*. Both animals died in the fight.

STAGES OF DEVELOPMENT
The frill on the *Protoceratops's* head grew with age. Several fossils at different stages of growth have been found to prove this. The females' frills were probably smaller.

Possibly female

HATCHLING BABY JUVENILE SUB-ADULT SUB-ADULT ADULT ADULT

275

Additional pictures highlight interesting facts about the animal

CLADOGRAM PAGES
Each cladogram shows the chain of evolution for a particular animal group.

ANIMAL PAGES
The main sections consist mostly of animal pages, which focus on individual prehistoric animals. On the page shown at left, you learn about *Protoceratops*—its looks, lifestyle, and interesting habits.

Each strip depicts the animals and plants of a certain timeline

FOSSIL TIMELINE
A fossil timeline feature at the beginning of the book provides a period-by-period look at prehistoric life. It traces the evolution of plants and animals, both on the land and in the water. A map shows what Earth was like during each period.

REFERENCE PAGES
This section tells you about famous dinosaur-hunters and their finds. It also explains how fossils are found and preserved. Finally, it gives you a list of meanings, or glossary, of the difficult words.

9

FINDING OUT ABOUT THE PAST

SINCE IT WAS REALIZED that fossils are the remains of once-living things, people have strived to interpret these clues to the past. Paleontology, the study of ancient life, involves reconstructing the former appearance, lifestyle, behavior, and evolution of vanished organisms. It shows how modern organisms arose, and how they relate to each other.

EARLY FINDS AND THEORIES
Paleontology as we recognize it today arose in the late 18th century. The discovery of fossil mastodons (relatives of elephants) and of *Mosasaurus*, a Cretaceous marine reptile, firmly established that species became extinct.

PALEONTOLOGISTS AT WORK IN MONGOLIA

FOSSILS AND THEIR SURROUNDINGS
Most fossils are found when they appear on the surface at places where there is continual erosion of rock by wind and water. Excavators need to study the sedimentary layer in which a fossil is found to learn about its history.

THE STUDY OF DEATH
Taphonomy is the study of how animals died and what happened to their bodies between death and discovery. It reveals much about ancient environments.

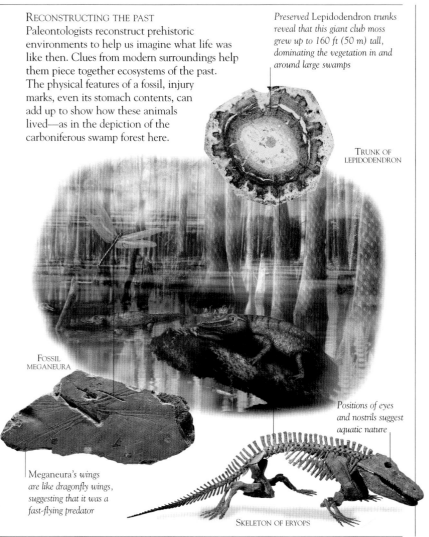

RECONSTRUCTING THE PAST

Paleontologists reconstruct prehistoric environments to help us imagine what life was like then. Clues from modern surroundings help them piece together ecosystems of the past. The physical features of a fossil, injury marks, even its stomach contents, can add up to show how these animals lived—as in the depiction of the carboniferous swamp forest here.

Preserved Lepidodendron trunks reveal that this giant club moss grew up to 160 ft (50 m) tall, dominating the vegetation in and around large swamps

TRUNK OF
LEPIDODENDRON

FOSSIL
MEGANEURA

Meganeura's wings are like dragonfly wings, suggesting that it was a fast-flying predator

Positions of eyes and nostrils suggest aquatic nature

SKELETON OF ERYOPS

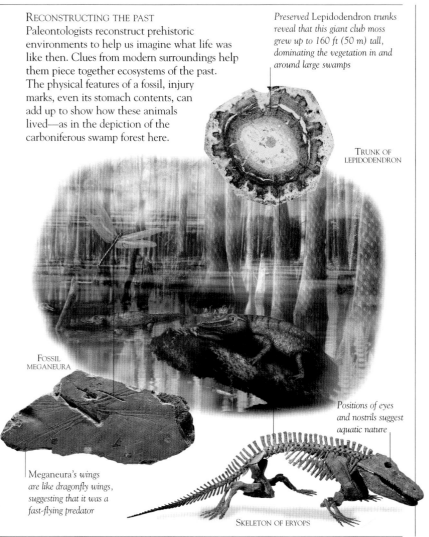

FOSSILS

NATURALLY PRESERVED remains of once-living organisms, or the traces they left, are called fossils. They are first entombed in sediment and later mineralized. There are fossils of microscopic organisms, plants, and animals.

Animal dies and decomposes in a riverbed

A skeleton buried by sediment is protected from scavengers

Rocks are condensed layers of sediments such as sand or mud

This armor plate comes from a sauropod

FOSSILIZED
SALTASAURUS
SKIN

Tracks formed on soft mud

Three-toed tracks were made by predatory dinosaurs

TYPES OF FOSSIL

The remains of plants and animals (shells, teeth, bones, or leaves) are called body fossils. Traces left behind by organisms (footprints, nests, droppings) are called trace fossils.

THEROPOD
TRACKWAY

HOW FOSSILS FORM

Fossilization occurs when an organism, or something produced by it, is buried in sediment and then becomes mineralized. Some fossils, however, are formed when the original object has been destroyed by acidic groundwater, and minerals have later formed a natural replica of the object.

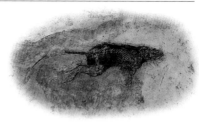

FOSSILIZED
HEDGEHOG PHOLIDOCERCUS

EXCEPTIONAL FOSSILS

Soft parts of organisms are usually lost before fossilization. However, rapid burial in soft sediment sometimes allows soft parts to become fossilized.

More sediments may bury the fossil deeper

Erosion at the surface of Earth reveals fossils

The skeleton may be partially decomposed underground

Minerals may change the fossil's composition

Moving continental plates may carry sediments far from their original location

Many exposed fossils are destroyed by wind and water

RESULTS OF FOSSILIZATION

Some fossils change color due to the replacement minerals. This ammonite fossil is gold because it is composed of iron pyrite, also called fool's gold.

EVOLVING LIFE

THE FOSSIL RECORD preserves the history of life from the earliest single-celled organisms to the complex multicellular creatures—including plants, fungi, and animals—of more recent times. It traces the the history of life from 3.8 billion years ago to a few centuries past.

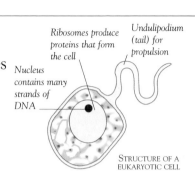

Ribosomes produce proteins that form the cell

Undulipodium (tail) for propulsion

Nucleus contains many strands of DNA

STRUCTURE OF A EUKARYOTIC CELL

ORIGIN OF EUKARYOTES
More complex single-celled organisms, called eukaryotic cells, evolved as a result of cooperative functioning. Fossil records of these appear 2 billion years ago.

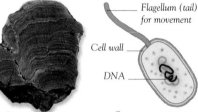

Flagellum (tail) for movement

Cell wall

DNA

FOSSIL STROMATOLITE   SINGLE-CELLED LIFE FORM

FOSSIL MAWSONITES

FIRST LIFE
The earliest forms of life were prokaryotes. These small, single-celled life forms contained DNA, a chemical that codes genetic information. Prokaryotes developed a wide range of metabolisms (chemical reactions to generate energy). Huge fossilized mats of prokaryotic cells, called stromatolites, show how widespread they were early in Earth's history.

VENDIAN LIFE
Multicellular organisms arose in the Late Precambrian, which witnessed a rapid growth of complex life forms. Fossilized remains of the Vendian fauna, discovered in South Australia, are an example of such life forms. Disc- and leaf-shaped fossils such as *Mawsonites* comprise some of these organisms.

THE BURGESS SHALE

The Burgess Shale of British Columbia, Canada, is a famous rock site composed of layers of siltstone deposited on the floor of a shallow Cambrian sea. Discovered in 1909 by Charles Walcott, it contains thousands of well-preserved animal fossils, and gives a unique insight into the "Cambrian explosion" of life.

Sponges grew on the sea floor, but the reefs of the time were mostly formed by algae

Marrella *was a tiny swimming arthropod*

Pikaia, *an early chordate, was a wormlike swimmer with tail fins*

Anomalocaris *was a large predatory arthropod*

Hallucigenia *was probably a bottom-dweller that fed on organic particles*

Priapulids *are burrow-dwelling worms abundant in Burgess Shale times*

METAZOAN DIVERSITY

The Burgess Shale shows how well metazoans (many-celled animals) diversified to fill different kinds of habitats. From the sea, animals spread through fresh water, colonized the land, and invaded the air.

DINOSAUR   BIRD   MAMMAL   ARTHROPOD

15

HOW EVOLUTION HAPPENS

AS ORGANISMS change to adapt to new ways of life, they give rise to new species. The inheritance of certain features by a species' descendants is a main component of evolutionary change. The key to interpreting the fossil record is to learn about evolution.

FISHING ABOARD THE BEAGLE

THE THEORY OF EVOLUTION

The theory that living things change to suit their environments was first presented by Charles Darwin. He argued that the fittest individuals survived and their features were inherited by future generations.

VOYAGE OF THE BEAGLE
Charles Darwin developed his theory of evolution by natural selection following his travels as ship's naturalist on HMS *Beagle* during the 1830s.

Low front of shell originally shared by all Galápagos tortoises

Tortoises on wet islands feed off the ground

Higher front of shell in dry island tortoises

EVOLUTION IN ACTION

On the Galápagos Islands, giant tortoises that feed off plant growth on the ground have shells with a low front opening. However, tortoises on dry islands have a tall front opening to their shells because there is no vegetation on the ground and they have to reach up to chew on higher branches. On the dry islands, individuals with taller front openings in their shells survived better and passed on their genes to future generations.

Tortoises on dry islands have to reach up to find food

EVOLUTION AND DIVERSIFICATION

Evolution is not as simple as was once thought—for example, organisms do not generally evolve in simple ladderlike progression. Instead, as new species evolve from old ones, they tend to branch out and diversify, forming complex patterns. Evolution also does not always lead to increasing complexity. Some living things have become less complex over time.

The gar fish demonstrates punctuated equilibrium—the last time it changed was 60 million years ago

EVOLUTION BY JUMPS

The old view that evolution is a slow and continuous process has been challenged by fossil evidence. Many species have remained the same for a long period and then seen sudden change; this is known as "punctuated equilibrium." If conditions stay the same, so does the species. But if conditions change rapidly, the species may need to change rapidly as well.

Humans and chimpanzees evolved in the Pliocene

Chimpanzees and humans share an enlarged canal in the palate

All great apes (hominids) have an enlarged thumb and other derived characters

HUMAN

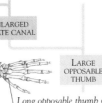

CHIMPANZEE

ORANGUTAN

DERIVED CHARACTERS

Scientists reveal evolutionary relationships by looking for shared features, called "derived characters." The presence of certain unique characters seen in one group of species but not in others shows that all the species within that group share a common ancestor. Such groups are called clades, as in the case of humans, chimpanzees, and orangutans.

ENLARGED PALATE CANAL

LARGE OPPOSABLE THUMB

Canal passing through palate in upper jaw

Long opposable thumb gives an evolutionary advantage

17

CLASSIFICATION OF LIFE

AN ACCURATE UNDERSTANDING of living things and how they have evolved relies on their being classified into groups according to their similarity. Animals are classified in groups of decreasing diversity. The diagram on the right outlines the evolution of the major groups of vertebrates through time, from the very primitive jawless fishes to mammals. This is based on an analysis of features shared by species and their ancestors.

THE LINNAEAN SYSTEM

Devised by Karl von Linné (Carolus Linnaeus), this system subdivides all living things into ever more specific groups down to species level. Many paleontologists prefer to use cladistic analysis to describe the relationships between species, but the Linnaean system of Latin species names remains standard throughout the scientific community. The Linnaean classification of *Tyrannosaurus rex* is shown below.

KINGDOM : Animalia	
PHYLUM : Chordata	
CLASS : Reptilia	
ORDER : Saurischia	
FAMILY : Tyrannosauridae	
GENUS : Tyrannosaurus	
SPECIES : Tyrannosaurus rex	

THE CLADISTIC SYSTEM

Cladistic analysis shows the closeness of a relationship between a species and its most recent ancestor in a branching diagram called a cladogram. This is constructed by assessing characteristics that are shared by species and the order in which these arise.

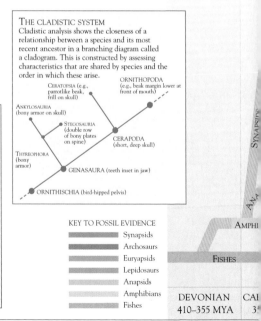

CERATOPSIA (e.g., parrotlike beak, frill on skull)

ORNITHOPODA (e.g., beak margin lower at front of mouth)

ANKYLOSAURIA (bony armor on skull)

STEGOSAURIA (double row of bony plates on spine)

CERAPODA (short, deep skull)

THYREOPHORA (bony armor)

GENASAURA (teeth inset in jaw)

ORNITHISCHIA (bird-hipped pelvis)

KEY TO FOSSIL EVIDENCE

- Synapsids
- Archosaurs
- Euryapsids
- Lepidosaurs
- Anapsids
- Amphibians
- Fishes

SYNAPSIDS

AMPHI

FISHES

DEVONIAN
410–355 MYA

CA
3

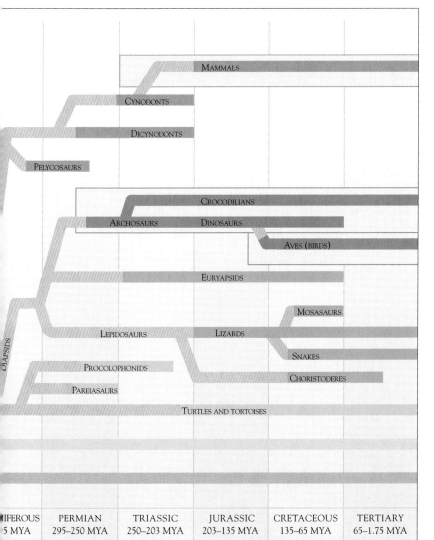

MAMMALS

CYNODONTS

DICYNODONTS

PELYCOSAURS

CROCODILIANS

ARCHOSAURS   DINOSAURS

AVES (BIRDS)

EURYAPSIDS

MOSASAURS

LEPIDOSAURS   LIZARDS

SNAKES

PROCOLOPHONIDS

CHORISTODERES

PAREIASAURS

DIAPSIDS

TURTLES AND TORTOISES

IFEROUS 5 MYA	PERMIAN 295–250 MYA	TRIASSIC 250–203 MYA	JURASSIC 203–135 MYA	CRETACEOUS 135–65 MYA	TERTIARY 65–1.75 MYA

GEOLOGICAL TIME

GEOLOGISTS subdivide the history of Earth into very long time intervals called eons. Eons are, in turn, subdivided into eras, eras into periods, and periods into epochs. The oldest surviving rocks to be excavated were formed about 4 billion years ago, in the Archean eon. The earliest fossils come from rocks of about this age.

ROCK	ENVIRONMENT	PERIOD
Shale, siltstone, mudstone	Tidal flat	Triassic
Limestone	Marine	Permian
Sandstone	Desert	
Shale	Savanna	
Mixed strata—shales, sandstones, limestones	Flood plain	Permian and Late Carboniferous
Limestone	Marine	Early Carboniferous
Limestone	Marine	Devonian
Limestone	Marine	Cambrian
Shale	Marine	
Sandstone	Marine	
Complex mixed strata	Marine and volcanic	Precambrian

ROCKS OF AGES
Where rock strata have remained undisturbed, a vertical section through the layers can reveal the rock types laid down during each time period. From these, it is possible to identify the environment (such as desert) and sometimes the age of fossils embedded in that rock, as shown at left for rock strata in the Grand Canyon.

CENOZOIC ERA	1.75 MYA–present
	23.5–1.75 MYA
MESOZOIC ERA	135–65 MYA
	203–135 MYA
	250–203 MYA
PALEOZOIC ERA	295–250 MYA
	355–295 MYA
	410–355 MYA
	435–410 MYA
	500–435 MYA
	540–500 MYA
	4,600–540 MYA

4,600 MYA	4,000 MYA	3,000 MYA

QUATERNARY	0.01 MYA – present Holocene epoch 1.75-0.01 MYA Pleistocene epoch	MACRAUCHENIA	The ice ages of the Quaternary period led to the evolution of many mammals that adapted to cold climates, such as mammoths and woolly rhinoceroses. Modern humans also evolved in this age.
TERTIARY	5.3-1.75 MYA Pliocene epoch 33.7-5.3 MYA Oligocene, Miocene epochs 65-33.7 MYA Paleocene, Eocene epochs		Large expanses of grassland, inhabited by grazing mammals and predatory giant birds. The first humans evolved from primate ancestors. After the end-Cretaceous extinctions, mammals evolved into large forms. Giant flightless birds also evolved. TITANIS

CRETACEOUS ALPHADON This was a time of flowering plants, duck-billed dinosaurs, immense tyrannosaurid predators, armored ankylosaurs, and horned ceratopsians.

JURASSIC The land was dominated by huge sauropods and large predators. A wide variety of pterosaurs evolved. Mammals remained small. BAROSAURUS

TRIASSIC The age of dinosaurs began. Advanced synapsids died out after giving rise to mammals. HERRERASAURUS

PERMIAN Synapsids became the dominant land animals. The period ended with the largest mass extinction event ever, and thousands of species were lost. DIMETRODON

CARBONIFEROUS GRAEOPHONUS Tropical forests flourished. The first four-limbed animals and, later, the first reptiles moved onto the land.

DEVONIAN A time of rapid evolution; ammonoids and bony fishes diversified. Trees appeared on land, as did insects. EASTMANOSTEUS

SILURIAN SAGENOCRINITES Invertebrates recovered rapidly during the Silurian, and the first jawed fishes appeared. Primitive lycopods and myriapods became the first land organisms.

ORDOVICIAN The seas teemed with primitive fishes, trilobites, corals, and shellfish. Plants spread onto land. The period ended with mass extinctions. ESTONIOCERAS

CAMBRIAN XYSTRIDURA The first animals with skeletons evolved during the Cambrian "explosion of life." These included trilobites and jawless fishes.

PRECAMBRIAN Life arose in the oceans—first as single-celled bacteria and algae, then as soft, multicellular animals, such as jellyfish and worms. CHARNIODISCUS

2,000 MYA	1,000 MYA	500 MYA	250 MYA	0

PRECAMBRIAN TIME

PLANET EARTH IS about 4.6 billion years old. The years from that point to 542 million years ago are known as the Precambrian. At first, the world was hot and molten. As it cooled, gases and water vapor formed the atmosphere and the oceans. Before about 3 billion years ago, most of Earth's surface was volcanic rock. Stable continental areas then began to form. Fossil evidence of life is first seen in rocks dated at 3.8 million years old.

VENDIAN LIFE

Impression of early jellyfish burrow or track of simple worm

Fossils in Precambrian rocks of the Vendian period are thought to be those of the earliest multicellular animals.

4,600 MYA   4,000 MYA   3,000 MYA

PRECAMBRIAN LANDMASSES

Landmasses began to form about 3,000 MYA. About 900 MYA they formed the first supercontinent, Rodinia. The southward movement of Rodinia triggered the Verangian Ice Age. Later, Rodinia split into two halves (see map), but by the end of the Precambrian again formed a single mass.

PRECAMBRIAN LIFE
The first living cells were microscopic organisms possibly living in hot springs. By about 3,500 MYA algae may have formed.

STROMATOLITES
These layered silica or limestone structures were created by colony-forming algae.

FIRST ANIMALS
Late in the Precambrian, the first true animals and plants appeared. *Spriggina* (above) was a strange, long, tapering animal, with V-shaped segments.

Charniodiscus looked like the modern sea pen

FILTER-FEEDER
The feather-shaped fossil of *Charniodiscus* is thought to represent an early filter-feeding animal that lived on the sea floor late in the Precambrian.

2,000 MYA   1,000 MYA   500 MYA   250 MYA   0

CAMBRIAN PERIOD

AQUATIC ANIMALS

EXPLOSION OF LIFE
Most of today's major
animal groups evolved in the
Cambrian. This huge growth
in diversity occurred only
in the seas. Soft-bodied
animals were largely
replaced by animals with
hard parts, many of whose
fossils were found in the
Burgess Shale in Canada.

METALDETES
These were early shell fossils shaped
like cones. Mollusks in coiled shells
and worms in tubes were other
early hard-shelled animals.

*Metaldetes probably
resembled a sponge*

METALDETES
TAYLORI

XYSTRIDURA
Trilobites were an
enormously successful
and diverse group and
make up one-third
of all fossils from
the Cambrian.
Xystridura, with
many legs and
complex eyes,
is one example
of this species.

Large eyes

*Each body segment
supported a walking leg
and a gill-bearing leg*

XYSTRIDURA

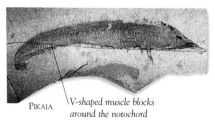

PIKAIA

*V-shaped muscle blocks
around the notochord*

PIKAIA
Chordates, the group
that includes vertebrates,
evolved in the Middle Cambrian.
One of the first was *Pikaia*, a
swimming eel-like animal, 2 in (5 cm)
in length. *Pikaia* had a flexible rod
called a notochord stiffening its body.
In later animals this developed into
the backbone.

WIWAXIA
Perhaps distantly related to the mollusks, *Wiwaxia* was 1¼ in (3 cm) long, dome-shaped, and covered in scales. It had long spines, probably for self-defense.

Ridged scale

Wiwaxia probably ate algae

MARRELLA
The most common arthropod in the Burgess Shale is *Marrella*—more than 13,000 specimens have been collected to date. Up to ¾ in (2 cm) long, this animal had a large head shield and two pairs of long antennae.

The head shield supported large backward-pointing horns

Indentations may have been sites of muscle attachment

Concave inner surface indicates an older individual

MOBERGELLA
Among the early shelled fossils of the Cambrian are tiny limpetlike forms, such as *Mobergella* from Scandinavia. These might have been not separate, individual animals but scalelike structures that covered the bodies of larger species. Members of another Cambrian group with hard parts, the halkieriids, were elongate with scaly bodies. It is possible that *Mobergella* may actually have been covered in halkieriid body scales.

EARTH FACTS

During the Cambrian, most of the world's landmasses were united as the supercontinent Gondwana. This was surrounded by the Iapetus Ocean. Smaller landmasses that today form Europe, North America, and Siberia lay in tropical and temperate zones.

ORDOVICIAN PERIOD

FILTER-FEEDERS
Another burst of evolution in the Ordovician gave rise to thousands of new animals. Many were filter-feeders that fed on plankton. These included bivalves and corals, which formed reefs that were home to mollusks and other animals. Vertebrates with jaws may have appeared.

ESTONIOCERAS
This mollusk belonged to the nautiloid group and hunted in deep waters. *Estonioceras* was 4 in (10 cm) across, but some of its relatives had shells 16 ft (5 m) in diameter.

ESTONIOCERAS PERFORATUM

Uncoiled final whorl of shell

STROPHOMENA
Strophomena was a small brachiopod (two-shelled animal) that lived on sand or mud.

Shell could be locked shut with internal pegs

ALGAE AND LIFE ON LAND
Blue-green algae of the Precambrian were still widespread during the Ordovician. True algae, including round forms that resembled sponges, lived alongside other reef-builders, such as corals, while green algae, the ancestors of land plants, took over freshwater habitats. Plants similar to liverworts and mosses evolved late in the Ordovician and began to colonize the land.

MASTOPORA
This reef-forming green alga grew in rounded clusters with a characteristic honeycomb surface. Fossils, each about 3 in (8 cm) across, are found worldwide. Hard limestone secretions on the surface protected *Mastopora* from hungry animals.

Honeycomb surface

MASTOPORA FAVUS

Colony about 3 in (8 cm) long

Serrated teeth to cut up prey

CONODONT
Conodonts were eel-like relatives of vertebrates. With large eyes, they hunted and ate small animals. *Promissum*, from South Africa, was the largest known conodont at 16 in (40 cm) in length.

ORTHOGRAPTUS
Graptolites formed colonies of linked cuplike structures called thecae, each inhabited by a soft-bodied filter-feeding animal called a zooid.

Surface strengthened by calcium carbonate

EARTH FACTS

The Gondwanan supercontinent remained separate from the smaller landmasses, although the Iapetus Ocean had started to close. The Ordovician was a time of global cooling, with a huge ice sheet covering much of the Southern Hemisphere toward the end.

Alga 2 in (5 cm) in diameter

ACANTHOCHONIA
The surface of *Acanthochonia* was made up of many diamond-shaped cells arranged in a spiral pattern. All the cells originated from a single central stem, which anchored the alga to rocks or corals.

SILURIAN PERIOD

AQUATIC ANIMALS

NEW LIFE
The end of the
Ordovician witnessed
a large-scale extinction
event. However, surviving
groups, such as rachiopods,
mollusks, and trilobites,
soon recovered and
increased in diversity
in the warm continental
seas. Invertebrates, such
as primitive sea urchins,
appeared for the first time.
Jawless fishes still thrived,
while jawed fishes
diversified. The first
land-living animals—
arthropods—evolved
from aquatic ancestors
in the Silurian.

Small body, about 2½ in (6 cm) in length

BIRKENIA ELEGANS

BIRKENIA
The small, spindle-shaped *Birkenia* lived
in European lakes and rivers. Like other
jawless fishes, it lacked paired fins, making
it unstable when swimming. It probably
foraged in mud for tiny food particles.

LAND PLANTS

THE PIONEERS
The Silurian marks the
appearance of the first
true land plants. Mosses
and liverworts grew
along the edges of
ponds and streams.
Later Silurian plants
had a woody lining, for
support and for carrying
water around the body
(vascular plants).
Thus the plant could
survive farther from
the water.

COOKSONIA
HEMISPHAERICA

COOKSONIA
Best known from
Silurian rocks of
southern Ireland, *Cooksonia*
was the first upright vascular
plant. Lacking leaves and
roots, it was composed of
cylindrical stems that
branched into two.

Branching stems formed Y-shapes

PARKA
Green algae are simple plants
that grow close to or in water.
Parka was a green alga from
the Silurian and Devonian.

Each arm was free and could be moved

The legs could have been used for walking or for handling prey

SAGENOCRINITES
Crinoids, or sea lilies, were important animals of the Silurian seas. Many species survive today in deeper waters. They collected plankton with their tentacles. *Sagenocrinites* was one of the smaller crinoids.

Stem base attached to the sea floor

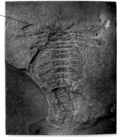

PARACARCINOSOMA
Sea scorpions were Silurian arthropods—relatives of the spiders. They had long tails and large pincers. *Paracarcinosoma* was a sea scorpion 2 in (5 cm) long.

Stem covered with fine leaves

BARAGWANATHIA
Closely resembling a club moss, *Baragwanathia* was a complex Silurian plant. Its "furry" stems spread across the ground and branched upward.

Distinct rounded spore capsules grew on its surface

PARKA
DECIPIENS

BARAGWANATHIA
LONGIFOLIA

EARTH FACTS

During the Silurian, Gondwana was fringed by smaller landmasses. These moved northward and collided, producing new mountain ranges in North America and Europe. Sea levels rose as ice melted and the climate became warmer and less changeable.

DEVONIAN PERIOD

LAND ANIMALS

LIMBS ON LAND
The first vertebrates with four limbs and distinct digits evolved during this period and spread around the world. Land-living arthropods diversified, and primitive insects forms appeared.

Sharp teeth suggest a diet of fish and other animals

ACANTHOSTEGA
Among the earliest of four-limbed vertebrates was *Acanthostega* from Greenland. Like its lobe-finned fish relatives, it was a pond-dwelling predator.

AQUATIC ANIMALS

DEVONIAN DIVERSITY
Armored jawless fishes flourished, and jawed fishes were also abundant. Bony, lobe-finned fishes were diverse, while ray-finned fishes gained importance. Ammonoids and horseshoe crabs also appeared.

Pointed fins

Prominent central row of bones

DIPTERUS
Lungfish such as *Dipterus* were an abundant group of the Devonian. Five species of these lobe-finned fishes survive today. *Dipterus* swam in European waters and, like all lungfish, had large crushing teeth.

LAND PLANTS

LEAVES AND ROOTS
The Devonian saw the most important steps so far in the development of land plants. Leaves and roots evolved in a number of different groups. Plant stems grew not only in length, but also in diameter. The early reedlike plants gave way to gigantic trees and species with complex leaves.

ARCHAEOPTERIS
This widespread Late Devonian plant was the first to resemble modern trees. It had an extensive root system and its trunk had branches.

Branching, fernlike leaves   ARCHAEOPTERIS

Seven toes on each foot

Used limbs to walk on land

ICHTHYOSTEGA FOSSIL
Ichthyostega was an early four-footed vertebrate. It probably hunted in shallow pools. Its multi-jointed limbs suggest that it was relatively advanced and was related to the ancestor of all later four-footed vertebrates.

Large eye for excellent vision

EASTMANOSTEUS
Placoderms were jawed fishes that included predators, armored bottom-dwellers, and flattened raylike forms. They were the largest vertebrates to have evolved so far.

PHACOPS
Each body segment of this small trilobite supported two sets of limbs. Seven out of eight trilobite groups died out at the end of the Devonian.

PHACOPS

Clusters of spore-bearing stems

ZOSTEROPHYLLUM
Lacking roots and leaves, this was a primitive land plant. Its erect, branching stems grew not from roots, but from a complex underground rhizome (stem).

ZOSTEROPHYLLUM
LLANOVERANUM

EARTH FACTS

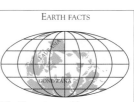

The Devonian world was warm and mild. The huge continent Gondwana lay over the South Pole while modern Europe and North America were positioned close to the equator. Much of the land lay under shallow seas.

CARBONIFEROUS PERIOD

LAND ANIMALS

ORIGIN OF THE AMNIOTES
Amniotes, vertebrates whose
embryos are enclosed by a
watertight membrane, evolved
in this period. Both reptiles and
the mammal-like synapsids
appeared, while other more
primitive vertebrates diversified.
Flying insects also evolved.

WESTLOTHIANA
Primitive four-footed
vertebrates are well known from
fossils in North America and
Europe. *Westlothiana* was
discovered in Scotland, in
rocks formed in a lake fed
by hot volcanic springs.

*Sharp teeth
suggest a
diet of
insects*

WESTLOTHIANA
LIZZIAE

AQUATIC ANIMALS

DIVERSE DEPTHS
Sharks and bony fish
dominated Carboniferous
seas, but ray-finned fish,
the actinopterygians, also
diversified greatly during this
period. Crinoids, brachiopods,
echinoderms, and swimming
mollusks inhabited the
coral reefs.

SYMMORIUM
Many of the Carboniferous sharks were bizarre
compared with modern ones. Some were
decorated with spiky crests and spines.
Stethacanthus and
Symmorium were a
few examples.

*Pointed teeth
of a predator*

LAND PLANTS

FORESTS AND FLOODPLAINS
Lush tropical forests forming
vast swamps and forested
deltas were widespread in the
Carboniferous. Club mosses
and horsetails were important
plants of these forests, and
some grew to immense sizes.
Gymnosperms—the group
that includes conifers and
cycads—began to diversify.
Toward the end of the
period, the huge floodplains
began to shrink as the
climate became drier.

EQUISETITES
Equisetites is an
extinct horsetail
that came from a
group that survives
worldwide today in the
form of *Equisetum*. It
grew to a height of
around 20 in (50 cm)
from underground stems
(tubers), and its straight
stem carried leaves
arranged in whorls.
Equisetites dominated
the river banks.

*Fossilized tubers and
roots of* Equisetites

GRAEOPHONUS

Arachnids, the arthropod group that includes spiders, scorpions, and their relatives, are well represented in the Carboniferous fossil record, and many new kinds made their first appearance at this time. *Graeophonus* was an early member of a group that survives to this day—the whip scorpions. These have six walking legs and a front pair of pincers.

Two eyes on a bump

GONIATITES

This animal is a type of swimming mollusk with a coiled shell. It was a member of a group of ammonoids that was dominant in the Paleozoic. Like all ammonoids, *Goniatites* had gas-filled shell chambers that allowed it to float. It had complex eyes and beaklike mouthparts and lived in large swarms over reefs in shallow seas.

Growth lines, or sutures, on shell

Forked tail suggests speed

CORDAITES

This conifer-like land plant grew in Carboniferous mangrove swamps, but died out in the Permian. It had characteristic long, leathery leaves, and its straight main trunk grew to a height of up to 100 ft (30 m), although other species of *Cordaites* were shrublike. It produced seeds in loose cones.

Straplike leaves

EARTH FACTS

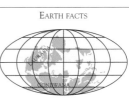

The Carboniferous is known as the "age of coal" because decaying vegetation from the vast forests was transformed into coal. The main landmasses present were the two huge continents of Gondwana and Laurasia.

33

PERMIAN PERIOD

LAND ANIMALS

SYNAPSIDS
The most important land vertebrates of the Permian were the primitive synapsids. Most were small flesh-eaters with powerful skulls and sharp teeth.

Palate fragment with teeth

EDAPHOSAURUS
This synapsid had a broad, rounded body with a tall fin on its back. It fed on ferns and tough Permian plants.

EDAPHOSAURUS

AQUATIC ANIMALS

SEAS OF LIFE
This period saw immense reefs teeming with marine life, shelled animals called brachiopods, and new fish groups. However, it ended with the biggest mass extinction of all time.

DERBYIA
Brachiopods were shelled, filter-feeding animals. Their larvae could swim, but adults were static. *Derbyia* was a large species of the Carboniferous and Permian seas.

LAND PLANTS

NAKED SEEDS
Plant communities in the Permian were basically similar to those of today. Club mosses and horsetails that had formed the Carboniferous forests were replaced by conifers, cycads and ginkgoes—gymnosperms or plants that have "naked" seeds not enclosed within a fruit.

Sword-shaped leaves

GLOSSOPTERIS

GLOSSOPTERIS
One of the important Permian gymnosperms was *Glossopteris*. This tree grew to 26 ft (8 m) tall, and its close relatives dominated the southern part of the supercontinent Pangaea.

Eye socket

295–250 MYA

DIMETRODON SKULL

DIMETRODON
Dimetrodon was an awesome predator. This fin-backed synapsid grew to 10 ft (3 m) long. It ran fast to catch its prey. Animals like *Dimetrodon* were important because they gave rise to an entirely new group of synapsids, the therapsids.

DIMETRODON LOOMISI SKULL

PALAEONISCUS
Ray-finned fishes diversified in the Permian, and a major new group—the neopterygians—appeared. *Palaeoniscus* was a primitive ray-finned fish.

PALAEONISCUS
MAGNUS

Long, streamlined body suited to fast swimming

Overlapping scales

MARIOPTERIS
Found in early Permian swamps, *Mariopteris* grew to a height of around 16 ft (5 m). Some species were tree-like, while others may have been climbing plants.

Small, pointed leaflets

MARIOPTERIS
MARICATA

EARTH FACTS

Two major landmasses—Laurasia in the north and Gondwana in the south—collided late in the Permian to form the supercontinent Pangaea. The climate became hotter and drier. The south was cool, while tropical conditions prevailed in the north.

PERMIAN EXTINCTION

THE END OF THE Permian saw the greatest mass extinction of all time. Perhaps only five percent of all species survived. In the seas, trilobites, scorpions, and key coral groups disappeared. On land, synapsids and many reptile groups vanished.

FIERY END
A possible cause of the end-Permian extinction is volcanic activity. Eruptions of volcanic material may have blotted out all sunlight.

CLIMATIC CRISIS
Climate change characterized the end of the Permian. Rocks from the period indicate that cooling occurred in some areas and ice sheets built up at the poles, causing the global sea level to drop.

Branching colonies of bryozoans, or moss animals

Rugose corals completely disappeared

Brachiopods grew on the tops of reefs

DESERT DEVASTATION
The vast continent of Pangaea was formed and parts of the world became drier. Deserts grew larger, and certain species of animals became extinct.

Corythosaurus
Among the most common Cretaceous dinosaurs were hadrosaurs—the duck-billed dinosaurs—which evolved from *Iguanodon*-like ancestors. With batteries of chewing teeth and powerful jaws, they were successful browsing herbivores. *Corythosaurus* had a hollow bony crest on its head to amplify its calls.

Hollow crest on head

Large, powerful legs

Protostega
Turtles first evolved in the Triassic, but forms specialized for life at sea, such as *Protostega*, did not appear until the Cretaceous.

Rubbery skin covered ribs

Strong flippers for fast swimming

Spore capsules were carried on the fronds

Onychiopsis
Ferns were important low-growing plants in the Mesozoic but became less widespread as flowering plants increased in importance during the Cretaceous. *Onychiopsis*, a small fern from the Northern Hemisphere, had delicate, feathery leaves and reached 20 in (50 cm) in height.

Onychiopsis
Psilotoides

Earth Facts

By the Cretaceous, Pangaea had split into Laurasia in the north and Gondwana in the south. These continents were themselves breaking apart into the continents that exist today. Madagascar and India separated from Gondwana and moved north. Large inland seas covered parts of Laurasia.

END OF THE DINOSAURS

THE END OF THE Cretaceous saw the most famous mass extinction event of all time—although it was not the biggest in terms of species lost. All large land animals disappeared, as did many marine invertebrate groups. The theropods survived as birds, but all other dinosaurs became extinct. In the seas, plesiosaurs and mosasaurs died out, as did many kinds of bivalves, swimming mollusks, and plankton.

AFTER THE ASTEROID

Some evidence indicates that a large asteroid struck Earth at this time. Experts speculate that such an impact would have thrown up enough dust to block out light from the Sun for years or even decades. Perhaps this prolonged cold, dark phase caused Cretaceous plants and animals to die off. The impact would have thrown up tidal waves that would have washed ashore on the North American continent, destroying coastal habitats. Hot debris thrown into the atmosphere by the impact may later have rained down to Earth and started huge wildfires.

LAST SURVIVORS

Triceratops and *Tyrannosaurus* were among the last of the dinosaurs, but many animal groups survived, including insects, mammals, reptiles, and fishes.

Triceratops *was one of the very last dinosaurs*

PALEOCENE & EOCENE EPOCHS

LAND ANIMALS

LARGE LANDLUBBERS
At the start of the Paleocene, there were no large animals on the land. But they soon began to evolve from the small survivors of the Cretaceous extinction. Bats, rodents, and true primates made their appearance, together with many birds, crocodiles, lizards, snakes, turtles, and frogs.

PALAEOCHIROPTERYX
Bats probably evolved from tree-climbing ancestors that leaped to catch insect prey. Early true bats, such as *Palaeochiropteryx* from Eocene Europe, had wings formed from enlarged hands.

AQUATIC ANIMALS

SEA MAMMALS
Modern forms of marine life became established. Fishes took on now-familiar forms. The first penguins appeared, including giant forms. Aquatic mammals such as whales and sea cows evolved.

WETHERELLUS
This Eocene mackerel was around 1 ft (25 cm) in length. Mackerels are fast-swimming marine fishes that belong to a group called the scombroids.

LAND PLANTS

TROPICAL TIMES
The world was dominated by tropical forests. Even Europe had tropical swamps where ferns, horsetails, and palms formed the undergrowth and vines and citrus trees grew overhead. Trees included forms as diverse as hazel, chestnut, magnolia, poplar, and walnut. Toward the end of the Eocene, the world cooled. Deciduous and coniferous trees became dominant at higher latitudes and tropical forests retreated to the equatorial regions.

Wide jaws lined with rows of pointed teeth

NIPA
BURTINII

NIPA
This palm, which survives only in the mangrove swamps of southeast Asia, was widespread in the Northern Hemisphere. Its coconut-like seeds grew at its base.

Rounded fruit with protective woody shell

GASTORNIS

Gastornis was a giant, flightless, land bird of Paleocene and Eocene North America and Europe. It stood 7 ft (2 m) high and had short, largely useless wings, but its long, sturdy legs would have made it a fast runner and a powerful kicker. Its massive, deep beak was very strong, suggesting that it could break open bones.

Beak well suited to crushing

BASILOSAURUS

One of the best-known prehistoric whales is *Basilosaurus*, a gigantic predator that grew to more than 66 ft (20 m) in length. It had a big skull with massive teeth for slicing prey. Its relatives were ancestors of modern whales.

Large brain, though smaller than that of living whales

Figs were an important food for animals

FICUS

Ficus, or figs, are widespread flowering plants and are part of the same group as oaks. They can be trees, shrubs, or climbers. Their fossils are first seen in Eocene rocks.

Ficus fruit with woody covering

FICUS

EARTH FACTS

The climate cooled late in the Eocene. North America and Europe were still linked, but a seaway separated Europe from Asia. India and Africa were isolated island continents, while Australia broke away from Antarctica late in the Eocene.

OLIGOCENE & MIOCENE EPOCHS

LAND ANIMALS

THE MODERN AGE
Many modern animals evolved during this period. Monkeys and apes replaced primitive primates. Mammals similar to today's horses, elephants, and camels, and new forms of carnivores, birds and reptiles also arose.

AEGYPTOPITHECUS
This primate from Egypt was about the size of a pet cat. It resembled a modern monkey and probably climbed in trees, feeding on fruit and leaves.

HIPPARION
With the spread of grasslands in the Miocene, horses such as *Hipparion* emerged as important herbivores.

AQUATIC ANIMALS

FAMILIAR WATERS
By the Miocene, well-known types of fishes such as mackerel, flatfish, and advanced sharks, including the great white, swam the seas, while carp, catfish, and other groups evolved in fresh water. Modern whales and the first seals evolved.

LEUCISCUS
PACHECOI

LEUCISCUS
The freshwater fish *Leuciscus* appeared in the Oligocene and survives to this day in North America, Asia, Europe, and Africa.

These Leuciscus *died as their home lake dried up*

LAND PLANTS

TEMPERATE LANDS
The tropical forests of the Eocene gave way to drier grasslands. The lower temperatures of the Oligocene allowed temperate woodlands to spread across the continents. The warmer and drier conditions of the Miocene coincided with the evolution of grasses, which spread across the landscape, forming vast savanna and prairie environments in the south.

ACER
The maples (*Acer*) and their relatives first evolved in the Oligocene, and many species survive today in temperate forests around the world. These deciduous trees grow to 80 ft (25 m) in height.

Typical winged fruit of Acer *preserved in limestone*

ACER

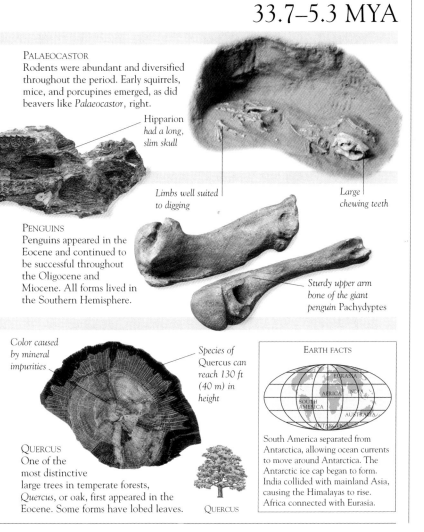

PALAEOCASTOR
Rodents were abundant and diversified throughout the period. Early squirrels, mice, and porcupines emerged, as did beavers like *Palaeocastor*, right.

Hipparion
had a long,
slim skull

Limbs well suited
to digging

Large
chewing teeth

PENGUINS
Penguins appeared in the Eocene and continued to be successful throughout the Oligocene and Miocene. All forms lived in the Southern Hemisphere.

Sturdy upper arm
bone of the giant
penguin *Pachydyptes*

Color caused
by mineral
impurities

Species of
Quercus can
reach 130 ft
(40 m) in
height

QUERCUS
One of the most distinctive large trees in temperate forests, *Quercus*, or oak, first appeared in the Eocene. Some forms have lobed leaves.

QUERCUS

EARTH FACTS

South America separated from Antarctica, allowing ocean currents to move around Antarctica. The Antarctic ice cap began to form. India collided with mainland Asia, causing the Himalayas to rise. Africa connected with Eurasia.

49

PLIOCENE EPOCH

LAND ANIMALS

GRASSLAND GRAZERS
Pliocene animals were
similar to today's forms.
Hoofed mammals such
as horses, elephants, and
antelopes diversified. Large
cats hunted the plains and
forests, and humans evolved
from chimplike ancestors.

TETRALOPHODON
LONGIROSTRUS

TETRALOPHODON
During this time,
advanced elephant
forms, closely related
to today's species,
spread worldwide.
Tetralophodon was an
elephant that lived in
Africa, Asia, and Europe.

AQUATIC ANIMALS

WHALE DIVERSITY
By the Pliocene, modern
whales such as sperm whales,
humpbacks, killer whales,
and many modern dolphin
species had evolved.
Numerous fishes and animals
unique to the Caribbean
Sea also evolved during
this time.

BALAENA
The bowhead whale
(*Balaena*) grows to 65 ft
(20 m) in length and has
been hunted to near-
extinction by humans.
Its ear bone often
drops away from
the carcass.

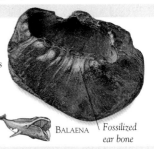

BALAENA   \ Fossilized
                ear bone

LAND PLANTS

RETREATING TROPICS
Conditions became drier and
cooler during the Pliocene
and arid grasslands spread,
replacing the more wooded
savannas of the Miocene. As
a result, grazing animals
flourished at the expense of
browsers. Tropical plants started
to disappear from high latitudes,
and bands of cool-adapted
forests, made up of conifers,
birches, and other trees,
began to spread across the
northern regions.

GRASSES
Grasses are a very important
group of plants today. They
provide shelter and food
for countless animal
species. The spread and
diversification of grasses
started in the Miocene
and continued through
the Pliocene as the
climate became drier.

*Grasses produce huge
quantities of pollen
and seed*

5.3–1.75 MYA

Body about 4 ft (1.2 m) long

Short tail

Retractable claws, like those of a living cat

Deep, powerful lower jaw

SMILODON
The famous saber-toothed cat, *Smilodon*, lived in the Americas. It hunted horses, camels, and other hoofed mammals that thrived during the epoch. *Smilodon* probably killed its prey by biting it in the throat.

MACRONES
All the familiar kinds of living fishes had evolved by the Pliocene. *Macrones* was a fish that resembled the catfish of today.

Sensitive barbels grew from the upper jaw

Long, toothed skull, ideal for a diet of invertebrates

Macrones was about 20 in (50 cm) long

LIQUIDAMBAR
These trees, sometimes called sweetgum, grew to about 80 ft (25 m) in height. They formed an important part of Pliocene forests worldwide.

Distinctive star-shaped, five-lobed leaf

Leaves were shed in the fall

LIQUIDAMBAR EUROPEANUM

EARTH FACTS

In the Pliocene, a land bridge formed between North and South America. Animals could move from one continent to the other. India continued to push the Himalayas higher. The climate grew cooler and Antarctica froze.

PLEISTOCENE EPOCH

LAND ANIMALS

MAMMALS AND HUMANS
During the Pleistocene, temperatures dropped in the Northern Hemisphere. Numerous large, fur-covered mammals, such as new mammoths, giant rhinos, cave lions, and giant deer, evolved. New human species emerged in Africa, Europe, and Asia.

HOMO SAPIENS
Our own species—*Homo sapiens*—emerged in Africa. It soon spread to Europe and Asia and even crossed over to the Americas and Australasia.

AQUATIC ANIMALS

COLD WATERS
Marine invertebrate life in the Pleistocene was largely unchanged from the Miocene and Pliocene. However, corals and other reef animals were affected as sea levels fell. The colder climate worldwide meant that cold-water sea birds and marine mammals were far more widely distributed.

GREAT AUK
The great auk, *Pinguinus impennis*, was a flightless sea bird that inhabited the seas of the Northern Hemisphere as far south as North Africa and Florida. Like the modern-day penguin (left), the great auk chased its prey underwater. The last great auks died by 1860.

LAND PLANTS

GRASSLANDS AND TAIGA
Grasslands developed in the northern latitudes. These also supported lichens, mosses, dwarf sedges, and miniature willows and birches. Taiga—a new kind of coniferous forest—colonized the area between the cold northern grasslands (steppes) and the temperate deciduous forests farther south. Tropical forests retreated, and the South American and African rainforests may have existed as small "islands."

PICEA
Spruces (*Picea*) are conifers that formed much of the taiga—the vast forests that spread through the Northern Hemisphere in the Pleistocene. More than 30 species of spruce exist today.

Cones release winged seeds

Woody cone covered with bracts in diamond pattern

Small brain

Some skeletons have marks indicating that they were hunted by prehistoric people

Strong, heavy, columnlike limbs

Short feet suited to bearing the animal's weight

DIPROTODON
Herds of this giant marsupial roamed the Australian grasslands of the Pleistocene. This herbivore had large chewing teeth set into thick, heavy jaws. *Diprotodon* declined as Australia became drier, and was replaced by the large grazing kangaroos of today.

HYDRODAMALIS
Steller's sea cow (*Hydrodamalis gigas*) was a marine mammal related to the modern dugong. It lived in the Arctic seas, protected from the icy water by layers of fat beneath its barklike skin. It survived into the Holocene and was hunted to extinction by 1767.

Blunt and stumplike flippers

Ranunculus spread across North America, Europe, and Asia

Buttercups can have yellow, white, red, or blue flowers

RANUNCULUS
Buttercups (*Ranunculus*) are flowering plants that grow in temperate grassland, wetland, and woodland environments. They are among the oldest groups of flowering plants and were widespread in the Pleistocene. About 2,000 members of the buttercup family are found today.

EARTH FACTS

Northern North America, Europe, and Asia were covered by ice. Southern South America, Australia, and Antarctica were also icier than today. Dry land linked North America to eastern Asia and Australia to New Guinea.

HOLOCENE EPOCH

LAND ANIMALS

THE GREATEST DIVERSITY EVER
With the formation of the
continents as they exist now, and
the clearly differentiated climatic
zones, Earth witnessed greater
biodiversity than at any other
time in the past. However,
increasing human presence and
pollution has taken its toll on
animal life and natural habitats.

*Prominent curved beak
and naked facial skin*

DODO
The dodo was a giant
flightless pigeon that
lived on the island of
Mauritius in the Indian
Ocean. Hunted mercilessly,
it was extinct by about 1680.

AQUATIC ANIMALS

WATER LOSSES
In the Holocene seas, some species of
seals and sea cows have been hunted
to extinction. Whaling has almost
wiped out certain whale species,
and industrial fishing has
changed the balance of life
in the seas. The waters
are also polluted.

SALMON
Today, wild salmon are hunted
for sport, while some species
are farmed. Salmon numbers have
been hit by water pollution
and by the construction of
dams, which prevent the
fish from migrating upstream
to breed.

LAND PLANTS

HUMAN INFLUENCE
At the start of the Holocene,
elm, birch, and conifer woodlands
colonized much of the Northern
Hemisphere. Vast tracts of
these woodlands, as well as
wetlands and tropical forests,
were later cleared by humans
for farming cereal crops. Other
apparently natural habitats,
such as moorlands, heaths, and
grasslands, are actually created
and maintained by human
activity, such as deliberate
burning and grazing of livestock.

*Branching, leafy
thallus (body)*

OAK MOSS
Oak moss is a lichen—an alga and a fungus growing
together. Some scientists believe that lichens may have
been the first multicellular organisms on Earth. Today,
many lichens are dying off as a result of pollution.

GIANT PANDA

Giant pandas are Asian bears that live on a diet of bamboo. Only one out three species survives today, and it is highly endangered.

DOLLY THE SHEEP

Advances in genetics now allow biologists to manipulate genetic material and clone (duplicate) embryos. Dolly the sheep, born in 1997, was the world's first successfully cloned animal.

BLUE WHALE

The invention of the explosive harpoon in the late 1800s enabled humans to hunt the blue whale, the largest animal that has ever lived, to near-extinction. It is still endangered.

DUCKS

Ducks are omnivorous water birds that evolved at the end of the Cretaceous. The mallard is a domesticated duck, different types of which have been introduced worldwide.

WHEAT

Early in the Holocene, people began to domesticate wild grasses to produce food grains. They deliberately cross-bred the types that produced the most seeds, or grew the fastest. Wheat is one such cereal, first domesticated in the Middle East.

Wheat is milled to produce flour

EARTH FACTS

Sea levels rose in the Holocene as the large ice caps retreated. Global warming continues this trend today. The land bridge that linked Asia with North America was submerged, and New Guinea was separated from Australia.

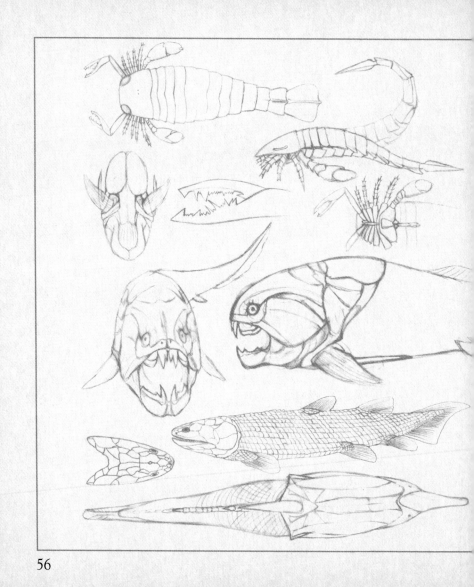

FISHES AND INVERTEBRATES

STARTING WITH a strange collection of invertebrates (animals without backbones), this section moves on to a fantastic variety of fishes, the first animals to have backbones. Little fishes with ever-open mouths, armored and spiny fishes, sharks, and finally, lobe-finned fishes, an ancient group that is ancestral to humans, are all exhibited here.

TRILOBITES

BEFORE FISHES BECAME dominant, the
seas teemed with trilobites. They
were among the earliest arthropods
(creatures that possess external
skeletons) and ranged in size
from microscopically tiny to
larger than a dinner plate.
With over 15,000 species,
trilobites outnumber any other
known extinct creature.

TRILOBITE BODY PLAN
Trilobite means "three-lobed," which
describes its body's lengthwise division into
three parts. A tough outer casing protected the
body. After a trilobite died, the casing often
broke apart into the three lobes.

*A knobbly shield
guarded the head*

*Middle lobe,
flanked by two
side lobes*

DEFENSE
Phacops curled
up in a tight ball or
burrowed if attacked. The
12 plates of its thorax
(middle region) overlapped
like a Venetian blind to protect
the legs and underside. Fish were
probably *Phacops*'s worst enemies.

PHACOPS ROLLED
UP IN DEFENSE

Tail

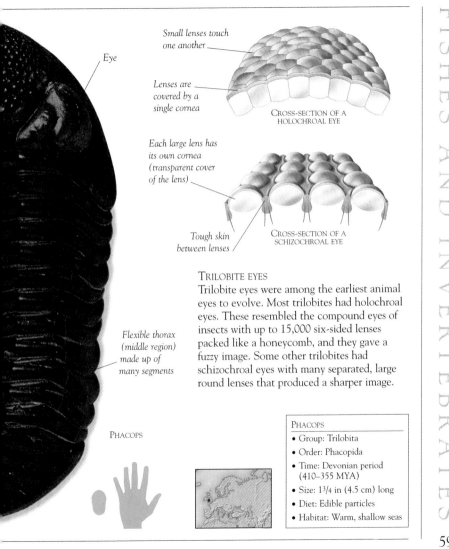

Eye

Small lenses touch
one another

Lenses are
covered by a
single cornea

CROSS-SECTION OF A
HOLOCHROAL EYE

Each large lens has
its own cornea
(transparent cover
of the lens)

Tough skin
between lenses

CROSS-SECTION OF A
SCHIZOCHROAL EYE

Flexible thorax
(middle region)
made up of
many segments

TRILOBITE EYES

Trilobite eyes were among the earliest animal
eyes to evolve. Most trilobites had holochroal
eyes. These resembled the compound eyes of
insects with up to 15,000 six-sided lenses
packed like a honeycomb, and they gave a
fuzzy image. Some other trilobites had
schizochroal eyes with many separated, large
round lenses that produced a sharper image.

PHACOPS

PHACOPS
- Group: Trilobita
- Order: Phacopida
- Time: Devonian period
  (410–355 MYA)
- Size: 1³/₄ in (4.5 cm) long
- Diet: Edible particles
- Habitat: Warm, shallow seas

SEA SCORPIONS

EURYPTERIDS (SEA SCORPIONS) were the largest-ever arthropods. They belong to the chelicerates ("pincered creatures"), a group that includes spiders and scorpions. Among the largest sea scorpions was *Pterygotus*, which lived more than 400 million years ago, and could grow longer than a man. Before hunting fish evolved, sea scorpions were among the most dominant hunters of shallow seas.

Large ey

Small eye

METHOD OF ATTACK

Pterygotus could spot prey a long
way off using its big, sharp eyes. It
swam slowly toward its victim, and
with a final burst of speed grabbed it
between its pincers. After crushing
the struggling fish in its great claw,
it would put it in its mouth.

Walking leg

*Pterygotus
swam by
beating its
broad paddles
up and down*

PTERYGOTUS
- Group: Chelicerata
- Subclass: Eurypterida
- Time: Silurian period
  (435–410 MYA)
- Size: Up to 7 ft 4 in (2.3 m)
  long
- Diet: Fish
- Habitat: Shallow seas

AMMONITES AND BELEMNITES

THE COILED SHELLS called ammonites were
named after Ammon, an Egyptian
god with coiled horns, while the
long, tapering belemnites take
their name from the Greek
word for darts. Both groups
were cephalopods—soft
bodied mollusks—and
they lived in the sea.

ECHIOCERAS
The ammonite *Echioceras* lived in
shallow seas around the world in
Jurassic times. In life, its tentacled
head poked out of the shell's open
end as it searched for food.

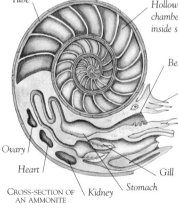

Tube

Hollow
chamber
inside shell

Beaklike jaws

Tentacle

Ovary

Heart

Gill

Stomach

CROSS-SECTION OF
AN AMMONITE

Kidney

INSIDE AN AMMONITE
When the young ammonite outgrew its
home, it built a bigger chamber next to
it, which it moved into. This process was
repeated as the ammonite grew, and a
shell with many chambers was created.

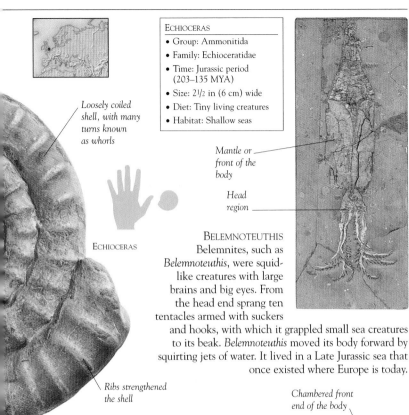

Loosely coiled shell, with many turns known as whorls

ECHIOCERAS
- Group: Ammonitida
- Family: Echioceratidae
- Time: Jurassic period (203–135 MYA)
- Size: 2½ in (6 cm) wide
- Diet: Tiny living creatures
- Habitat: Shallow seas

Mantle or front of the body

Head region

ECHIOCERAS

BELEMNOTEUTHIS
Belemnites, such as *Belemnoteuthis*, were squid-like creatures with large brains and big eyes. From the head end sprang ten tentacles armed with suckers and hooks, with which it grappled small sea creatures to its beak. *Belemnoteuthis* moved its body forward by squirting jets of water. It lived in a Late Jurassic sea that once existed where Europe is today.

Ribs strengthened the shell

INSIDE A BELEMNITE
This *Cylindroteuthis* fossil shows the main parts of a belemnite's internal shell. The chambered front end helped the body float while the tapering rear end fitted into a hard, narrow guard.

Chambered front end of the body

Long, pointed guard or pen

EVOLVING INSECTS

THE FIRST INSECTS were tiny, wingless arthropods that lived in the Devonian. By 320 million years ago, some insects had developed wings. The flowering plants of the Cretaceous provided food for butterflies and bees. By 220 million years ago, termites were forming colonies; they were followed by ants, bees, and wasps. The world now teems with millions of insect species.

HYDROPHILUS

Fine veins stiffened the wings

Hard wing case preserved in a fossil

MEGANEURA FOSSIL

WINGS AS SHIELDS
Beetles almost identical to this *Hydrophilus* fossil still swim in ponds today. Their forewings form hard protective cases.

HAWKLIKE HUNTERS
Meganeura was a gigantic, primitive dragonfly with two pairs of wings that were 27 in (70 cm) wide. It hunted insects above tropical forests in the Late Carboniferous. Its swiveling eyes were like headlights, sharp enough to allow it to spot and pounce on flying prey.

Six jointed legs, as found in other insects

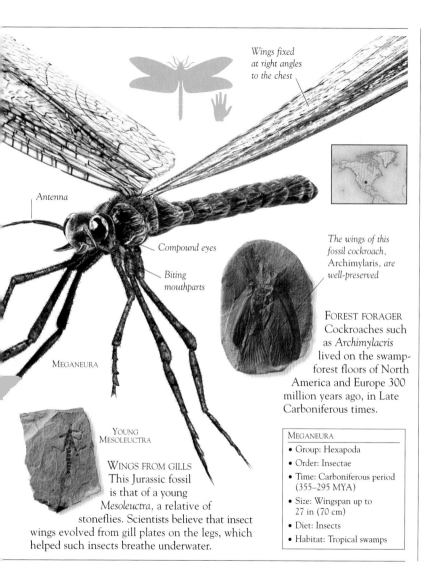

*Wings fixed
at right angles
to the chest*

Antenna

Compound eyes

*Biting
mouthparts*

MEGANEURA

*The wings of this
fossil cockroach,*
Archimylaris, *are
well-preserved*

FOREST FORAGER
Cockroaches such
as *Archimylacris*
lived on the swamp-
forest floors of North
America and Europe 300
million years ago, in Late
Carboniferous times.

YOUNG
MESOLEUCTRA

WINGS FROM GILLS
This Jurassic fossil
is that of a young
Mesoleuctra, a relative of
stoneflies. Scientists believe that insect
wings evolved from gill plates on the legs, which
helped such insects breathe underwater.

MEGANEURA	
• Group: Hexapoda	
• Order: Insectae	
• Time: Carboniferous period (355–295 MYA)	
• Size: Wingspan up to 27 in (70 cm)	
• Diet: Insects	
• Habitat: Tropical swamps	

65

VERTEBRATES CLADOGRAM

ALL VERTEBRATES possess an internal skeleton. The
evolution of the skeleton allowed vertebrates to
support their weight on land better than any other
animal group. Vertebrates have grown
larger and adopted more complex
lifestyles than other animals.

Eusthenopteron

Dunkleosteus

COELACANTHS,
LUNGFISH, AND
THEIR RELATIVES

ARMORED FISH

Lepidotes fossil

LAMPREY

JAWLESS FISH

RAY-FINNED FISH

CARTILAGINOUS FISH

SARCOPTERYGIANS
Muscular fin base

SPINY SHARKS

BONY FISH
Bony fin skeleton

Muscle

LOBE-FINNED
FISH'S FIN

GNATHOSTOMES
Jaws

BONY FIN SKELETON
All bony fishes have
fin bones, with
muscles attached
for better control.

MUSCULAR FINS
Sarcopterygians
have muscles at
the base of their
fins, and strong
fin bones, which
allowed some of
them to clamber
on to land.

VERTEBRATES
Vertebral column
and brain case

BARRACUDA
JAWS

JAWS
The evolution
of jaws allowed
vertebrates to
eat a varied diet.

*Bones in
bony fish's
fin*

BRAIN CASE AND
VERTEBRAL COLUMN
These structures protect
the brain and main
nervous system.

*Vertebral column and skull
in a simple vertebrate*

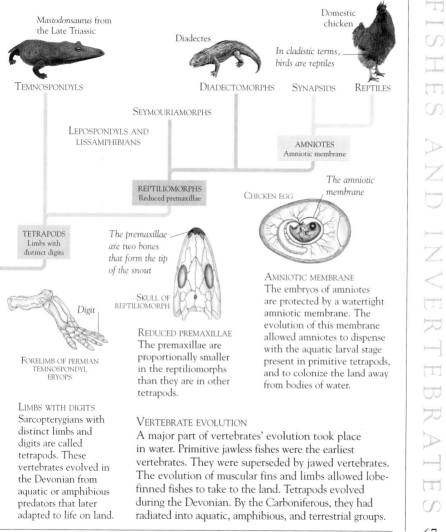

Mastodonsaurus from the Late Triassic

TEMNOSPONDYLS

Diadectes

DIADECTOMORPHS

Domestic chicken

In cladistic terms, birds are reptiles

SYNAPSIDS

REPTILES

SEYMOURIAMORPHS

LEPOSPONDYLS AND LISSAMPHIBIANS

AMNIOTES
Amniotic membrane

REPTILIOMORPHS
Reduced premaxillae

The amniotic membrane

CHICKEN EGG

TETRAPODS
Limbs with distinct digits

The premaxillae are two bones that form the tip of the snout

SKULL OF REPTILIOMORPH

Digit

FORELIMB OF PERMIAN TEMNOSPONDYL ERYOPS

REDUCED PREMAXILLAE
The premaxillae are proportionally smaller in the reptiliomorphs than they are in other tetrapods.

AMNIOTIC MEMBRANE
The embryos of amniotes are protected by a watertight amniotic membrane. The evolution of this membrane allowed amniotes to dispense with the aquatic larval stage present in primitive tetrapods, and to colonize the land away from bodies of water.

LIMBS WITH DIGITS
Sarcopterygians with distinct limbs and digits are called tetrapods. These vertebrates evolved in the Devonian from aquatic or amphibious predators that later adapted to life on land.

VERTEBRATE EVOLUTION
A major part of vertebrates' evolution took place in water. Primitive jawless fishes were the earliest vertebrates. They were superseded by jawed vertebrates. The evolution of muscular fins and limbs allowed lobe-finned fishes to take to the land. Tetrapods evolved during the Devonian. By the Carboniferous, they had radiated into aquatic, amphibious, and terrestrial groups.

TOWARD THE FIRST FISHES

THE EARLIEST sea creatures were sponges with a single type of cell in their bodies. Gradually, cells became specialized and bodies more complex, giving rise to bilaterians—creatures with left and right sides. About 535 million years ago, bilaterians called chordates developed a stiffening rod (notochord) that would eventually become a true skeleton. These became the first fishes.

Inlet for food and water

COTHURNOCYSTIS

Cothurnocystis was a strange, bootlike animal. Its tail might have had a notochord, and the small slits in its body might have filtered food. It had a hard outer shell like a sea urchins.

COTHURNOCYSTIS

Hard protective covering on the body

Hard plates framing the head

Slits for expelling waste

COTHURNOCYSTIS FOSSIL

A *Cothurnocystis* fossil lies embedded in an ancient piece of Scottish rock. *Cothurnocystis* belonged to the carpoids—small, oddly flattened creatures that lived on Early Paleozoic seabeds—and may have been the ancestors of fishes.

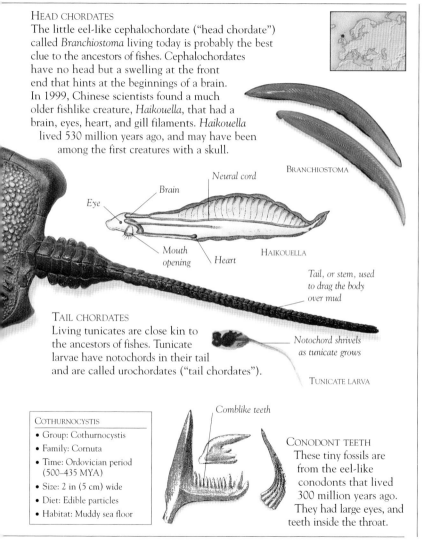

HEAD CHORDATES

The little eel-like cephalochordate ("head chordate") called *Branchiostoma* living today is probably the best clue to the ancestors of fishes. Cephalochordates have no head but a swelling at the front end that hints at the beginnings of a brain. In 1999, Chinese scientists found a much older fishlike creature, *Haikouella*, that had a brain, eyes, heart, and gill filaments. *Haikouella* lived 530 million years ago, and may have been among the first creatures with a skull.

BRANCHIOSTOMA

Neural cord

Brain

Eye

Mouth opening

Heart

HAIKOUELLA

Tail, or stem, used to drag the body over mud

TAIL CHORDATES

Living tunicates are close kin to the ancestors of fishes. Tunicate larvae have notochords in their tail and are called urochordates ("tail chordates").

Notochord shrivels as tunicate grows

TUNICATE LARVA

COTHURNOCYSTIS
- Group: Cothurnocystis
- Family: Cornuta
- Time: Ordovician period (500–435 MYA)
- Size: 2 in (5 cm) wide
- Diet: Edible particles
- Habitat: Muddy sea floor

Comblike teeth

CONODONT TEETH

These tiny fossils are from the eel-like conodonts that lived 300 million years ago. They had large eyes, and teeth inside the throat.

JAWLESS FISHES

AGNATHANS ("WITHOUT JAWS") were the most primitive fishes. Their mouths were fixed open because they lacked jaws, they had no bony internal skeleton, and they lacked paired fins. Early jawless fishes lived in the seas, but they later invaded rivers and lakes. They swam by waggling their tails, and sucked in small food particles from the mud or water around them.

Backswept horns helped with balance

The long lower lobe of the tail lifted the fish as it swam

PTERASPIS

Bony armor protected it from sea scorpions and other predators

VERTEBRATE PIONEER
Sacabambaspis was a tadpole-shaped fish that lived 450 million years ago. It swam by waggling its tail, but had no fins, which would have made braking and steering very difficult. Two tiny, headlightlike eyes gazed from the front of its armored head as it sucked in water and food through its always-open mouth.

Large bony plates protected the head and chest

SACABAMBASPIS

A tall, bony spine at the back of the head shield served as a dorsal fin

Small eyes set in a head shield made of several bony plates

Long, pointed snout

WING SHIELD
Pteraspis ("wing shield") is named after the winglike armored spines sticking out from its sides. Its head ended in a long, sharp snout. Its mouth was fixed open and the animal might have swum near the surface, guzzling shrimplike creatures.

Bony head shield with eyes on top

Upturned tail tilted the head downward

BETTER BALANCE
Cephalaspis was an advanced jawless fish that had a big, bony head with sense organs on the sides and top, a mouth below the head, and paired flaps that provided lift and balance.

PTERASPIS
- Group: Agnatha
- Order: Heterostraci
- Time: Devonian period (410–355 MYA)
- Size: 8 in (20 cm) long
- Diet: Tiny water animals
- Habitat: Shallow seas

ARMORED FISHES

PLACODERMS ("PLATED SKINS") were primitive jawed fishes named after the protective bony plates on their head and body. Some lived in the sea, some in fresh water, and they ranged in size from a few inches up to 26 ft (8 m)—the first fishes to grow to such a large size. Placoderms were a very successful group. It is possible that they may have shared a common ancestor with sharks.

BOTHRIOLEPIS

Each jointed "arm" was a fin inside a bony tube

Preserved head and trunk shields

ROCK SLAB CONTAINING MANY FOSSILS OF BOTHRIOLEPIS

FISH WITH "ARMS"
Bothriolepis was among the strangest of placoderms. Up to 3 ft 3 in (1 m) in length, it possessed jointed "arms" made of bony tubes that enclosed its long, narrow pectoral fins. It might have used these arms to dig for food in the mud or to even drag itself over dry land as it migrated from one pool to another.

FLAT OUT
The flat-bodied fish *Gemuendina* belonged to an ancient group of placoderms called rhenanids. Much like living rays, it swam with rippling movements of its broad, winglike pectoral fins. A short, bony shield guarded its foreparts, and tiny bony plates ran down its slender tail. It thrust out its jaws and caught shellfish for food.

GEMUENDINA FOSSIL IN FINE-GRAINED ROCK

Head and chest shields
connected by
flexible joint

*Dorsal
fin*

*Unprotected
scaleless tail*

DUNKLEOSTEUS
One of the largest
placoderms, *Dunkleosteus* was
named after paleontologist
D.H. Dunkle. With massive head and
jaws, it reached a size of around 16 ft
(5 m). Only its head and shoulders were
covered by a protective shield, leaving
the big pectoral fins free to
help it move. Scientists are
unsure about the shape and
habits of *Dunkleosteus*. It may
have been sharklike, or it may have
had an eel-shaped body.

*Bony plates served
as teeth*

*Razor sharp
"teeth"*

HUGE HEAD AND
CHEST SHIELD OF
DUNKLEOSTEUS

DUNKLEOSTEUS
- Group: Arthrodira
- Family: Diniochtyloidea
- Time: Devonian period
  (410–355 MYA)
- Size: 16 ft (5 m)
  or more long
- Diet: Fish
- Habitat: Oceans

73

SHARKS AND RAYS

SHARKS HAVE BEEN among the top ocean predators for over 400 million years. Their basic features—a streamlined shape and jaws bristling with razor-sharp fangs—have changed little in this time, although many different kinds of sharklike fishes have evolved. These include rat fish, skates, and rays. Sharks and their relatives are known as Chondrichthyes ("cartilage fishes") because their skeletons are made of cartilage.

Streamlined, torpedo-shaped body

CLADOSELACHE
Well-preserved fossils of *Cladoselache*, one of the earliest known sharks, have been found in Late Devonian rocks. This carnivore hunted fish, squid, and crustaceans.

CLADOSELACHE

The fin rays radiated like the rays of the sun

SUN RAY
The stingray *Heliobatis* ("sun ray") was a flat-bodied, freshwater fish that lived in North America about 50 million years ago. Up to 1 ft (30 cm) in length, its flat, round body had a long whiplike tail armed with spines.

CLADOSELACHE
- Group: Elasmobranchii
- Family: Cladoselachidae
- Time: Devonian period (410–355 MYA)
- Size: Up to 6 1/2 ft (2 m) long
- Diet: Fish and crustaceans
- Habitat: Seas

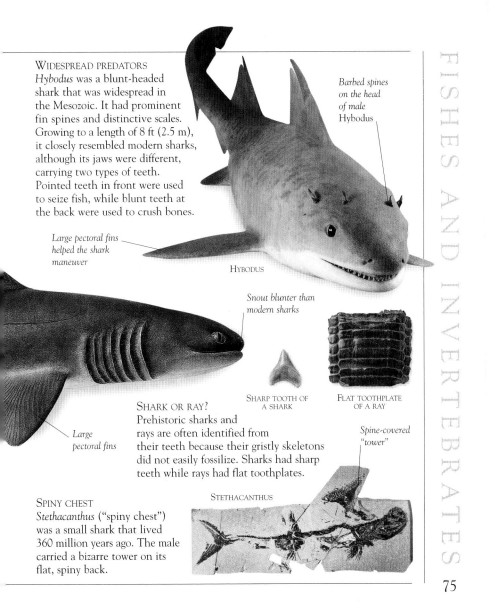

WIDESPREAD PREDATORS
Hybodus was a blunt-headed
shark that was widespread in
the Mesozoic. It had prominent
fin spines and distinctive scales.
Growing to a length of 8 ft (2.5 m),
it closely resembled modern sharks,
although its jaws were different,
carrying two types of teeth.
Pointed teeth in front were used
to seize fish, while blunt teeth at
the back were used to crush bones.

*Barbed spines
on the head
of male
Hybodus*

*Large pectoral fins
helped the shark
maneuver*

HYBODUS

*Snout blunter than
modern sharks*

*Large
pectoral fins*

SHARK OR RAY?
Prehistoric sharks and
rays are often identified from
their teeth because their gristly skeletons
did not easily fossilize. Sharks had sharp
teeth while rays had flat toothplates.

SHARP TOOTH OF
A SHARK

FLAT TOOTHPLATE
OF A RAY

*Spine-covered
"tower"*

STETHACANTHUS

SPINY CHEST
Stethacanthus ("spiny chest")
was a small shark that lived
360 million years ago. The male
carried a bizarre tower on its
flat, spiny back.

SPINY SHARKS

ACANTHODIANS OR "SPINY SHARKS" may have predated placoderms as the first fishes with jaws. They got their name from their sharklike bodies with upturned tails, and the sharp spines at the tip of their fins. Although their cartilage backbone reminds us of a shark's, acanthodians had a braincase, gills, and other features more like those of bony fishes that are common today.

Large eyes suggest that Climatius *hunted by sight, not scent*

Distinctive ridges on surface

SPINY PROTECTION

Fin spines up to 16 in (40 cm) long are the best known remains of the spiny shark *Gyracanthus*. Fossils of this well-defended animal are found in Carboniferous rocks of North America and Europe. Some acanthodians had spines that were half their body length as protection against large, fierce predators.

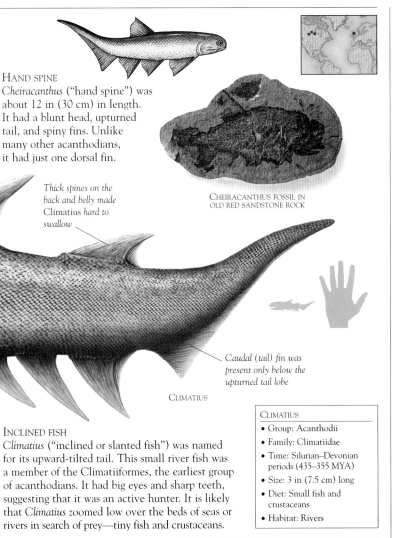

HAND SPINE
Cheiracanthus ("hand spine") was
about 12 in (30 cm) in length.
It had a blunt head, upturned
tail, and spiny fins. Unlike
many other acanthodians,
it had just one dorsal fin.

Thick spines on the
back and belly made
Climatius *hard to
swallow*

CHEIRACANTHUS FOSSIL IN
OLD RED SANDSTONE ROCK

Caudal (tail) fin was
present only below the
upturned tail lobe

CLIMATIUS

INCLINED FISH
Climatius ("inclined or slanted fish") was named
for its upward-tilted tail. This small river fish was
a member of the Climatiiformes, the earliest group
of acanthodians. It had big eyes and sharp teeth,
suggesting that it was an active hunter. It is likely
that *Climatius* zoomed low over the beds of seas or
rivers in search of prey—tiny fish and crustaceans.

CLIMATIUS
- Group: Acanthodii
- Family: Climatiidae
- Time: Silurian–Devonian
  periods (435–355 MYA)
- Size: 3 in (7.5 cm) long
- Diet: Small fish and
  crustaceans
- Habitat: Rivers

EARLY RAY-FINNED FISHES

BONY FISHES ARE the most numerous and diverse of all living vertebrates and more than 20,000 of them belong to one giant group known as actinopterygians or "ray fins." They are named after the straight bony rays that jut out from their body and stiffen the fins. The earliest known ray fins lived 410 million years ago.

LIVING FOSSILS
Bichirs are ray-finned fish that live in Africa. They can be traced back to ancestors that lived 400 MYA.

HAND FIN
Cheirolepis ("hand fin") was one of the earliest ray-finned fishes. Only parts of its backbone were actually made of bone; the rest was made of gristle and so not often preserved in fossils. This wide-jawed fish was a good hunter, swimming fast to catch prey in freshwater pools and streams.

Relatively large eyes

Long jaws equipped with many tiny teeth

Pectoral fins on fleshy lobes

REDFIELDIUS
About 8 in (20 cm) in length, *Redfieldius* lived about 210 million years ago. Its group, the redfieldiids, are thought to have evolved in Australia or South Africa and then spread to North Africa and North America in Early Mesozoic times.

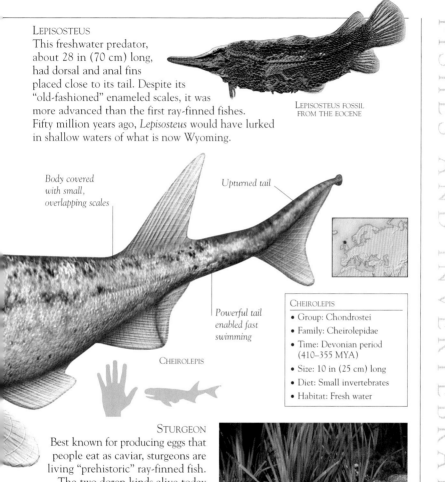

LEPISOSTEUS

This freshwater predator, about 28 in (70 cm) long, had dorsal and anal fins placed close to its tail. Despite its "old-fashioned" enameled scales, it was more advanced than the first ray-finned fishes. Fifty million years ago, *Lepisosteus* would have lurked in shallow waters of what is now Wyoming.

LEPISOSTEUS FOSSIL FROM THE EOCENE

Body covered with small, overlapping scales

Upturned tail

Powerful tail enabled fast swimming

CHEIROLEPIS

CHEIROLEPIS
- Group: Chondrostei
- Family: Cheirolepidae
- Time: Devonian period (410–355 MYA)
- Size: 10 in (25 cm) long
- Diet: Small invertebrates
- Habitat: Fresh water

STURGEON

Best known for producing eggs that people eat as caviar, sturgeons are living "prehistoric" ray-finned fish. The two dozen kinds alive today live in northern seas and swim up rivers to lay eggs. Several species are endangered by fishing, dam construction, and pollution.

ADVANCED RAY-FINNED FISHES

IMPROVED TYPES of ray-finned fishes called the neopterygians ("new fins") began to appear in Mesozoic times. Their mouths could open wider and had tooth plates to grind up food. Changes in the fins and tail made them better swimmers. The most advanced of this group were the teleosts or "complete bones."

Body made inflexible by thick layer of scales

SCURFY SCALES

Lepidotes ("covered in scurfy scales") was a bony fish nearly as long as a human. Like early ray-finned fishes, its body had a coat of thick and hard scales, although it was far bigger in size. *Lepidotes* swam in shallow coastal waters, hunting for shellfish. However, it too was sometimes eaten by a fish-eating dinosaur called *Spinosaur*.

Relatively deep body

LEPIDOTES

Leptolepides, a teleost fossil of the Late Jurassic

PRIMITIVE TELEOST

As big as a human hand, *Leptolepides* was a bony fish that lived about 150 million years ago. It swam in shoals in tropical lagoons where Germany now stands. It is the ancestor of carp and other modern teleosts.

LEPIDOTES

- Group: Neopterygii
- Family: Semionotidae
- Time: Triassic–Cretaceous periods (250–65 MYA)
- Size: Up to 5 ft 6 in (1.7 m) long
- Diet: Shellfish
- Habitat: Lakes and shallow seas

OLD ACARA

Priscacara was a small, perch-like teleost. It lived in North America 45 million years ago. It had spiny fins, and its jaws were crammed with tiny teeth with which it ate snails.

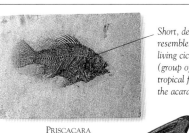

Short, deep body resembles a living cichlid (group of tropical fishes), the acara

PRISCACARA

Top and bottom tail lobes of equal length

Heavily enameled, overlapping scales resembled rows of shiny tiles

SWORD RAY

Xiphactinus was a primitive teleost that swam in Late Cretaceous seas. It grew up to 14 ft (4.2 m) in length and could swallow fish as long as a human—the guts of one fossil *Xiphactinus* have the remains of *Gillicus*, a neopterygian, which was 6 ft (1.8 m) long.

"Bulldog" jaw

XIPHACTINUS

LOBE-FINNED FISHES

THE BONY FISHES OF 400 million years ago belonged to two large groups—lobe-fins and ray-fins. Lobe-finned fishes, or sarcopterygians, had fins that sprouted from fleshy lobes. Many also had a type of lung in addition to gills and so could breathe in air. There were two main groups of lobe-fins—lungfish and crossopterygians. The latter group included the coelacanths ("hollow spines") and rhipidistians ("fan sails"), which have an important place in evolutionary history.

PANDER'S FISH
In the 1990s, scientists made an important discovery about the Late Devonian fan sail *Panderichthys*. Their studies revealed that this freshwater rhipidistian was one of the closest known ancestors of four-limbed vertebrates.

RIDGED UPPER AND
LOWER TOOTHPLATES
OF CERATODUS

Broad, flat head of Panderichthys with eyes located on top

HORN TEETH
Ceratodus ("horn teeth") was a lungfish that lived in the Age of Dinosaurs. It had gills, but could also breathe through its nostrils at the water surface, using its swim bladder as a kind of lung.

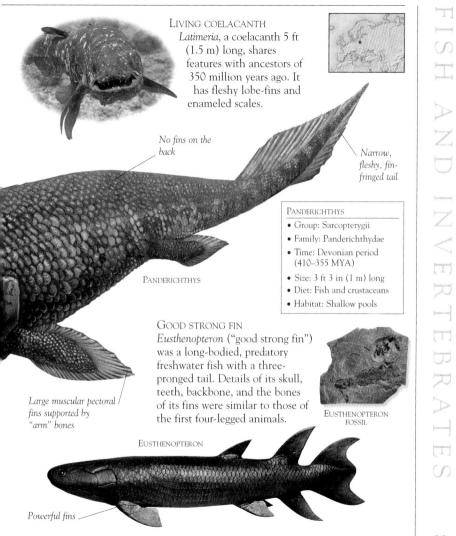

LIVING COELACANTH
Latimeria, a coelacanth 5 ft (1.5 m) long, shares features with ancestors of 350 million years ago. It has fleshy lobe-fins and enameled scales.

No fins on the back

Narrow, fleshy, fin-fringed tail

PANDERICHTHYS

PANDERICHTHYS
- Group: Sarcopterygii
- Family: Panderichthydae
- Time: Devonian period (410–355 MYA)
- Size: 3 ft 3 in (1 m) long
- Diet: Fish and crustaceans
- Habitat: Shallow pools

GOOD STRONG FIN
Eusthenopteron ("good strong fin") was a long-bodied, predatory freshwater fish with a three-pronged tail. Details of its skull, teeth, backbone, and the bones of its fins were similar to those of the first four-legged animals.

EUSTHENOPTERON FOSSIL

Large muscular pectoral fins supported by "arm" bones

EUSTHENOPTERON

Powerful fins

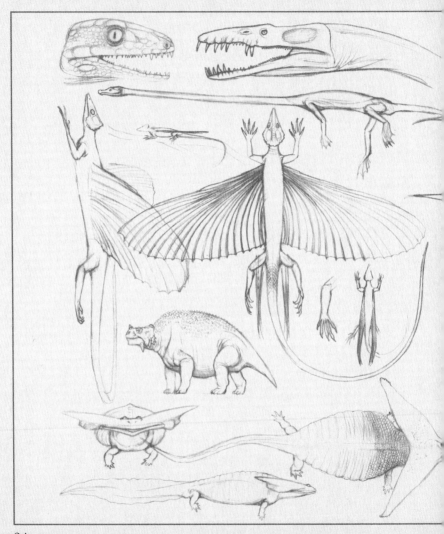

AMPHIBIANS AND REPTILES

ABOUT 360 MILLION years ago, a fish with lungs crawled ashore on stubby fins. So vertebrates began their great adventure on dry land. From early amphibians that laid small, unprotected eggs in water, eventually reptiles began to breed on land with eggs that were protected by a shell. An incredible variety of prehistoric reptiles began to rule land, sea, and air.

EARLY TETRAPOD AND AMPHIBIAN CLADOGRAM

TETRAPODS, the limb-bearing vertebrates, gradually adapted to life on land. They evolved stronger limbs, each with five digits, and some of the skull bones seen in their fish ancestors were lost. They also developed a stronger link between their hips and vertebrae.

Eucritta from the Carboniferous

BAPHETIDS

Acanthostega was a primitive tetrapod that lived among water plants

ICHTHYOSTEGA

Ichthyostega's limbs could bear more weight

Five digits or fewer on hand

Ventastega's body and tail were fish-like, and its limbs were used as paddles

ACANTHOSTEGA

Olecranon process

ICHTHYOSTEGA FORELIMB

Olecranon process

VENTASTEGA

Interlocking vertebral pegs

OLECRANON PROCESS
This bony region on the lower arm unites tetrapods higher than *Acanthostega*.

Limbs with distinct digits

Digit

VERTEBRAL PEGS
Interlocking pegs called zygapophyses project from the ends of vertebrae. They help stiffen the spine.

ERYOPS FORELIMB

LIMBS WITH DISTINCT DIGITS
Well-formed limbs with distinct digits (fingers and toes) unite the tetrapods.

VENTASTEGA FORELIMB

HUMAN VERTEBRAE

FIVE-DIGIT HAND
The presence of five digits on the hand unites the tetrapods at the higher end of the evolutionary scale.

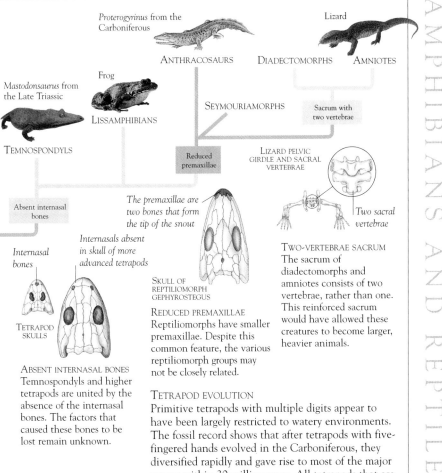

Proterogyrinus from the Carboniferous

Lizard

ANTHRACOSAURS   DIADECTOMORPHS   AMNIOTES

Frog

Mastodonsaurus from the Late Triassic

SEYMOURIAMORPHS

Sacrum with two vertebrae

LISSAMPHIBIANS

TEMNOSPONDYLS

Reduced premaxillae

LIZARD PELVIC GIRDLE AND SACRAL VERTEBRAE

Absent internasal bones

The premaxillae are two bones that form the tip of the snout

Two sacral vertebrae

Internasals absent in skull of more advanced tetrapods

Internasal bones

SKULL OF REPTILIOMORPH GEPHYROSTEGUS

TWO-VERTEBRAE SACRUM
The sacrum of diadectomorphs and amniotes consists of two vertebrae, rather than one. This reinforced sacrum would have allowed these creatures to become larger, heavier animals.

TETRAPOD SKULLS

REDUCED PREMAXILLAE
Reptiliomorphs have smaller premaxillae. Despite this common feature, the various reptiliomorph groups may not be closely related.

ABSENT INTERNASAL BONES
Temnospondyls and higher tetrapods are united by the absence of the internasal bones. The factors that caused these bones to be lost remain unknown.

TETRAPOD EVOLUTION
Primitive tetrapods with multiple digits appear to have been largely restricted to watery environments. The fossil record shows that after tetrapods with five-fingered hands evolved in the Carboniferous, they diversified rapidly and gave rise to most of the major groups within 30 million years. All tetrapods that are not amniotes were formerly called amphibians. However, many fossil animals that have been called amphibians were not in fact related to each other.

EARLY TETRAPODS

THE TETRAPODS, meaning "four feet," are a group that include all vertebrates with four limbs and distinct digits (fingers and toes). Early tetrapods were tied to life in water. They had paddlelike limbs, gills, and tail fins. They also possessed many features inherited by later types: digits, limbs with wrist and elbow joints, and vertebrae with interlocking pegs, which all seem to have evolved in the water.

Bony rays supported the tail fins

Early tetrapods were quite large—between 20 in (50 cm) and 40 in (1 m) long

Hind limbs were directed sideways and backward, to help in swimming

ELGINERPETON

Paddlelike limbs

TETRAPOD ORIGINS

Among the earliest tetrapods is *Elginerpeton* from Devonian Scotland. The very first tetrapods, which include *Obruchevichthys* from Latvia and *Metaxygnathus* from Australia, are from the late Devonian (about 365 MYA). Footprints found in Australia show that four-footed animals were walking on land even at this time.

ACANTHOSTEGA

- Group: Labyrinthodontia
- Order: Acanthostegidae
- Time: Devonian period (410–355 MYA)
- Size: 3 ft 4 in (1 m) long
- Diet: Insects, fish, smaller animals of its own kind
- Habitat: Lakes and ponds

Patterned skull surface
seen in all early
limbed vertebrates

ACANTHOSTEGA
SKULL

FISHLIKE SKULL
The skull of *Acanthostega* was
designed for grabbing fish and
other aquatic prey. This well-
preserved skull is similar to that
of the lobe-finned fishes, ancestors
of the earliest limbed vertebrates.

ACANTHOSTEGA
Tetrapods like *Ichthyostega* and *Acanthostega* from
Late Devonian Greenland were aquatic predators
with fishlike features, including a tail fin, gill bones,
and paddlelike hind limbs. Intriguingly, their
multiple digits suggest that the evolution of limbs
and digits first occurred in the water, and not on
land. *Acanthostega* might have ventured
onto land, although
its limbs were not
suited to walking.

Acanthostega
had a stiff spine with
interlocking pegs on
the vertebrae

The eight fingers
were probably
webbed together to
form a paddle

Large eyes
directed upward
and sideway

EVOLUTION OF DIGITS
Digits evolved from the fin bones of
lobe-finned fishes. The early vertebrates
often had more than five digits. More
advanced tetrapods may have five digits
because this is best suited for walking.

Numerous small
bones form the
fin skeletons of
lobe-finned fishes

ICHTHYOSTEGA
FIN/HAND

TEMNOSPONDYLS

THESE WERE A LARGE group of animals that
lived in the water, on land, or both.
Most early temnospondyls were
aquatic, but some were
land-living predators with
short, scaly bodies and
sturdy limbs. Some later
land temnospondyls had
armor on their backs:
some that stayed in the
water became huge predators.

MASTODONSAURUS
PROBABLY SPENT ALL OF
ITS TIME IN THE WATER

RECONSTRUCTED
BUETTNERIA
SKELETON

*Small limbs suggest that it
did not often walk on land*

METOPOSAURS
Related to *Mastodonsaurus*, the
metoposaurs were a group of large, mostly
aquatic temnospondyls. All metoposaurs,
including this *Buettneria* from Late Triassic
North America, had large, flat skulls.

MASS DEATHS
Some temnospondyls perished in
hundreds and were preserved in mass
death fossils, as seen below in the
case of *Trimerorhachis*, a Permian
temnospondyl from North America.

TRIMERORHACHIS MASS-DEATH FOSSIL

Notches at the back of the skull captured vibrations for hearing

Mastodonsaurus could probably hide underwater with just its eyes above the surface

Skull up to 4 ft 6 in (1.4 m) long

Tusks could have been used to hold prey

MASTODON LIZARD
Mastodonsaurus was a large-headed temnospondyl that belonged to a group of advanced, mostly Triassic animals called capitosaurs. It had a short, massive body, sturdy limbs, a short tail, and a long-jawed, powerful skull. Two large triangular tusks pointed up from near the tip of its lower jaw. These protruded from holes on the top of the skull.

MASTODONSAURUS
- Group: Temnospondyli
- Family: Capitosauroidea
- Time: Triassic period (250–203 MYA)
- Size: 7 ft (2 m) long
- Diet: Other smaller temnospondyls, fish
- Habitat: Lakes, ponds, and swamps

SIDEROPS

The tail was short but may have served as a paddle

Siderops grew to 8 ft (2.5 m) long

Small teeth lined the jaws

CRETACEOUS SURVIVORS
Temnospondyls survived as late as the Early Cretaceous. *Siderops* from Jurassic Australia was an aquatic predator with a huge head and bladelike teeth.

LIFE IN A SWAMP FOREST

DURING THE CARBONIFEROUS
period, several new kinds of
terrestrial vertebrates evolved.
Lush, forested swamps with
an atmosphere rich in
oxygen favored the growth
of giant arthropods, as well
as different species of
amphibious, aquatic, and
land-dwelling predators.

GIANT ARTHROPODS
With a wingspan of 27 in
(70 cm), *Meganeura* was
the largest flying insect
ever. Other giant
arthropods included
scorpions and flat-
bodied millipedes.

*Eryops was an
aquatic hunter*

AQUATIC HUNTERS
Various large predators haunted
the dark waters of the Carboniferous
forests, including amphibious
temnospondyls called eryopids ("long-
faces") that survived into the Permian
period. Their long, flat skulls had
numerous sharp teeth, suggesting that
they were aquatic hunters. Eyes and
nostrils were located on the top of the
head, and were the only part of their
body exposed while they stalked prey.

*Early reptiles, such
as Hylonomus,
foraged in the leaf
litter for insects*

CARBONIFEROUS PLANTS
A number of plant groups,
including club mosses, horsetails,
and ferns, formed the swamp
forests. The largest club mosses,
such as *Lepidodendron*, reached
165 ft (50 m) in height, while
the biggest horsetails grew to
50 ft (15 m). Today such plants
are usually a few feet high.

ERYOPS
- Group: Temnospondyli
- Family: Eryopidae
- Time: Carboniferous period
  (355–295 MYA)
- Size: 6½ ft (2 m) long
- Diet: Fish, amphibious
  tetrapods
- Habitat: Swamps and lakes

*Eryops may have crawled onto
the shore or onto fallen tree
trunks to bask or rest*

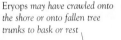

COAL FORMATION
Broken stems, branches,
and leaves of Carboniferous
plants would have lain in
the waters. The decaying
tissues built up in layers as
peat. Later, this became
compressed and fossilized
to produce lignite and,
eventually, coal.

LEPOSPONDYLS AND LISSAMPHIBIANS

LEPOSPONDYLS WERE A group of tetrapods that probably included the ancestors of lissamphibians, the group that includes frogs and salamanders. They lived in a warm, humid world. Some were well-adapted for life on land, while others were aquatic. Today there are more lissamphibian than mammal species.

SNAKELIKE AÏSTOPODS
One of the most bizarre groups of Paleozoic tetrapods were the limbless aïstopods, eel-like animals with more than 200 vertebrae.

Snakelike body with no sign of limbs

AÏSTOPOD AORNERPETON

BOOMERANG HEAD
Diplocaulus from the Permian of Texas was one of the most unusual lepospondyls. The "boomerang" shape of the skull was formed by hornlike extensions from the back of the skull. There were several bizarre features found among nectrideans—for example, some later species grew extremely elongated snouts.

GIANT SALAMANDER ANDRIAS

LISSAMPHIBIAN DIVERSITY
Lissamphibians have evolved into a wide variety of forms. Frogs have dramatically reduced skeletons—they lack ribs and a tail, and have a few vertebrae. Salamanders first appeared in the Jurassic, and modern groups, such as giant salamanders, are known from the Eocene. The wormlike caecilians also originated in the Jurassic.

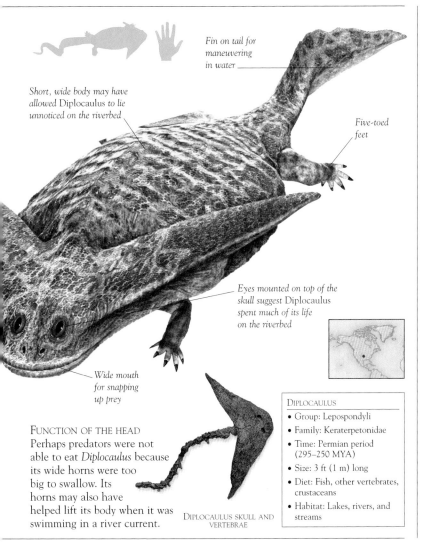

Fin on tail for
maneuvering
in water

Short, wide body may have
allowed Diplocaulus to lie
unnoticed on the riverbed

Five-toed
feet

Eyes mounted on top of the
skull suggest Diplocaulus
spent much of its life
on the riverbed

Wide mouth
for snapping
up prey

FUNCTION OF THE HEAD
Perhaps predators were not
able to eat *Diplocaulus* because
its wide horns were too
big to swallow. Its
horns may also have
helped lift its body when it was
swimming in a river current.

DIPLOCAULUS SKULL AND
VERTEBRAE

DIPLOCAULUS
- Group: Lepospondyli
- Family: Keraterpetonidae
- Time: Permian period
  (295–250 MYA)
- Size: 3 ft (1 m) long
- Diet: Fish, other vertebrates,
  crustaceans
- Habitat: Lakes, rivers, and
  streams

REPTILIOMORPHS

THE REPTILIOMORPHS include the amniotes—the group that includes reptiles—and the ancestors of amniotes. Although some reptiliomorphs were amphibious or aquatic, generally their skeletons became steadily better suited for carrying weight on land. Some reptiliomorphs have been found preserved in environments well away from water.

Tail was probably long and used in swimming

Barrel-shaped body

The back of the skull had large chewing muscles

Diadectes *had a sturdy skull*

Strong fingers to dig up plants

Front teeth were spoon-shaped

DIADECTES

Powerful limbs sprawled sideways

FIRST HERBIVORES

Diadectomorphs were reptilelike animals with short, strong limbs. *Diadectes* from North America and Europe is the best known of the diadectomorphs. Their teeth show that they were the first land vertebrates to evolve plant-eating habits.

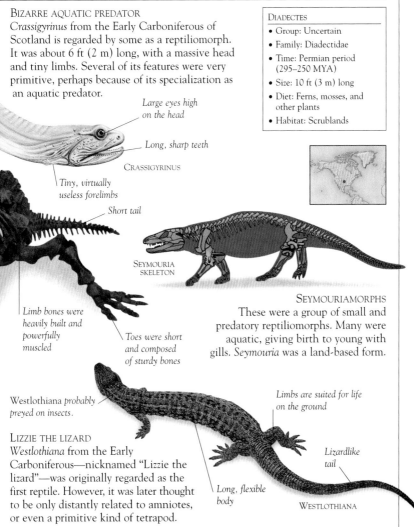

BIZARRE AQUATIC PREDATOR

Crassigyrinus from the Early Carboniferous of Scotland is regarded by some as a reptiliomorph. It was about 6 ft (2 m) long, with a massive head and tiny limbs. Several of its features were very primitive, perhaps because of its specialization as an aquatic predator.

Large eyes high on the head

Long, sharp teeth

CRASSIGYRINUS

Tiny, virtually useless forelimbs

Short tail

DIADECTES
- Group: Uncertain
- Family: Diadectidae
- Time: Permian period (295–250 MYA)
- Size: 10 ft (3 m) long
- Diet: Ferns, mosses, and other plants
- Habitat: Scrublands

SEYMOURIA SKELETON

SEYMOURIAMORPHS

These were a group of small and predatory reptiliomorphs. Many were aquatic, giving birth to young with gills. *Seymouria* was a land-based form.

Limb bones were heavily built and powerfully muscled

Toes were short and composed of sturdy bones

Westlothiana probably preyed on insects.

Limbs are suited for life on the ground

LIZZIE THE LIZARD

Westlothiana from the Early Carboniferous—nicknamed "Lizzie the lizard"—was originally regarded as the first reptile. However, it was later thought to be only distantly related to amniotes, or even a primitive kind of tetrapod.

Long, flexible body

Lizardlike tail

WESTLOTHIANA

INTRODUCING AMNIOTES

THE AMNIOTES WERE animals that dominated life on land in the Late Carboniferous. They were the first creatures to protect their unborn babies in an amniotic egg, which survived on land. Amniotes comprise two groups: synapsids (mammals and their relatives) and reptiles. Many later did away with the eggshell and retained their embryos inside the body.

Shell can breathe

Embryo is protected by the outer shell

Yolk feeds the embryo

waste collects in allantois

AMNIOTE EGGS
Amniotic eggs have a shell that can let gases in and out. It protects the embryo from drying out on land. The embryo is fed by the yolk, and a sac called the allantois stores waste.

SKULL OF
PALEOTHYRIS

EARLY FOSSIL AMNIOTES
Certain skeletal features unique to synapsids and reptiles, such as their teeth, allow scientists to recognize early fossil amniotes without direct proof that they laid amniotic eggs.

The rotten tree stumps that trapped Hylonomus *mostly belonged to Sigillaria, a giant club moss*

Hylonomus *was attracted by millipedes and other insects that fell into the hollow*

Trapped at the bottom of the hollow tree stump, Hylonomus *died of starvation*

Hylonomus *and other*
early reptiles had jaws
with muscles that were
more powerful than
earlier tetrapods'

Sturdy skull
and sharp
pointed teeth

HYLONOMUS
- Group: Captorhinomorpha
- Family: Protorothyrididae
- Time: Carboniferous period
  (355–295 MYA)
- Size: 8 in (20 cm) long
- Diet: Millipedes and other
  arthropods
- Habitat: Tropical forest floors

LIFE AND DEATH
OF HYLONOMUS
The early reptile *Hylonomus*
("forest mouse") comes from a
famous fossil site called Joggins
in Nova Scotia, Canada. Here,
specimens were preserved with
full skeletons including the
smallest bones. This remarkable
preservation occurred because
the remains were fossilized
inside forest-floor traps formed
from rotten tree stumps.

Repeated floods left mud
deposits at the base of a
tree. The sediments built up
and were later compressed
into rock.

REPTILE CLADOGRAM

REPTILES DOMINATED Earth during the Paleozoic and Mesozoic. First to appear were parareptiles, the ancestors of turtles, followed by the earliest reptiles, which were tiny insectivores. Diapsids, including lizards and snakes, evolved late in the Carboniferous. The late Permian saw the rise of the archosaurs: dinosaurs, birds, pterosaurs, and crocodiles.

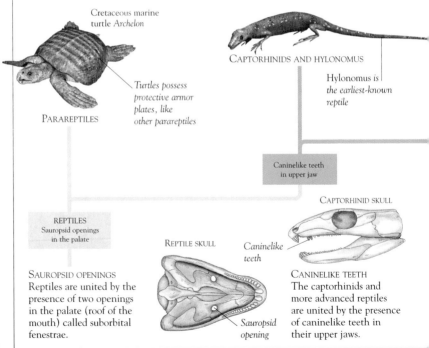

Cretaceous marine turtle *Archelon*

CAPTORHINIDS AND HYLONOMUS

Hylonomus is the earliest-known reptile

Turtles possess protective armor plates, like other parareptiles

PARAREPTILES

Caninelike teeth in upper jaw

CAPTORHINID SKULL

REPTILES
Sauropsid openings in the palate

REPTILE SKULL

Caninelike teeth

SAUROPSID OPENINGS
Reptiles are united by the presence of two openings in the palate (roof of the mouth) called suborbital fenestrae.

Sauropsid opening

CANINELIKE TEETH
The captorhinids and more advanced reptiles are united by the presence of caninelike teeth in their upper jaws.

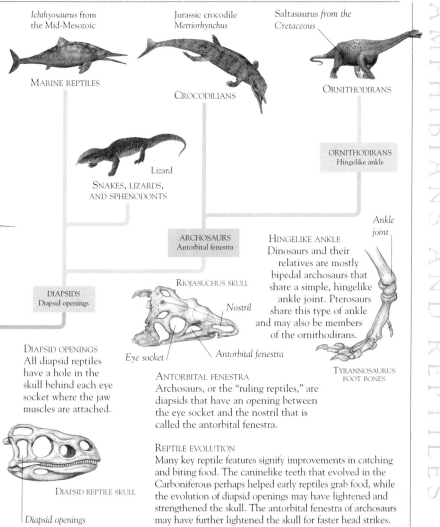

Ichthyosaurus from the Mid-Mesozoic

Jurassic crocodile *Metriorhynchus*

Saltasaurus from the Cretaceous

MARINE REPTILES

CROCODILIANS

ORNITHODIRANS

Lizard

SNAKES, LIZARDS, AND SPHENODONTS

ORNITHODIRANS
Hingelike ankle

Ankle joint

ARCHOSAURS
Antorbital fenestra

HINGELIKE ANKLE
Dinosaurs and their relatives are mostly bipedal archosaurs that share a simple, hingelike ankle joint. Pterosaurs share this type of ankle and may also be members of the ornithodirans.

DIAPSIDS
Diapsid openings

RIOJASUCHUS SKULL

Nostril

Eye socket

Antorbital fenestra

TYRANNOSAURUS
FOOT BONES

DIAPSID OPENINGS
All diapsid reptiles have a hole in the skull behind each eye socket where the jaw muscles are attached.

ANTORBITAL FENESTRA
Archosaurs, or the "ruling reptiles," are diapsids that have an opening between the eye socket and the nostril that is called the antorbital fenestra.

REPTILE EVOLUTION
Many key reptile features signify improvements in catching and biting food. The caninelike teeth that evolved in the Carboniferous perhaps helped early reptiles grab food, while the evolution of diapsid openings may have lightened and strengthened the skull. The antorbital fenestra of archosaurs may have further lightened the skull for faster head strikes.

DIAPSID REPTILE SKULL

Diapsid openings

101

PARAREPTILES

THIS GROUP OF unusual reptiles includes small lizardlike forms as well as larger animals. Unlike most reptiles, many parareptiles lack holes, called fenestrae, at the back of their skulls. Many parareptiles appear to have been herbivorous, while others probably ate insects and other arthropods.

Conical defensive spikes covering back

PROCOLOPHONIDS
The procolophonids were parareptiles that lived worldwide from the Late Permian to the Late Triassic. They were shaped like chunky lizards, with broad-cheeked skulls and backward-pointing spikes on their cheeks.

Short tail

Large eyes suggest good vision

Strong limbs perhaps used for digging

FRAGMENTED
PROCOLOPHON
FOSSIL

Robust, rounded body

SCUTOSAURUS

Skull surface covered in bumps

ARMORED SKULL
Elginia was a Late Permian parareptile that had a pair of long horns and a head covered in spikes.

Short legs and toes suggest that Procolophon *was not a fast runner*

ELGINIA SKULL

Large, projecting cheek flanges (plate-like projections), perhaps for defense

Nasal horn developed in adults

Blunt, broad snout with broad mouth

Large spikes growing from lower jaw

PAREIASAURS

Giant pareiasaurs like *Scutosaurus* ("shield lizards") were parareptiles with massive, rounded bodies. Their sawlike teeth were good for chewing tough foliage. *Scutosaurus* and its relatives were covered with bony spikes, bumps, and horns.

Powerfully muscled limbs for supporting weight

MESOSAURS

Distant relatives of the parareptiles, and all other reptiles, were the mesosaurs, small aquatic reptiles from Permian times. They preyed on fish and arthropods.

FOSSIL MESOSAURS

SCUTOSAURUS

- Group: Procolophonia
- Family: Pareiasauridae
- Time: Permian period (295–250 MYA)
- Size: 8 ft (2.5 m) long
- Diet: Ferns and other plants
- Habitat: Marshes and floodplains

TURTLES

TURTLES, OR CHELONIANS, are unique
reptiles that first appeared in the Triassic
as small amphibious omnivores (eaters of a
varied diet, including plants and animals).
During the Mesozoic, they diverged into land-
dwelling herbivores, freshwater omnivores and
predators, and giant, fully marine creatures
with a diet of sponges and jellyfish. Today
they flourish as more than 250 species.

*The largest
meiolaniids had
skulls more than
12 in (30 cm)
wide*

MEIOLANIID
SKULL

*Large side
horns, perhaps
used in fighting*

*Nostrils high
up on the
snout*

HORNED LAND TURTLES
The meiolaniids were a group
of giant land turtles that lived
from the Cretaceous to the
recent past. Large horns on their
skulls meant that they could not
pull their heads into their shells.

MARINE GIANT
Seagoing turtles first evolved in the Early
Cretaceous, and are just one of many groups
that developed into giant forms. *Archelon*,
among the biggest of all, reached nearly 13 ft
(4 m) long—twice the length of a large modern
marine turtle. Turtles never grew much larger
than this because they still needed to come
ashore and lay eggs, and this meant they had to
be able to support their weight on land.

SHELL STRUCTURE

All turtles possess a shell—their most distinctive feature. This is actually a modified rib cage covered by armor plates. Unlike any other vertebrate, turtles have modified their skeletons so that their shoulder and hip girdles are inside their rib cage.

Hind flippers shorter and broader than the front ones

Male turtles have shorter tails than female ones

INTERIOR OF ARARIPEMYS SHELL

ARCHELON

Female sea turtles use their hind paddles to dig nests

Shell may have been covered in thick skin, rather than armor plates

Of five fingers in the paddle, the third and fourth were longest

Large winglike paddles used for underwater flight

ARCHELON

- Group: Testudinata
- Family: Chelonoidea
- Time: Cretaceous period (135–65 MYA)
- Size: 13 ft (4 m) long
- Diet: Probably jellyfish
- Habitat: Warm, shallow seas

DIVERSIFYING DIAPSIDS

LATE IN THE PERMIAN, the diapsids—the reptilian group that includes lizards, archosaurs, and marine ichthyosaurs and plesiosaurs—underwent a burst of evolution. Evolving from small insect-eating ancestors of the Carboniferous, the diapsids soon produced gliders, swimmers, and diggers. Many of the new diapsids were grouped together as the neodiapsids.

Each wing was supported by 22 curving, rodlike bones

Serrated crest

The back of the skull resembles that of lizards. This once led experts to think that lizards descended from younginiforms

Long, narrow snout

YOUNGINA SKULL

Sharp, conical teeth for catching insects

COELUROSAURAVUS
- Group: Diapsida
- Family: Coelurosauravidae
- Time: Permian period (295–250 MYA)
- Size: 2 ft (60 cm) long
- Diet: Insects
- Habitat: Open forests

YOUNGINA AND RELATIVES

The younginiforms were among the most primitive neodiapsids. They were agile Permian reptiles with short necks and large holes at the back of the skull. Some were aquatic, but most were land-dwellers.

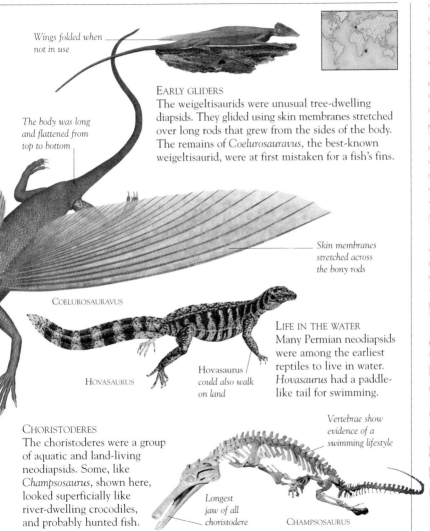

Wings folded when not in use

The body was long and flattened from top to bottom

EARLY GLIDERS

The weigeltisaurids were unusual tree-dwelling diapsids. They glided using skin membranes stretched over long rods that grew from the sides of the body. The remains of *Coelurosauravus*, the best-known weigeltisaurid, were at first mistaken for a fish's fins.

Skin membranes stretched across the bony rods

COELUROSAURAVUS

HOVASAURUS

Hovasaurus could also walk on land

LIFE IN THE WATER

Many Permian neodiapsids were among the earliest reptiles to live in water. *Hovasaurus* had a paddle-like tail for swimming.

CHORISTODERES

The choristoderes were a group of aquatic and land-living neodiapsids. Some, like *Champsosaurus*, shown here, looked superficially like river-dwelling crocodiles, and probably hunted fish.

Vertebrae show evidence of a swimming lifestyle

Longest jaw of all choristodere

CHAMPSOSAURUS

107

MOSASAURS

SEA LIZARDS called mosasaurs ruled the continental seas of the Cretaceous. These creatures grew to more than 50 ft (15 m) long and were among the most awesome marine predators of all time. With their strong jaws, mosasaurs preyed on fish, turtles, and plesiosaurs.

Deep but narrow tail like a living sea snake's

TYLOSAURUS
This giant, long-skulled mosasaur was part of a group called the varanoids. One of its most distinctive features was a hard, bony tip to the snout, which it may have used to hit and stun its prey.

Like modern sea creatures, Tylosaurus probably had a dark upper surface and a light underside

Mosasaurs had scales covering their body

TYLOSAURUS

Bony tip to snout

Mosasaurs not only had teeth lining their jaws, they also had teeth on the bones of their palate

MOSASAUR SENSES
Like their land relatives, such as gila monsters and monitor lizards, mosasaurs probably had long, forked tongues. Their skulls show that they had Jacobson's organ, used by snakes and lizards to detect scent particles in air or water.

MONITOR LIZARD

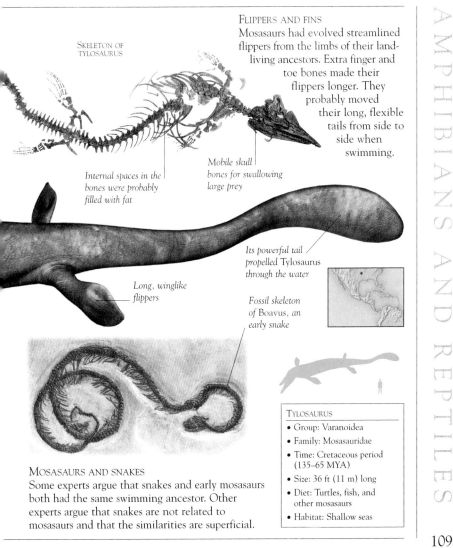

SKELETON OF
TYLOSAURUS

FLIPPERS AND FINS
Mosasaurs had evolved streamlined
flippers from the limbs of their land-
living ancestors. Extra finger and
toe bones made their
flippers longer. They
probably moved
their long, flexible
tails from side to
side when
swimming.

*Internal spaces in the
bones were probably
filled with fat*

*Mobile skull
bones for swallowing
large prey*

*Its powerful tail
propelled Tylosaurus
through the water*

*Long, winglike
flippers*

*Fossil skeleton
of Boavus, an
early snake*

MOSASAURS AND SNAKES
Some experts argue that snakes and early mosasaurs
both had the same swimming ancestor. Other
experts argue that snakes are not related to
mosasaurs and that the similarities are superficial.

TYLOSAURUS

- Group: Varanoidea
- Family: Mosasauridae
- Time: Cretaceous period
  (135–65 MYA)
- Size: 36 ft (11 m) long
- Diet: Turtles, fish, and
  other mosasaurs
- Habitat: Shallow seas

PLACODONTS AND NOTHOSAURS

THESE TWO GROUPS of creatures were marine reptiles. They were related to plesiosaurs and formed part of a larger group called the sauropterygia. Placodonts and nothosaurs were largely restricted to the warm, shallow seas of Triassic Europe, northern Africa, and Asia, and most were about 3 ft (1 m) long.

Fanglike teeth

NOTHOSAURUS
Nothosaurs were amphibious predators. The best-known of them is *Nothosaurus*, of which eight species have been found in Europe and the Middle East. In the Early Triassic, *Nothosaurus* lived in a shallow sea over what is now Israel.

Shoulder and chest bones formed large, flattened plates

NOTHOSAURUS

SHELLFISH DIET
Some placodonts, such as *Placodus*, had peglike teeth, which they probably used to pluck shellfish from the sea floor.

Flattened teeth for crushing food

Peglike teeth stuck out of the front of the jaws

The lower-jaw teeth were wide and rounded

UPPER JAW OF PLACODUS

LOWER JAW OF PLACODUS

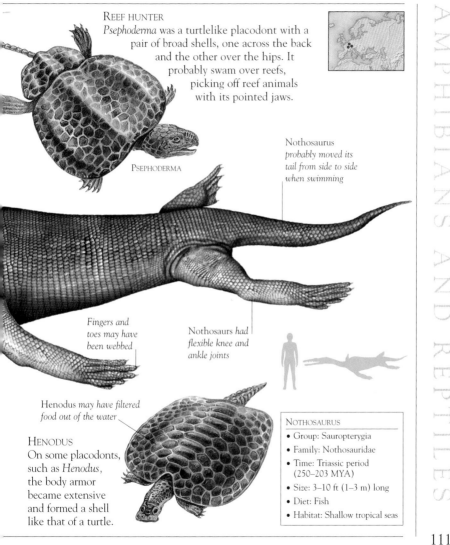

REEF HUNTER
Psephoderma was a turtlelike placodont with a pair of broad shells, one across the back and the other over the hips. It probably swam over reefs, picking off reef animals with its pointed jaws.

PSEPHODERMA

Nothosaurus *probably moved its tail from side to side when swimming*

Fingers and toes may have been webbed

Nothosaurs *had flexible knee and ankle joints*

Henodus *may have filtered food out of the water*

HENODUS
On some placodonts, such as *Henodus*, the body armor became extensive and formed a shell like that of a turtle.

NOTHOSAURUS
- Group: Sauropterygia
- Family: Nothosauridae
- Time: Triassic period (250–203 MYA)
- Size: 3–10 ft (1–3 m) long
- Diet: Fish
- Habitat: Shallow tropical seas

SHORT-NECKED PLESIOSAURS

PLESIOSAURS WERE MARINE REPTILES that belonged to the sauropterygia group. All plesiosaurs had four winglike flippers, which they probably used to "fly" underwater in much the same way as marine turtles or penguins do. While many plesiosaurs had long necks and small skulls, others, the pliosaurs, were short-necked and had enormous skulls.

SOUTHERN-HEMISPHERE GIANT
Kronosaurus was a giant pliosaur found in Australia and South America. It is best known from the reconstructed skeleton displayed at the Harvard Museum in Cambridge, MA. Pliosaurs like *Kronosaurus* lived worldwide throughout the Jurassic and Cretaceous periods.

Flippers formed of numerous finger and toe bones

Large eye socket

Water flows out from external nostrils

Water enters mouth into the internal nostrils

PLESIOSAURUS SKULL

UNDERWATER SNIFFING
Plesiosaurs had "internal nostrils" separate from external ones, which were used for "sniffing" the water, as sharks do, to detect prey.

The biggest teeth were 10 in (25 cm) long

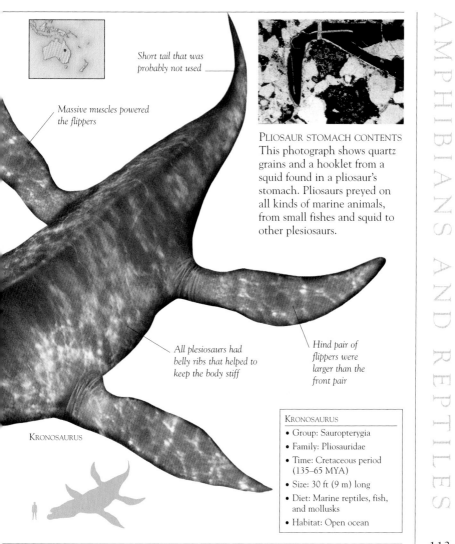

Short tail that was probably not used

Massive muscles powered the flippers

PLIOSAUR STOMACH CONTENTS
This photograph shows quartz grains and a hooklet from a squid found in a pliosaur's stomach. Pliosaurs preyed on all kinds of marine animals, from small fishes and squid to other plesiosaurs.

All plesiosaurs had belly ribs that helped to keep the body stiff

Hind pair of flippers were larger than the front pair

KRONOSAURUS

KRONOSAURUS
- Group: Sauropterygia
- Family: Pliosauridae
- Time: Cretaceous period (135–65 MYA)
- Size: 30 ft (9 m) long
- Diet: Marine reptiles, fish, and mollusks
- Habitat: Open ocean

LONG-NECKED PLESIOSAURS

WHILE SOME PLESIOSAURS were large-headed predators, others had small skulls and very long necks. One group of plesiosaurs, the elasmosaurs, had necks up to 16 ft (5 m) long. Most long-necked plesiosaurs fed on fish and mollusks, though some may have eaten sea-floor invertebrates; others perhaps preyed on other marine reptiles. Both short- and long-necked plesiosaurs became extinct at the very end of the Cretaceous.

LONG NECKS
Elasmosaurus had 72 vertebrae in its neck, more than any other plesiosaur, or indeed any other animal. Studies suggest that its neck was fairly flexible, but experts are still unsure about the way it was used.

Light skull with interlocking teeth

PLATE LIZARD

Elasmosaurus was a Late Cretaceous representative of the elasmosaurs, a group of long-necked plesiosaurs that originated in the Jurassic. Its name means "plate lizard" and comes from the platelike shoulder bones that covered its chest and formed its arm sockets. The huge muscles that powered its flippers were anchored to these bones.

ELASMOSAURUS
- Group: Plesiosauria
- Family: Elasmosauridae
- Time: Cretaceous period (135–65 MYA)
- Size: 46 ft (14 m) long
- Diet: Fish and swimming mollusks
- Habitat: Shallow seas

Flippers with pointed tips

ICHTHYOSAURS

THESE MESOZOIC MARINE REPTILES resemble sharks or dolphins. Fossils preserved with impressions of skin show that ichthyosaurs such as *Ichthyosaurus* had a triangular dorsal fin and a forked, vertical tail like a shark's. While smaller ichthyosaurs were about 3 ft (1 m) long, giant ichthyosaurs grew to over 65 ft (20 m), making them the largest marine reptiles ever.

SHARK-SHAPED REPTILE
Many fossils of *Ichthyosaurus*, the best-known ichthyosaur, have been found in Jurassic rocks in England and Germany.

Small, pointed teeth

Nostril was positioned close to the eye

ICHTHYOSAURUS

Long, slim jaws

This ichthyosaur fossil is preserved with its babies

BIRTH AND BABIES
Some ichthyosaurs have been found with the bones of babies preserved in their abdominal region. At first, experts thought that these babies were stomach contents.

FOSSIL OF PREGNANT STENOPTERYGIUS

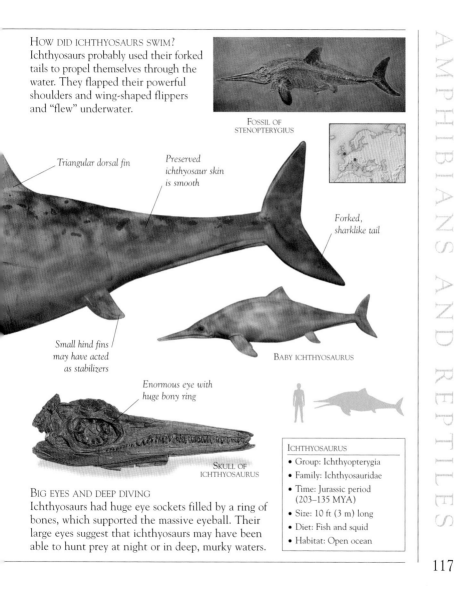

HOW DID ICHTHYOSAURS SWIM?
Ichthyosaurs probably used their forked
tails to propel themselves through the
water. They flapped their powerful
shoulders and wing-shaped flippers
and "flew" underwater.

FOSSIL OF
STENOPTERYGIUS

Triangular dorsal fin

*Preserved
ichthyosaur skin
is smooth*

*Forked,
sharklike tail*

*Small hind fins
may have acted
as stabilizers*

BABY ICHTHYOSAURUS

*Enormous eye with
huge bony ring*

SKULL OF
ICHTHYOSAURUS

BIG EYES AND DEEP DIVING
Ichthyosaurs had huge eye sockets filled by a ring of
bones, which supported the massive eyeball. Their
large eyes suggest that ichthyosaurs may have been
able to hunt prey at night or in deep, murky waters.

ICHTHYOSAURUS
- Group: Ichthyopterygia
- Family: Ichthyosauridae
- Time: Jurassic period
  (203–135 MYA)
- Size: 10 ft (3 m) long
- Diet: Fish and squid
- Habitat: Open ocean

EARLY RULING REPTILE GROUPS

ARCHOSAURS—THE GROUP OF animals that includes crocodiles, dinosaurs, and birds—belong to a larger group called the archosauromorphs or "ruling reptile forms." Out of the many archosauromorph groups evolved the lizard-like meat-eating prolacertiforms, and the plant-eating trilophosaurs and rhynchosaurs.

GIRAFFE-NECKED FISHER
The Triassic reptile *Tanystropheus* had a neck twice as long as its body. Most of its fossils are found in marine rocks, so it may have swum or caught fish at the water's edge.

Lizardlike body shape

Tanystropheus had long legs

Toes may have been webbed for swimming

All trilophosaurs were less than 3 ft (1 m) in length

TRILOPHOSAURS
This was an archosauromorph with a robust skull and beaklike snout tip. It had broad teeth for slicing and chewing tough plants.

Long limbs suited to running and digging

SKELETON OF
TRILOPHOSAURUS

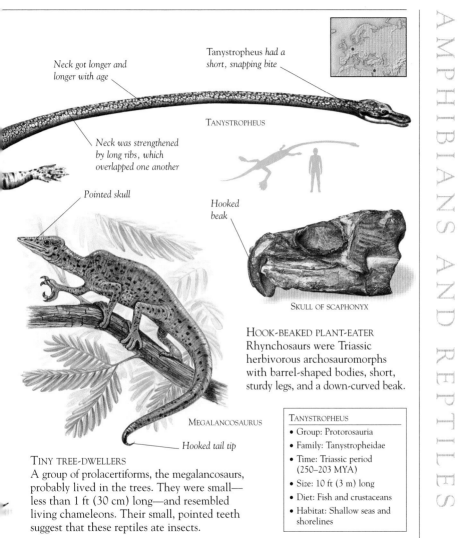

*Neck got longer and
longer with age*

*Tanystropheus had a
short, snapping bite*

TANYSTROPHEUS

*Neck was strengthened
by long ribs, which
overlapped one another*

Pointed skull

*Hooked
beak*

SKULL OF SCAPHONYX

HOOK-BEAKED PLANT-EATER
Rhynchosaurs were Triassic
herbivorous archosauromorphs
with barrel-shaped bodies, short,
sturdy legs, and a down-curved beak.

MEGALANCOSAURUS

Hooked tail tip

TINY TREE-DWELLERS
A group of prolacertiforms, the megalancosaurs,
probably lived in the trees. They were small—
less than 1 ft (30 cm) long—and resembled
living chameleons. Their small, pointed teeth
suggest that these reptiles ate insects.

TANYSTROPHEUS
- Group: Protorosauria
- Family: Tanystropheidae
- Time: Triassic period
  (250–203 MYA)
- Size: 10 ft (3 m) long
- Diet: Fish and crustaceans
- Habitat: Shallow seas and
  shorelines

119

CROCODILE-GROUP REPTILES

ARCHOSAURS—CROCODILES, PTEROSAURS, dinosaurs, and their relatives—diversified into many groups during the Triassic. Early on, archosaurs split into two groups, both of which have living members today. Ornithodirans included pterosaurs, dinosaurs, and birds. Crocodylotarsians included numerous extinct groups and crocodiles.

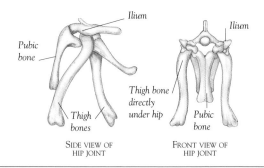

Long, slender tail

Powerful leg bones suggest that Prestosuchus *could run at high speeds*

DEEP-SKULLED GIANTS
Many crocodile-group reptiles were land-living predators, called rauisuchians. Some were huge, reaching lengths of up to 33 ft (10 m). *Prestosuchus* was from Triassic Brazil. Similar rauisuchians lived in Europe, Argentina, and elsewhere.

HOW RAUISUCHIANS WALKED
Rauisuchians had a stance that was similar to that of the dinosaurs, with their legs held beneath the body. The flexibility of the backbone shows that they ran with a bounding gait.

Ilium

Pubic bone

Thigh bones

SIDE VIEW OF
HIP JOINT

Ilium

Thigh bone directly under hip

Pubic bone

FRONT VIEW OF
HIP JOINT

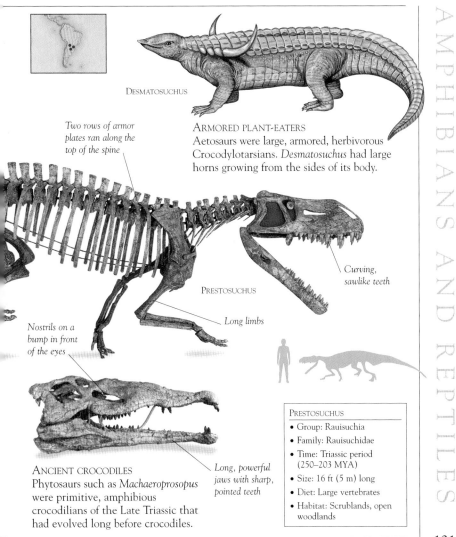

DESMATOSUCHUS

Two rows of armor plates ran along the top of the spine

ARMORED PLANT-EATERS

Aetosaurs were large, armored, herbivorous Crocodylotarsians. *Desmatosuchus* had large horns growing from the sides of its body.

Curving, sawlike teeth

PRESTOSUCHUS

Long limbs

Nostrils on a bump in front of the eyes

ANCIENT CROCODILES

Phytosaurs such as *Machaeroprosopus* were primitive, amphibious crocodilians of the Late Triassic that had evolved long before crocodiles.

Long, powerful jaws with sharp, pointed teeth

PRESTOSUCHUS
- Group: Rauisuchia
- Family: Rauisuchidae
- Time: Triassic period (250–203 MYA)
- Size: 16 ft (5 m) long
- Diet: Large vertebrates
- Habitat: Scrublands, open woodlands

CROCODILIANS

APART FROM BIRDS, crocodilians are the last surviving archosaurs. They evolved at about the same time as the dinosaurs and have a 200-million-year history. In the dinosaur age, when climates were warm, these cold-blooded creatures spread throughout the world. Some lived on land, others in the sea.

Body lacked armor of other crocodilians

Skull broader behind the eyes than in front

Long, thin jaw with pointed teeth

Small but sharp teeth

SEA CROCODILIAN
Metriorhynchus was a seagoing crocodilian from the Mesozoic. Its webbed toes and fingers formed paddles for efficient swimming, and its jaws bristled with razor-sharp teeth for seizing fish and squid.

Slender jaws

SLENDER-JAWED FISH-EATER
Gavials are crocodilians dating back 50 million years. They are now only found in India.

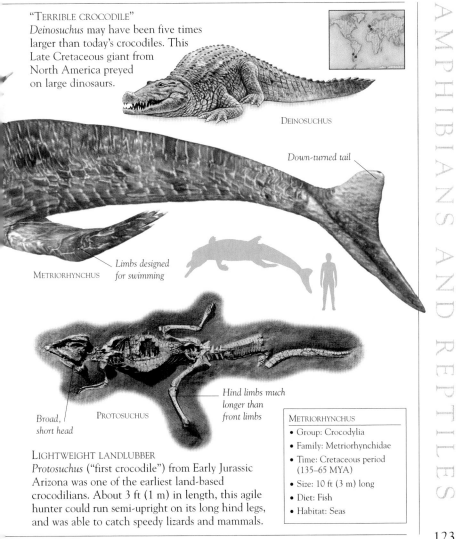

"TERRIBLE CROCODILE"
Deinosuchus may have been five times
larger than today's crocodiles. This
Late Cretaceous giant from
North America preyed
on large dinosaurs.

DEINOSUCHUS

Down-turned tail

METRIORHYNCHUS

*Limbs designed
for swimming*

*Hind limbs much
longer than
front limbs*

*Broad,
short head*

PROTOSUCHUS

LIGHTWEIGHT LANDLUBBER
Protosuchus ("first crocodile") from Early Jurassic
Arizona was one of the earliest land-based
crocodilians. About 3 ft (1 m) in length, this agile
hunter could run semi-upright on its long hind legs,
and was able to catch speedy lizards and mammals.

METRIORHYNCHUS
- Group: Crocodylia
- Family: Metriorhynchidae
- Time: Cretaceous period
  (135–65 MYA)
- Size: 10 ft (3 m) long
- Diet: Fish
- Habitat: Seas

EARLY PTEROSAURS

PTEROSAURS WERE flying archosaurs that may have been closely related to dinosaurs. A pterosaur's wings were made of skin that stretched from the end of its incredibly long fourth finger to its body and back legs. Fossils show that some pterosaurs had furry bodies and may have been warm-blooded. Early pterosaurs were small compared to later types, with a wingspan of up to 10 ft (3 m).

Fossil skeleton of Dimorphodon

PRIMITIVE PTEROSAURS
Dimorphodon was an Early Jurassic pterosaur, notable for its huge skull and large, pointed teeth at the front of its jaw.

EXCELLENT FLIERS
Pterosaurs had large eyes with excellent vision. The parts of the brain responsible for sight and control of movement were well developed and similar to those of modern birds.

Short wrist bones of early pterosaurs

ANUROGNATHUS

INSECT CATCHERS
Anurognathids had short, high skulls, sharply pointed teeth, and long, slim wings. These features suggest that they were fast-flying predators that fed on insects.

ANUROGNATHUS
- Group: Pterosauria
- Family: Rhamphorhynchoidea
- Time: Jurassic period (203–135 MYA)
- Size: Wingspan 2 ft 6 in (50 cm)
- Diet: Insects, possibly lacewings
- Habitat: Seashores, riverbanks, and woodlands

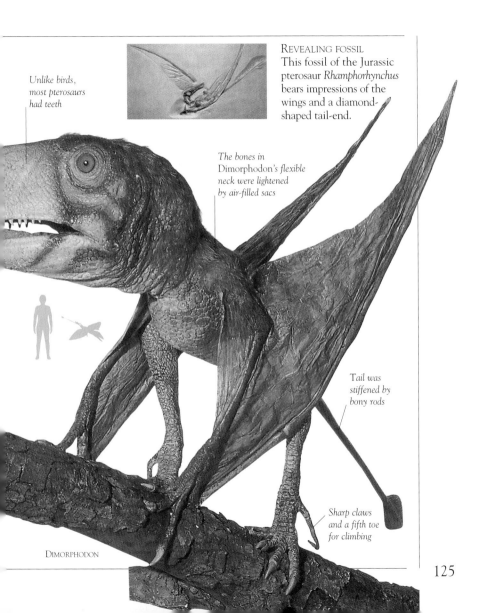

Unlike birds, most pterosaurs had teeth

This fossil of the Jurassic pterosaur *Rhamphorhynchus* bears impressions of the wings and a diamond-shaped tail-end.

The bones in Dimorphodon's *flexible neck were lightened by air-filled sacs*

Tail was stiffened by bony rods

Sharp claws and a fifth toe for climbing

DIMORPHODON

125

DIMORPHODON

THE MOST STRIKING feature of *Dimorphodon* ("two-form tooth") was its enormous puffinlike head. It had a short neck, and a long tail that ended in a diamond shape. The tail could only be moved near the base, helping to steer the animal. *Dimorphodon* had two types of teeth—long front ones and small cheek teeth. It may have been a clumsy walker.

Leathery wings

Large, toothed beak

Diamond-shaped flap of skin at tail end used as a rudder

DIMORPHODON

- Group: Rhamphorhynchoidea
- Family: Dimorphodontidae
- Time: Jurassic period (203–135 MYA)
- Size: 4 ft (1.4 m) long
- Diet: Small animals and fish
- Habitat: Shores, river banks

OPPORTUNISTIC HUNTER

Remains of *Dimorphodon* and related pterosaurs have been found in former sea and riverside areas, so they may have lived in a variety of habitats. This group probably preyed on small animals, such as insects, lizards and other small reptiles, fish, and crustaceans. Experts do not know whether they caught their prey on the wing, or while standing on all fours. It is possible that *Dimorphodon* spent most of its time on cliffs or branches, from which it launched itself into flight.

127

ADVANCED PTEROSAURS

PTERODACTYLOIDS WERE advanced pterosaurs that came to rule the Cretaceous skies. However, by the end of this period, only one or two species survived. Pterosaurs may have died out as newly evolving water birds took over their habitats.

WINGS AND NO TEETH
Pteranodon, meaning "wings and no teeth," is one of the most famous pterosaurs that inhabited North America. It had a large head crest, and the shape of its lower jaw suggests that it had a pouch under its bill like a pelican's.

Long, backward-pointing crest

MALES AND FEMALES
Different specimens of *Pteranodon* have differently shaped head crests. Some have a large, very prominent crest, others a small crest. These two kinds have been found together, so it seems that they are males and females of the same species. The males are probably the ones with the bigger crests, which they used to attract females.

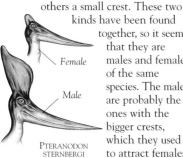

Female

Male

PTERANODON
STERNBERGI

PTERODAUSTRO
Some pterodactyloids had long jaws and hundreds of slim teeth. The best example is *Pterodaustro* from South America. Its lower jaws were filled with about 1,000 bristlelike teeth, through which it strained out plankton from the water.

Bristle-like teeth

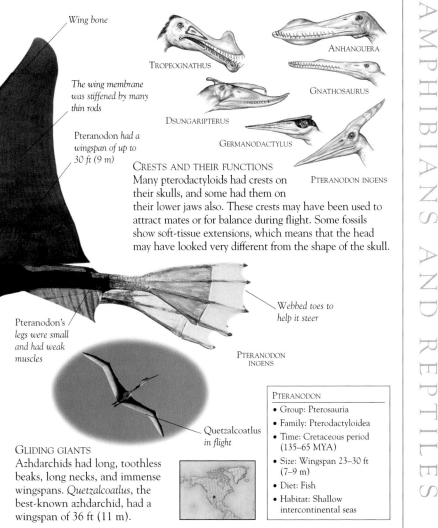

Wing bone

TROPEOGNATHUS

ANHANGUERA

The wing membrane was stiffened by many thin rods

GNATHOSAURUS

DSUNGARIPTERUS

Pteranodon had a wingspan of up to 30 ft (9 m)

GERMANODACTYLUS

PTERANODON INGENS

CRESTS AND THEIR FUNCTIONS

Many pterodactyloids had crests on their skulls, and some had them on their lower jaws also. These crests may have been used to attract mates or for balance during flight. Some fossils show soft-tissue extensions, which means that the head may have looked very different from the shape of the skull.

Webbed toes to help it steer

Pteranodon's legs were small and had weak muscles

PTERANODON INGENS

Quetzalcoatlus in flight

GLIDING GIANTS

Azhdarchids had long, toothless beaks, long necks, and immense wingspans. *Quetzalcoatlus*, the best-known azhdarchid, had a wingspan of 36 ft (11 m).

PTERANODON
• Group: Pterosauria
• Family: Pterodactyloidea
• Time: Cretaceous period (135–65 MYA)
• Size: Wingspan 23–30 ft (7–9 m)
• Diet: Fish
• Habitat: Shallow intercontinental seas

DINOSAURS AND BIRDS

A BEE-SIZED hummingbird seems worlds apart from a dinosaur that is as heavy as a whale. Yet birds almost certainly evolved from feathered dinosaurs. This section brings to life those ancient reptiles that between them dominated life on land for an astonishing 160 million years.

WHAT ARE DINOSAURS?

ABOUT 225 MILLION YEARS AGO, a new group of reptiles appeared on Earth. Like all reptiles, they had waterproof, scaly skin and young that hatched from eggs. These were the dinosaurs. For the next 160 million years they ruled the world, before finally becoming extinct.

Powerful neck muscles were needed for ripping flesh from prey

LAND LEGS
Dinosaurs were land animals—they could not swim or fly. All dinosaurs had four limbs, but many, such as this *Tyrannosaurus*, walked on only their two back legs, leaving the front legs free for other tasks.

Tyrannosaurus killed prey with its strong jaws and sharp teeth

Clawed hands

TYRANNOSAURUS
(LIZARD-HIPPED)

DINOSAUR DIVISIONS
Dinosaurs are divided into two groups based on the shape of their hips: saurischians (lizard-hipped) and ornithischians (bird-hipped). Saurischians had one lower hip-bone pointing downward and forward, and the other downward and backward. Ornithischians had their two lower hipbones pointing downward and backward.

IGUANODON
(BIRD-HIPPED)

Period	Millions of years ago	Examples of dinosaurs from each period	
CRETACEOUS	65–145		Triceratops
JURASSIC	145–208		Stegosaurus
TRIASSIC	208–245		Herrerasaurus

TIMELINES
Dinosaurs lived through three periods in Earth's history—Triassic, Jurassic, and Cretaceous. Different species of dinosaurs lived and died throughout these three periods. Each species may have survived for only 2–3 million years.

Waterproof skin was covered in scales

Muscular tail balanced the front of the body

LIVING REPTILES
Modern reptiles, such as this iguana, have many features in common with dinosaurs, such as scaly skin and sharp claws. But many scientists believe that birds, rather than modern reptiles, are the closest living relatives of the dinosaurs.

Powerful legs

TYPES OF DINOSAURS

DINOSAUR DESIGNS were varied
and spectacular. A group of dinosaurs
called the sauropods were the largest
land animals that ever lived. The
smallest dinosaurs were chicken-
sized. Some dinosaurs had armored
skin for protection;
others could run
fast to escape
being hunted.

DINOSAUR TERROR
Tyrannosaurus
and other fierce
meat-eaters had
huge, sharp teeth
with which they
killed prey.

HERBIVORES
There were many more
herbivores (plant-eaters) than
carnivores (meat-eaters) in the
dinosaur world. A herbivore
called *Stegosaurus* had a sharp
beak for cropping leaves
off plants.

ONE OF THE BIGGEST
Heavier than eight elephants and more than
80 ft (24 m) long, *Barosaurus*, a sauropod, was
one of the biggest dinosaurs.

Compsognathus
reached just below
Barosaurus' ankle

Barosaurus' *tail*
was about 42 ft
(13 m) long

Compsognathus *had long legs for running fast*

See the size of Compsognathus compared to Barosaurus *at the bottom of page 134*

Barosaurus' *extremely long neck was balanced by its very long tail*

Rows of thick plates

ONE OF THE SMALLEST
At 3 ft (1 m) long, *Compsognathus* was among the smallest dinosaurs.

Sharp spines at the side

Thick legs

DINOSAUR FACTS

• There were about thirty times more herbivores than carnivores.

• The fastest dinosaurs were the theropods, which ran on two legs.

• Dinosaurs did not fly or live in the sea.

• The sauropods were the largest dinosaurs.

SPIKY PROTECTION
The plant-eating, slow-moving ankylosaurs had armored skin for protection from sharp-toothed meat-eaters. *Edmontonia* had bony plates and spikes on its skin. It lived at the same time and in the same places as *Tyrannosaurus*, so it needed all the protection its armor could give.

135

MORE TYPES OF DINOSAURS

WE WILL NEVER KNOW how many kinds of dinosaurs existed over the 160 million years of their existence. We do know that some fossils belong not to the dinosaurs but to swimming and flying relatives.

Strong, plant-chewing jaws

Arms sometimes used for walking

IGUANODON TRAVELED AROUND IN HERDS

Flexible neck

Long jaws

Hooked claw on each hand

Baryonyx walked on two legs

BARYONYX WAS ABOUT 33 FT (10 M) LONG

VERY COMMON *Iguanodon* was a common dinosaur. In one location, between 1878 and 1881, coal miners in Belgium dug up more than 39 *Iguanodon* skeletons.

VERY RARE *Baryonyx* is one of the rarest dinosaurs known. Only one specimen of this hook-clawed meat-eater has been found so far.

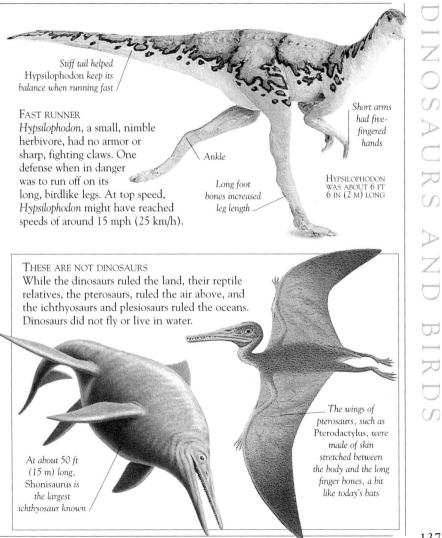

*Stiff tail helped
Hypsilophodon keep its
balance when running fast*

FAST RUNNER
Hypsilophodon, a small, nimble
herbivore, had no armor or
sharp, fighting claws. One
defense when in danger
was to run off on its
long, birdlike legs. At top speed,
Hypsilophodon might have reached
speeds of around 15 mph (25 km/h).

*Short arms
had five-
fingered
hands*

Ankle

*Long foot
bones increased
leg length*

HYPSILOPHODON
WAS ABOUT 6 FT
6 IN (2 M) LONG

THESE ARE NOT DINOSAURS
While the dinosaurs ruled the land, their reptile
relatives, the pterosaurs, ruled the air above, and
the ichthyosaurs and plesiosaurs ruled the oceans.
Dinosaurs did not fly or live in water.

*The wings of
pterosaurs, such as
Pterodactylus, were
made of skin
stretched between
the body and the long
finger bones, a bit
like today's bats*

*At about 50 ft
(15 m) long,
Shonisaurus is
the largest
ichthyosaur known*

DINOSAUR ANATOMY

THE SIZE AND SHAPE of a dinosaur's head, body, and legs help us to tell one dinosaur from another, and also tell us how the body parts were used. From the skeleton inside to the scaly skin outside, each part of a dinosaur helps build a picture of these amazing animals.

Neck muscles

BODY POWER
The shoulder and pelvic muscles were crucial areas of power for light, fast runners as well as slow, heavy plodders. The largest dinosaurs were not always the mightiest. Some of the smallest dinosaurs were powerful runners.

BRACHIOSAURUS

Pelvic muscles

Shoulder muscles

Rib cage

Elbow joint

Thigh bone

PROTECTIVE CAGE
Like all dinosaurs, *Brachiosaurus* had a cage, formed from vertebrae, ribs, and sheets of muscle, to protect the vital internal organs.

Wrist joint

Shin bone

Toe bone

FIGHTING MALES

Strength and power were not always used to kill. Male dinosaurs may have fought each other over females or to win or defend territory. Beaten, and possibly bruised, the loser would need to move on to other hunting grounds.

TWO MALE
CERATOSAURUS
FIGHTING

Hip muscles

Shoulder muscles

Muscles in neck frill

STRONG MUSCLES

Centrosaurus needed powerful muscles to move its heavy, bulky body. Muscles attached to the pelvis and shoulders pulled and lifted strong legs. When running fast, *Centrosaurus* would have been difficult to stop in its tracks.

Neck muscles

CENTROSAURUS

ORNITHOLESTES

Small and lightweight, *Ornitholestes* used much of its energy powering long legs when chasing small prey such as lizards and mammals.

Back vertebrae

Ribs

Clawed hands

ORNITHOLESTES
WAS 6 FT 6 IN
(2 M) LONG

Slender leg bones

139

HEADS

CRESTS, FRILLS, and horns adorned the heads of many dinosaurs. These helped dinosaurs identify one another or were used for signaling. A dinosaur with more spectacular headgear may have won in a fight for dominance, while horns may have been used by herbivores to ward off hungry carnivores.

Large eye socket

Toothless jaws

BIRD BEAK
Gallimimus ate plants, insects, and lizards with its long, toothless beak. Its large-eyed skull looks very much like that of a big bird.

The size of the head crest may have been recognized as a sign of strength

OVIRAPTOR

Strong jaws with beak

CENTROSAURUS
HEAD

HEAD CREST
Oviraptors may have used their head crests to signal to one another. Although toothless, their beaked jaws may have been powerful enough to crush shellfish.

HORNS AND FRILLS
The Ceratopsian group of dinosaurs had heads with a variety of frills and horns. These plant-eaters probably used such decorations to frighten off attackers as well as to attract a mate.

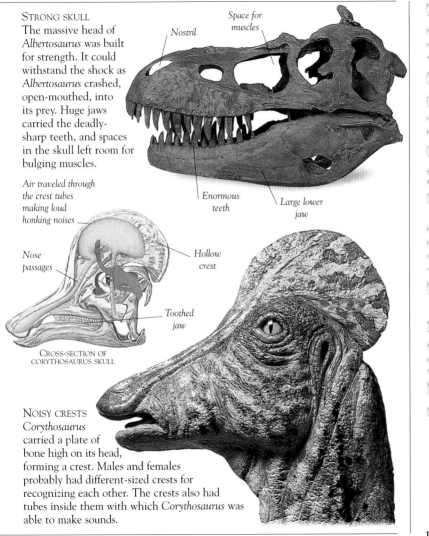

STRONG SKULL
The massive head of *Albertosaurus* was built for strength. It could withstand the shock as *Albertosaurus* crashed, open-mouthed, into its prey. Huge jaws carried the deadly-sharp teeth, and spaces in the skull left room for bulging muscles.

Space for muscles

Nostril

Air traveled through the crest tubes making loud honking noises

Enormous teeth

Large lower jaw

Nose passages

Hollow crest

Toothed jaw

CROSS-SECTION OF
CORYTHOSAURUS SKULL

NOISY CRESTS
Corythosaurus carried a plate of bone high on its head, forming a crest. Males and females probably had different-sized crests for recognizing each other. The crests also had tubes inside them with which *Corythosaurus* was able to make sounds.

NECKS

FOR DINOSAURS, the neck was a vital channel between the head and body. It carried food to the stomach and air to the lungs; nerves passed on messages to and from the brain and body, and blood traveled through the arteries and veins. All of these lifelines, as well as muscles, were supported by the neck vertebrae.

BAROSAURUS
NECK VERTEBRA

LONG AND FLEXIBLE

Plant-eating, long-necked dinosaurs like *Barosaurus* probably used their flexible necks to browse on leaves from a large area of low-lying foliage while standing still. But if they needed to, they could have reached up to the leaves in tall trees.

Muscles were attached to spines on the vertebrae

Barosaurus' neck was 30 ft (9 m) long

STRONG AND LIGHT

The long neck of *Diplodocus* was made up of 15 vertebrae. These bones had deep hollows inside them to make them lightweight, although they remained very strong. Notches on top of the vertebrae carried a strong ligament that supported the neck in the way that wires support a suspension bridge.

SHORT AND STOUT

Allosaurus, a fierce and terrifying carnivore, had a short and sturdy neck. The neck bones were cupped tightly together to give a very mobile and curved neck. When *Allosaurus*' jaws bit into prey, powerful neck muscles pulled the massive head up and back, tearing chunks of flesh from the victim.

Curved neck

Powerful jaws with huge, sharp teeth

LIKE AN OSTRICH

Gallimimus held its head high above its shoulders, like an ostrich. In this position, *Gallimimus* could swivel its head on its long neck to give good vision in all directions.

The skull may have weighed as much as 110 lb (50 kg)

Very short neck

Long, flexible neck

HEAD SUPPORT

Triceratops had an extension at the back of its skull made of solid bone. This made the skull very heavy. A short and very strong neck was needed to support the huge weight.

DINOSAUR LIMBS

Femur (thigh bone)

DINOSAURS HELD their legs directly beneath the body, unlike other reptiles, which crawl with their legs held out to the sides. Huge plant-eating dinosaurs, such as *Diplodocus*, walked on all fours, while most carnivores, such as *Albertosaurus*, walked on the two back legs, leaving the front limbs free for catching prey.

IGUANODON FOOT BONE

Knee

Muscle

Ankle

Metatarsals

Toe

MYSTERIOUS DINOSAUR

Almost all that is known of *Deinocheirus* is this huge pair of arms and hands. These forelimbs are 8 ft (2.4 m) long. It is thought that Deinocheirus belonged to a group of dinosaurs called ornithomimosaurs. The huge hands would have been used to catch and hold prey.

Long, slender arms

Fingers have 8-in (26-cm) claws

Three clawed fingers on each hand

FLESH AND BONE

The rear legs of *Albertosaurus* were powered by large muscles that pulled on the bones to make them move. The metatarsal foot bones worked as part of the leg, giving a longer stride.

Large claw on first toe

Ankle joint

Birdlike toes

GOOD SUPPORT

Five widely spread toes on the rear feet of *Diplodocus* helped support the dinosaur's enormous weight. The first three toes had claws. A padded heel, like that of an elephant, cushioned the thundering footsteps.

Foot bone extension

BRACHIOSAURUS

FLEET FOOT

Ornithomimus was one of the speediest dinosaurs. Its three foot bones were locked together, making a long extension to the leg. Running on the tips of its toes, it could take long strides. *Ornithomimus* may have reached top speeds of 37 mph (60 km/h)—fast enough to escape most predators.

Elephants are the biggest land animals alive today

ELEPHANT

LEGS LIKE PILLARS

The heaviest dinosaurs had pillarlike legs, like those of elephants. *Brachiosaurus* weighed about 50 tons, so it needed thick, strong legs to support its body.

Long rear leg

Sturdy front leg

Hoof-shaped claw

Widely spaced toes

MORE ABOUT LIMBS

THE SHAPE of a dinosaur's feet depended on whether it walked on two or four legs. Four-legged dinosaurs had similar front and rear feet, while two-legged dinosaurs could use their front feet like hands, grasping at prey or plant food.

STURDY LIMBS

Widely spaced toes and thick, sturdy limb bones helped *Triceratops* spread the weight of its massive body. The shorter forelimbs carried the weight of *Triceratops'* huge head. Much of the body weight was supported by the long and powerful rear legs. Short and stubby toes on all four feet ended in hoof-shaped claws.

The claw was the first part of Baryonyx to be discovered, giving the dinosaur the nickname "Claws"

GIANT CLAW

The powerful carnivore *Baryonyx* had one of the largest dinosaur claws known. The curved talon, which was 12 in (30 cm) long, formed a huge weapon on *Baryonyx's* hand.

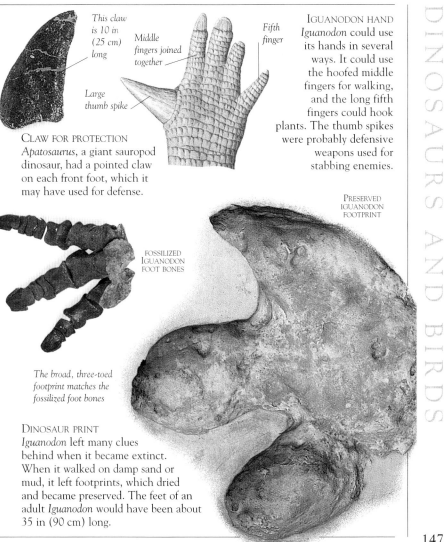

This claw is 10 in (25 cm) long

Middle fingers joined together

Fifth finger

Large thumb spike

CLAW FOR PROTECTION
Apatosaurus, a giant sauropod dinosaur, had a pointed claw on each front foot, which it may have used for defense.

IGUANODON HAND
Iguanodon could use its hands in several ways. It could use the hoofed middle fingers for walking, and the long fifth fingers could hook plants. The thumb spikes were probably defensive weapons used for stabbing enemies.

PRESERVED IGUANODON FOOTPRINT

FOSSILIZED IGUANODON FOOT BONES

The broad, three-toed footprint matches the fossilized foot bones

DINOSAUR PRINT
Iguanodon left many clues behind when it became extinct. When it walked on damp sand or mud, it left footprints, which dried and became preserved. The feet of an adult *Iguanodon* would have been about 35 in (90 cm) long.

TAILS

DINOSAUR TAILS had many uses, and tail bones can tell us a lot about them. The giant sauropods had long, tapering, flexible tails, while two-legged dinosaurs had tail bones that were locked stiffly to help give balance. Tails that ended in lumps and spikes were used as weapons.

Slender head perched on long neck

TROODON

Tail bones tightly locked together

BALANCING ACT
Scientists once believed that *Parasaurolophus* used its thick tail for swimming by sweeping it from side to side like a fish's tail. But they now think that the tail counterbalanced the front of the body.

TAIL WHIP
When defending itself, *Diplodocus* used its long tail like a huge whip to swipe at its attacker. The tail had 73 bones joined together, and made a powerful weapon with its thin, whiplike end.

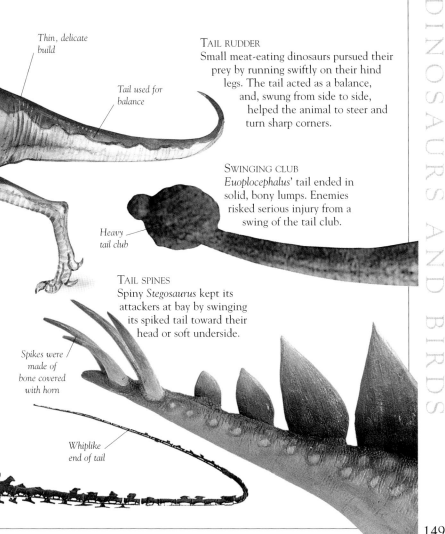

Thin, delicate
build

Tail used for
balance

TAIL RUDDER

Small meat-eating dinosaurs pursued their
prey by running swiftly on their hind
legs. The tail acted as a balance,
and, swung from side to side,
helped the animal to steer and
turn sharp corners.

SWINGING CLUB

Euoplocephalus' tail ended in
solid, bony lumps. Enemies
risked serious injury from a
swing of the tail club.

Heavy
tail club

TAIL SPINES

Spiny *Stegosaurus* kept its
attackers at bay by swinging
its spiked tail toward their
head or soft underside.

Spikes were
made of
bone covered
with horn

Whiplike
end of tail

SKIN SHAPE
Bony scutes, such as this one, were set in the skin of *Polacanthus*, an early relative of the ankylosaurs.

SKIN

TOUGH, SCALY SKIN is a trademark of all reptiles, and dinosaurs were no exception. Fossilized imprints of their skin shows patterns of big and small bumps. Some dinosaurs had spikes and scutes (plates or lumps of bone) embedded in their skin to give them protection.

WELL-ARMORED
Polacanthus' protective coat of horn-covered scutes was a barrier against the teeth of hungry predators. The arrangement of the scutes can be seen in fossil remains.

Fossilized scute

CROCODILE SCALES
Crocodiles have a leathery skin of lumpy scales. Like dinosaurs, they have scutes embedded in the back that add to the skin's toughness. The skin of crocodiles and other reptiles is also waterproof, keeping body moisture in but water out.

Crocodile skin in close-up

ARMOR-PLATED

Ankylosaurs were among the most heavily protected of all dinosaurs. Large, platelike scutes lay side by side on the upper part of its body.

SPIKES AND SCUTES

As well as scutes, the ankylosaur *Euoplocephalus* had thorn-shaped spikes across its shoulders for added protection.

FOSSIL ANKYLOSAUR
SCUTE

*Scutes were
ridged in the
middle*

*Shoulder
spike*

EUOPLOCEPHALUS

WRAPPED IN SKIN

In rare cases, a dinosaur's dead body dried up and shriveled instead of rotting away. This *Edmontosaurus* fossil has the skin impression preserved and wrapped around the skeleton.

*Small
bumps*

SKIN PATTERN

Corythosaurus had no protective armor. Its skin, a mosaic of small bumpy scales, was wrinkled and folded around the moving parts of the body.

*This fossil
is 65 million
years old*

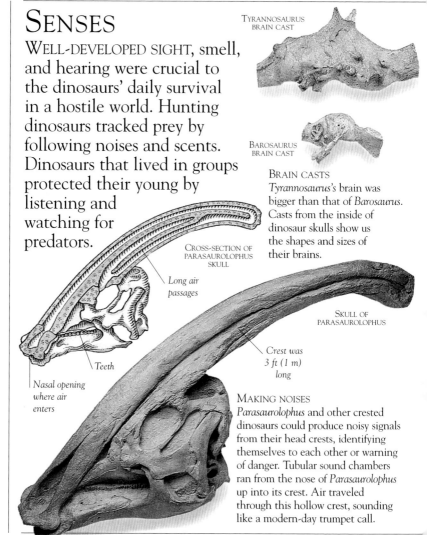

SENSES

WELL-DEVELOPED SIGHT, smell, and hearing were crucial to the dinosaurs' daily survival in a hostile world. Hunting dinosaurs tracked prey by following noises and scents. Dinosaurs that lived in groups protected their young by listening and watching for predators.

TYRANNOSAURUS
BRAIN CAST

BAROSAURUS
BRAIN CAST

BRAIN CASTS
Tyrannosaurus's brain was bigger than that of *Barosaurus*. Casts from the inside of dinosaur skulls show us the shapes and sizes of their brains.

CROSS-SECTION OF
PARASAUROLOPHUS
SKULL

Long air passages

Teeth

Nasal opening where air enters

SKULL OF
PARASAUROLOPHUS

Crest was 3 ft (1 m) long

MAKING NOISES
Parasaurolophus and other crested dinosaurs could produce noisy signals from their head crests, identifying themselves to each other or warning of danger. Tubular sound chambers ran from the nose of *Parasaurolophus* up into its crest. Air traveled through this hollow crest, sounding like a modern-day trumpet call.

VIEW FROM LEFT

VIEW FROM RIGHT

BLACK AND WHITE

VIEW FROM LEFT

VIEW FROM RIGHT

DOUBLE VISION

We do not know if dinosaurs could see in color, but the position of the eyes affected the kind of image seen. Eyes on the sides of the head, common in herbivores, sent two different pictures to the brain.

SINGLE VISION

Brain size is not always a sign of intelligence, but big-brained *Troodon* was probably one of the smartest dinosaurs. *Troodon* had large eyes and good vision. It benefitted from stereoscopic sight, which means it saw one image, the way that we do. Whether it could see in color or black and white, *Troodon* could judge distance when chasing or catching its prey.

COLOR

BLACK AND WHITE

WARM AND COLD BLOOD

REPTILES ARE COLD-BLOODED, which means that they depend on the sun's heat for warmth. Warm-blooded animals, such as mammals, produce heat from food energy within their body. Although dinosaurs were reptiles, much of their behavior was mammal-like. Scientists have wondered whether certain dinosaurs were indeed warm-blooded.

Skin "sail" was supported by spines projecting from the vertebrae

Blood vessels

CROSS-SECTION OF
MAMMAL BONE

Blood vessels

CROSS-SECTION OF
REPTILE BONE

BLOOD AND BONES
Dinosaurs had bones more like mammals than reptiles. Mammal bones contain far more blood vessels than reptile bones.

Side view of plate

Cross-section of plate

STEGOSAURUS BACK
PLATE FOSSILS

SAIL BACK
Spinosaurus had a large "sail," which may have been used for temperature control, absorbing the sun's warmth in the morning and cooling down in the breeze later in the day. *Stegosaurus* may have used its back plates in a similar way.

SPINOSAURUS

COLD-BLOODED SUNBATHER
A typical cold-blooded creature, such as a lizard, spends hours sunbathing to raise the body's temperature to a level where it can work effectively. To avoid overheating, the lizard can cool off in the shade. When it is cold at night, or in the winter, reptiles are inactive.

LIZARD SUNBATHING

Long jaws with small, pointed teeth for catching and eating fish

High blood pressure was needed to reach a brain 50 ft (15 m) above the ground

BLOOD PRESSURE
Tall dinosaurs needed high blood pressure to pump blood to their brain. But down at the level of their lungs, such high pressure would be fatal. Warm-blooded animals have a twin pressure system. Perhaps dinosaurs had a similar system.

Spinosaurus was about 40 ft (12 m) long

Feathered coat

VELOCIRAPTOR

GOOD EXAMPLE
Velociraptor is one of the best arguments for dinosaurs being warm-blooded animals. Fast and agile, *Velociraptor* had a lifestyle better suited to warm-blooded killers like wolves than to reptiles like lizards.

BRACHIOSAURUS

155

DINOSAUR LIFESTYLES

ALTHOUGH DINOSAURS died out 65 million years ago, we know a lot about their lifestyles. Some were herbivores, some carnivores, and others omnivores. Some dinosaurs lived in herds or families and cared for their young. But whether they were warm- or cold-blooded has yet to be established.

LIFESTYLE FACTS

- Some dinosaurs may have lived for 200 years.

- *Carcharodontosaurus* is the largest land-living carnivore found to date.

- The largest dinosaur eggs probably belonged to the sauropod *Hypselosaurus*.

- Dinosaur embryos have been found fossilized in their eggs.

CARNIVORES

Most carnivores had deadly-sharp teeth and claws. Some hunted in packs; some hunted alone; while others may have scavenged on dead animals that were possibly killed by disease.

FAST FOOD

Dromaeosaurus had features common to many carnivores. It was fast, agile, and armed with sharp teeth and claws. *Dromaeosaurus* may have hunted in packs, chasing and bringing down much larger animals.

Clawed hands gripped prey

Long, slender legs

Slashing talon flicked forward

BARYONYX
From the side, *Baryonyx's* skull appears crocodile-shaped. *Baryonyx* may have used its long, narrow snout for catching fish.

Sharp, serrated teeth lined the long jaws

Lethal claw

CUTTING CLAW
Like *Dromaeosaurus*, *Deinonychus* had a lethal weapon: a 6-in-(15-cm-) long curved claw on each foot. When *Deinonychus* caught prey, it flicked the claw forward to cut deep into its victim.

TERRIBLE TEETH
The teeth of carnivorous dinosaurs were sharp with serrated (sawlike) edges for cutting through flesh and bones.

LOWER JAW OF ALBERTOSAURUS

MEATY DIET
Tyrannosaurus was one of the fiercest carnivores. With its powerful body and massive head, it overwhelmed victims, delivering a fatal, biting blow with its deadly jaws.

Small hands could tear food apart

HERBIVORES

PLANT-EATING DINOSAURS had to eat
large amounts of plants to fuel
their bodies. Some herbivores'
teeth were shaped for chopping
or crushing. Other herbivores
had sharp beaks for snipping
leaves and twigs. Once
eaten, these plants may
have taken days to digest.

GRINDING GUT
Barosaurus did not
chew its food—it
swallowed tough
leaves and twigs
whole. In a part of
its stomach, stones
called gastroliths
ground the food
for digestion.

SMOOTH STONES
Gastroliths have been
found near the skeletons
of several dinosaurs.

HERBIVORE FACTS

• All ornithischian
dinosaurs were
herbivores.

• Some herbivores had
up to 960 teeth.

• There were no
flowers for dinosaurs
to eat until about
125 million years ago.

• Herds of herbivores
may have migrated
during dry seasons to
find fresh food supplies.

• Some of the plants
the dinosaurs ate, such
as pine trees, ferns, and
cycads, still grow today.

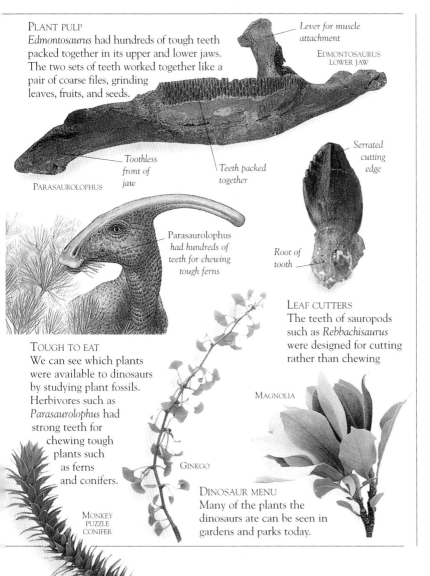

PLANT PULP

Edmontosaurus had hundreds of tough teeth packed together in its upper and lower jaws. The two sets of teeth worked together like a pair of coarse files, grinding leaves, fruits, and seeds.

Lever for muscle attachment

EDMONTOSAURUS LOWER JAW

Toothless front of jaw

PARASAUROLOPHUS

Teeth packed together

Serrated cutting edge

Parasaurolophus had hundreds of teeth for chewing tough ferns

Root of tooth

LEAF CUTTERS

The teeth of sauropods such as *Rebbachisaurus* were designed for cutting rather than chewing

MAGNOLIA

TOUGH TO EAT

We can see which plants were available to dinosaurs by studying plant fossils. Herbivores such as *Parasaurolophus* had strong teeth for chewing tough plants such as ferns and conifers.

GINKGO

MONKEY PUZZLE CONIFER

DINOSAUR MENU

Many of the plants the dinosaurs ate can be seen in gardens and parks today.

EGGS, NESTS, AND YOUNG

DINOSAURS laid eggs, like most other reptiles as well as birds. Scientists have discovered dinosaur nesting sites that show that some young were cared for by adults in their nests until they were old enough to leave. Other dinosaurs used the same nesting sites year after year.

Fossil egg with broken eggshell fragments

EGG FIND
Dinosaur eggs were first discovered in the 1920s in fossil nests in Mongolia. Once believed to be from *Proceratops*, the eggs are now known to belong to *Oviraptor*.

Hard snout for breaking out of egg

SMALL EGGS
These fossilized sauropod eggs, which are only 6 in (15 cm) in diameter, could have produced young that grew to an adult length of 40 ft (12 m). It probably took sauropods several years to reach their adult size.

HOME LIFE

Female *Maiasaura* laid about 25 eggs in a nest that was dug in the ground and lined with leaves and twigs. Young *Maiasaura* were about 12 in (30 cm) long when they hatched. They were reared in the nest until they grew to about 5 ft (1.5 m), when they would be old enough to start fending for themselves.

FOSSILIZED MAIASAURA EGG AND SKELETON OF YOUNG

Maiasaura hatchlings were very weak

EGGSHELLS

It was once thought that dinosaur eggs were soft and leathery, like those of snakes and other reptiles. Microscopic studies now show that dinosaur eggshells were hard and brittle like those of birds. The eggs of pterosaurs, on the other hand, seem to have had reptilian leathery shells.

Eggs left empty and broken

THE FIRST DINOSAURS

SEVERAL GROUPS of reptiles existed before the dinosaurs appeared. One group was the thecodonts. These were the ancestors of the dinosaurs, and they probably also gave rise to the pterosaurs and the crocodiles. Like the first dinosaurs, thecodonts were large carnivores that had straighter legs than other reptiles. The earliest known dinosaur, *Eoraptor*, first appeared 228 million years ago.

A VERY EARLY DINOSAUR
Eoraptor may have been the first dinosaur. It was discovered in 1992 in Argentina. *Eoraptor* had a crocodile-like skull with sharp, curved teeth.

Jaws were lined with sharp teeth

Long, stiff tail

Long tail acted as a counterbalance to the front of the body

STAURIKOSAURUS

Staurikosaurus was about 6 ft 6 in (2 m) long.

FAST HUNTER
Speedy *Staurikosaurus* was one of the first carnivorous dinosaurs. It had long, tooth-lined jaws for catching its prey, which it chased on its long and slender back legs.

Long, bird-like back legs

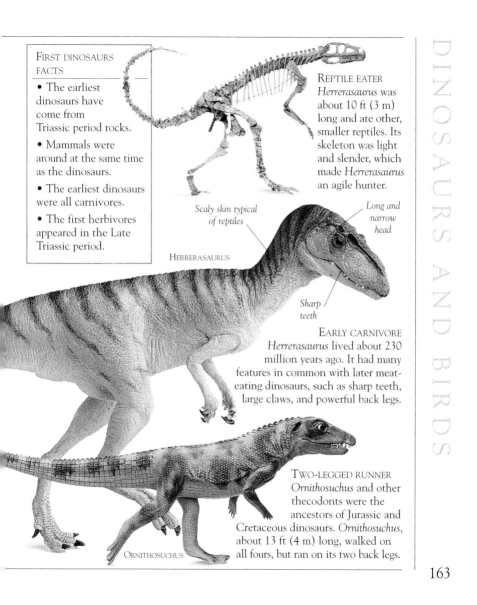

FIRST DINOSAURS
FACTS

• The earliest
dinosaurs have
come from
Triassic period rocks.

• Mammals were
around at the same time
as the dinosaurs.

• The earliest dinosaurs
were all carnivores.

• The first herbivores
appeared in the Late
Triassic period.

REPTILE EATER
Herrerasaurus was
about 10 ft (3 m)
long and ate other,
smaller reptiles. Its
skeleton was light
and slender, which
made *Herrerasaurus*
an agile hunter.

*Scaly skin typical
of reptiles*

*Long and
narrow
head*

HERRERASAURUS

*Sharp
teeth*

EARLY CARNIVORE
Herrerasaurus lived about 230
million years ago. It had many
features in common with later meat-
eating dinosaurs, such as sharp teeth,
large claws, and powerful back legs.

TWO-LEGGED RUNNER
Ornithosuchus and other
thecodonts were the
ancestors of Jurassic and
Cretaceous dinosaurs. *Ornithosuchus*,
about 13 ft (4 m) long, walked on
all fours, but ran on its two back legs.

ORNITHOSUCHUS

DINOSAUR EXTINCTION

AROUND 65 MILLION YEARS AGO, the dinosaurs became extinct. At the same time, other creatures, such as the sea and air reptiles, also died out. There are many theories for this extinction. But as with so many things about dinosaurs, no one really knows for sure what happened.

ASTEROID THEORY
At the end of the Cretaceous, a giant asteroid struck Earth. The impact resulted in a dust cloud that circled the globe, blocking out the sunlight and bringing cold, stormy weather.

Even the mighty Tyrannosaurus rex could not survive extinction

SLOW DEATH
Some experts are of the opinion that dinosaurs died out over a few million years.

MAGNOLIA

FLOWERS

Certain poisonous flowering plants may have contributed to the extinction of the dinosaurs. Herbivorous dinosaurs that ate these plants may have died. Many carnivores, which fed on herbivores, would then have died because of lack of prey to hunt and eat.

VOLCANO THEORY

Many volcanoes were active during the Cretaceous period. There were vast lava flows in the area that is now India. This would have poured huge amounts of carbon dioxide into the air, causing overheating, acid rain, and the destruction of the protective ozone layer.

Crocodiles have not changed much in appearance over the years

Megazostrodon *was a mammal that lived in the Triassic period*

MAMMALS

Mammals appeared during the Triassic period, when they lived alongside the dinosaurs. They became the dominant land animals after the dinosaurs' extinction.

SURVIVING REPTILES

Crocodiles were around before the dinosaurs, and are still alive today. The reason these reptiles survived while the dinosaurs died out is a complete mystery.

DINOSAURS TODAY

THE REMAINS OF DINOSAURS have been discovered on every continent. New dinosaur fossils are being discovered constantly by scientists, amateur fossil-hunters, or by accident in construction sites and mines. This map shows the major dinosaur finds.

NORTH AMERICA
Expeditions are always being organized to search for dinosaurs in North America, since rocks from the dinosaur age are exposed over vast areas. The dinosaurs discovered here include:

- *Allosaurus*
- *Triceratops*
- *Deinonychus*
- *Camarasaurus*
- *Parasaurolophus*
- *Corythosaurus*
- *Stegosaurus*
- *Apatosaurus*
- *Coelophysis*

ANTARCTICA
The climate in Antarctica was much warmer in the dinosaur age than it is today. The bones of several small Cretaceous-period dinosaurs have been found here, including a relative of the small ornithopod *Hypsilophodon*.

SOUTH AMERICA
Most South American dinosaurs have been found in Argentina and Brazil. Some of the earliest known dinosaurs have been found here. The South American dinosaurs include:

- *Saltasaurus*
- *Herrerasaurus*
- *Patagosaurus*
- *Staurikosaurus*
- *Piatnitzkyosaurus*

EUROPE
It was here in the 19th century that the first dinosaur fossils were collected and recorded, and where the name "dinosaur" was first used. Dinosaurs found in Europe include:

- *Hypsilophodon*
- *Iguanodon*
- *Plateosaurus*
- *Baryonyx*
- *Compsognathus*
- *Eustreptospondylus*

ASIA
Many exciting discoveries of dinosaurs have been made in the Gobi Desert. Scientists are still making new discoveries in China and India. Dinosaurs found in Asia include:

- *Velociraptor*
- *Oviraptor*
- *Protoceratops*
- *Tuojiangosaurus*
- *Mamenchisaurus*
- *Gallimimus*

AUSTRALIA AND NEW ZEALAND
There have been many fossil finds in Australia, and one in New Zealand. There are probably many sites rich in dinosaur fossils in these countries, but they have yet to be found. Dinosaurs found in these countries include:

- *Muttaburrasaurus*
- *Leaellynosaura*
- *Austrosaurus*
- *Rhoetosaurus*
- *Minmi*

AFRICA
Africa is a rich source of dinosaur fossils. A site in Tanzania has held some major discoveries. Dinosaurs found in Africa include:

- *Spinosaurus*
- *Brachiosaurus*
- *Barosaurus*
- *Massospondylus*

DINOSAURS CLASSIFIED

THE CLASSIFICATION OF DINOSAURS is controversial and continually being revised. In this chart, dinosaurs are subdivided into three main groups—Herrerasauria, Saurischia, and Ornithischia. Birds (Aves) also now come under dinosaurs, since they share many basic features.

ORNITHISCHIA

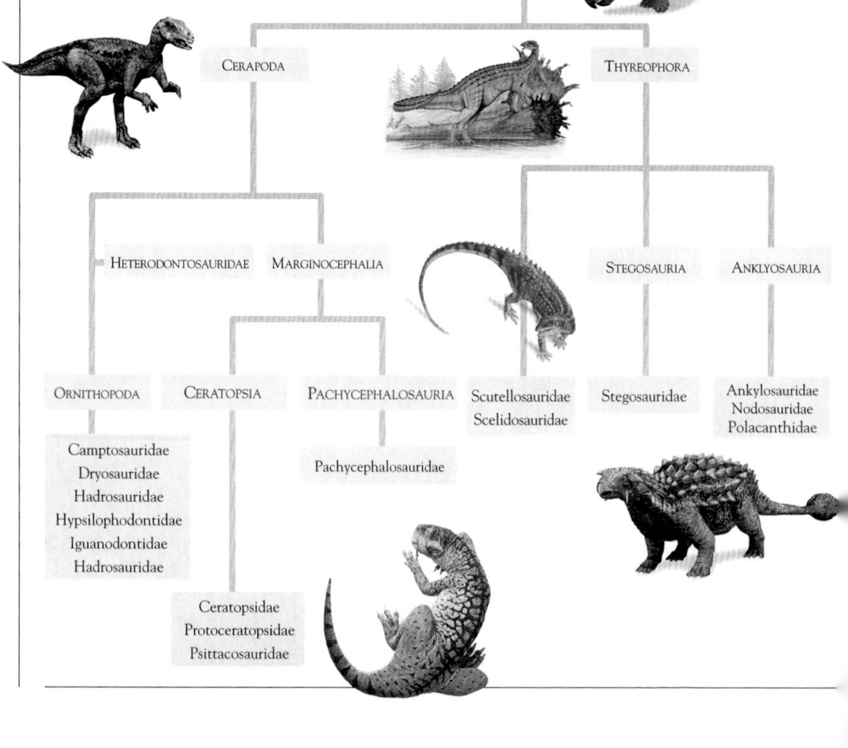

CERAPODA

THYREOPHORA

HETERODONTOSAURIDAE MARGINOCEPHALIA

STEGOSAURIA

ANKLYOSAURIA

ORNITHOPODA CERATOPSIA PACHYCEPHALOSAURIA

Scutellosauridae
Scelidosauridae

Stegosauridae

Ankylosauridae
Nodosauridae
Polacanthidae

Camptosauridae
Dryosauridae
Hadrosauridae
Hypsilophodontidae
Iguanodontidae
Hadrosauridae

Pachycephalosauridae

Ceratopsidae
Protoceratopsidae
Psittacosauridae

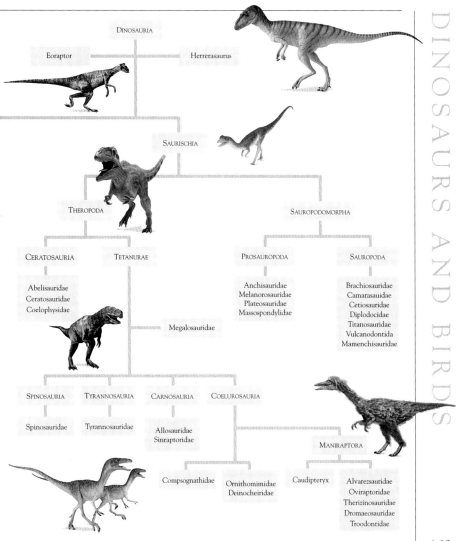

DINOSAURIA

Eoraptor

Herrerasaurus

SAURISCHIA

THEROPODA

SAUROPODOMORPHA

CERATOSAURIA

TETANURAE

PROSAUROPODA

SAUROPODA

Abelisauridae
Ceratosauridae
Coelophysidae

Anchisauridae
Melanorosauridae
Plateosauridae
Massospondylidae

Brachiosauridae
Camarasauridae
Cetiosauridae
Diplodocidae
Titanosauridae
Vulcanodontida
Mamenchisauridae

Megalosauridae

SPINOSAURIA

TYRANNOSAURIA

CARNOSAURIA

COELUROSAURIA

Spinosauridae

Tyrannosauridae

Allosauridae
Sinraptoridae

MANIRAPTORA

Compsognathidae

Ornithomimidae
Deinocheiridae

Caudipteryx

Alvarezsauridae
Oviraptoridae
Therizinosauridae
Dromaeosauridae
Troodontidae

ABOUT SAURISCHIANS

THERE WERE two main groups of saurischians— the theropods and the sauropodomorphs. The largest dinosaurs, and some of the smallest, were saurischians. This group differed from ornithischians mainly in the shape of the hip bones.

Sharp-toothed jaws typical of the meat-eating theropods

SAUROPODOMORPHS
Members of the sauropodomorph group were mainly herbivorous and quadrupedal (walked on four legs). The sauropodomorphs included the longest of all dinosaurs, *Seismosaurus*, which was about 130 ft (40 m) long.

TYRANNOSAURUS

BRACHIOSAURUS—A SAUROPODOMORPH

THEROPODS
All theropods were carnivores, and were bipedal (walked on two legs only). One of the smallest dinosaurs, *Compsognathus*, and the largest-ever land-based carnivore, *Tyrannosaurus*, both belonged in the theropod group.

COMPSOGNATHUS

170

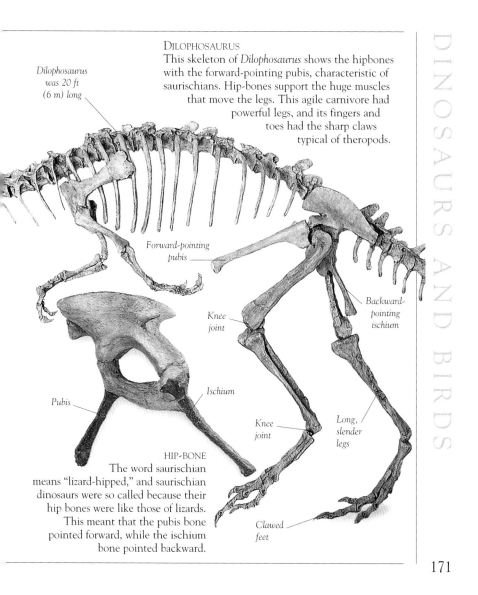

DILOPHOSAURUS
This skeleton of *Dilophosaurus* shows the hipbones
with the forward-pointing pubis, characteristic of
saurischians. Hip-bones support the huge muscles
that move the legs. This agile carnivore had
powerful legs, and its fingers and
toes had the sharp claws
typical of theropods.

*Dilophosaurus
was 20 ft
(6 m) long*

*Forward-pointing
pubis*

*Backward-
pointing
ischium*

*Knee
joint*

Pubis

Ischium

*Knee
joint*

*Long,
slender
legs*

HIP-BONE
The word saurischian
means "lizard-hipped," and saurischian
dinosaurs were so called because their
hip bones were like those of lizards.
This meant that the pubis bone
pointed forward, while the ischium
bone pointed backward.

*Clawed
feet*

THEROPODS

THIS GROUP comprised the killers of the dinosaur world. Often large and ferocious, these carnivores usually walked on their clawed rear feet. Theropod means "beast feet," but their feet were very birdlike. Each foot had three toes for walking on, with long foot bones that added to the length of the legs. Sharp-clawed hands were often used for attacking and catching hold of prey.

EARLY THEROPOD
Dilophosaurus lived during the early part of the Jurassic period. An agile predator, it was one of the first large carnivorous dinosaurs.

Tail

FOSSIL FIND
Coelophysis hunted lizards and small dinosaurs. But in this fossilized *Coelophysis* skeleton, there are skeletons of young of the same species among the ribs, indicating that *Coelophysis* was also a cannibal.

Coelophysis was 10 ft (3 m) long.

Bones of young in rib cage

THEROPOD FACTS

• All theropods were carnivores.

• *Coelophysis* was one of the first theropods, living about 220 million years ago.

• *Tyrannosaurus* was one of the last theropods, living 65 million years ago.

• Many theropods had no fourth or fifth fingers.

• At least five vertebrae supported the pelvis of theropods.

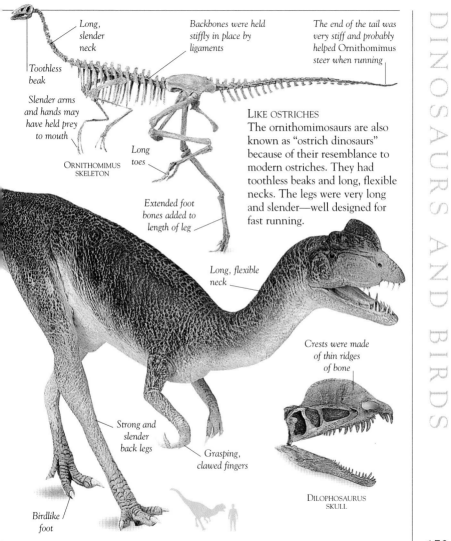

Long, slender neck

Toothless beak

Slender arms and hands may have held prey to mouth

ORNITHOMIMUS SKELETON

Long toes

Backbones were held stiffly in place by ligaments

The end of the tail was very stiff and probably helped Ornithomimus steer when running

Extended foot bones added to length of leg

LIKE OSTRICHES

The ornithomimosaurs are also known as "ostrich dinosaurs" because of their resemblance to modern ostriches. They had toothless beaks and long, flexible necks. The legs were very long and slender—well designed for fast running.

Long, flexible neck

Strong and slender back legs

Grasping, clawed fingers

Crests were made of thin ridges of bone

Birdlike foot

DILOPHOSAURUS SKULL

STAURIKOSAURUS

STAURIKOSAURUS ("Southern Cross lizard") was a primitive, bipedal dinosaur. It had the typical theropod body shape—long, slim tail, long, powerful hind legs, and short arms. The back was held horizontally, with the tail used for balance. The lower jaw had a joint that allowed the tooth-bearing part to move independently of the back part of the jaw.

LONG AND LIGHT
This lightly built hunter was relatively long in size, but would have been no heavier than a nine-year-old child—around 65 lb (30 kg). It ran swiftly on two legs.

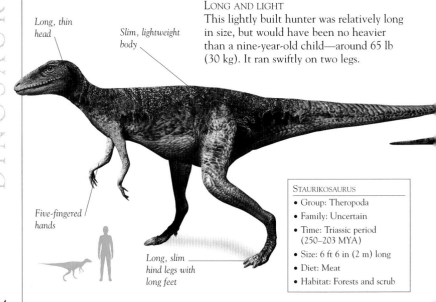

Long, thin head

Slim, lightweight body

Five-fingered hands

Long, slim hind legs with long feet

STAURIKOSAURUS
- Group: Theropoda
- Family: Uncertain
- Time: Triassic period (250–203 MYA)
- Size: 6 ft 6 in (2 m) long
- Diet: Meat
- Habitat: Forests and scrub

EORAPTOR

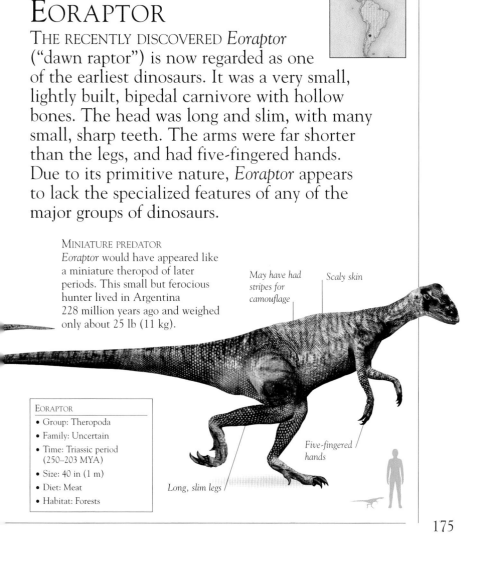

THE RECENTLY DISCOVERED *Eoraptor* ("dawn raptor") is now regarded as one of the earliest dinosaurs. It was a very small, lightly built, bipedal carnivore with hollow bones. The head was long and slim, with many small, sharp teeth. The arms were far shorter than the legs, and had five-fingered hands. Due to its primitive nature, *Eoraptor* appears to lack the specialized features of any of the major groups of dinosaurs.

MINIATURE PREDATOR
Eoraptor would have appeared like a miniature theropod of later periods. This small but ferocious hunter lived in Argentina 228 million years ago and weighed only about 25 lb (11 kg).

May have had stripes for camouflage

Scaly skin

Five-fingered hands

Long, slim legs

EORAPTOR
- Group: Theropoda
- Family: Uncertain
- Time: Triassic period (250–203 MYA)
- Size: 40 in (1 m)
- Diet: Meat
- Habitat: Forests

COELOPHYSIS

COELOPHYSIS ("hollow face") was a lightly built dinosaur with open skull bones (hence its name). Its body was long and slim, and the head was pointed, with many small, serrated teeth. The bones of young *Coelophysis* have been found in the stomachs of fossilized adults, suggesting that this dinosaur was a cannibal.

COELOPHYSIS
- Group: Theropoda
- Family: Coelophysidae
- Time: Triassic period (250–203 MYA)
- Size: 9 ft (2.8 m) long
- Diet: Lizards, fish
- Habitat: Desert plains

GHOST RANCH, NEW MEXICO
Coelophysis is one of the best-known dinosaurs, and many of its fossils have been found at this site.

Remains of own young in abdominal cavity

FOSSIL SKELETON EMBEDDED IN ROCK

LIGHT BONES
Although *Coelophysis* was as long as a small car, it was a light as an eight-year-old child.

Long, flexible tail

Long hind legs

Small, pointed teeth

Hands with three fingers and a fourth rudimentary digit

DILOPHOSAURUS

DILOPHOSAURUS ("two-ridged lizard") was named after the pair of bony crests that adorned its head. These were so fragile that they were probably used only for display, and not in fights. Not all specimens have the crest—they may have been evident only in males, which used them to attract a mate. *Dilophosaurus* had a large head, with a slender neck, body, and tail. It seems to have been closely related to *Coelophysis*.

DILOPHOSAURUS
- Group: Theropoda
- Family: Coelophysidae
- Time: Jurassic period (203–135 MYA)
- Size: 20 ft (6 m)
- Diet: Small animals, fish
- Habitat: Riverbanks

Flexible tail

Bony, semicircular crests

Long, slim, powerful hind legs

DANGEROUS DISPLAY
The male *Dilophosaurus* may have scared rivals away by standing and nodding its head up and down to appear bigger (and more dangerous) than it actually was.

Three long, forward-facing, clawed toes

CERATOSAURUS

CERATOSAURUS ("horned lizard") was named after the short horn above its nose. This dinosaur's other striking feature was the line of bony plates that ran down its back—the only theropod known to have had them. It had strong yet short arms, with four fingers on each hand. Three of the fingers were clawed. *Ceratosaurus's* teeth were long and bladelike. It had a deep and flexible tail.

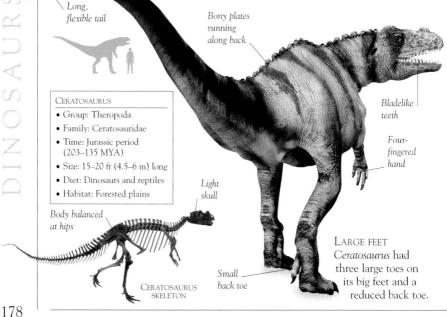

Long, flexible tail

Bony plates running along back

CERATOSAURUS
- Group: Theropoda
- Family: Ceratosauridae
- Time: Jurassic period (203–135 MYA)
- Size: 15–20 ft (4.5–6 m) long
- Diet: Dinosaurs and reptiles
- Habitat: Forested plains

Bladelike teeth

Four-fingered hand

Light skull

Body balanced at hips

Small back toe

CERATOSAURUS SKELETON

LARGE FEET
Ceratosaurus had three large toes on its big feet and a reduced back toe.

ABELISAURUS

THIS LARGE THEROPOD, named after its discoverer, Roberto Abel, is known only from a single skull. Its big head had a rounded snout, and its teeth were small for a carnivorous dinosaur of its size. Its skull is peculiar in that it has a huge opening at the side just above the jaws, which is much larger than in other dinosaurs.

CARNOTAURUS'S COUSIN

Abelisaurus was a primitive dinosaur related to another theropod known as *Carnotaurus*. Since there are no other bones except for the skull available, palaeontologists have had to imagine the rest of *Abelisaurus*'s body based on that of other, better-known abelisaurids.

Large head

Relatively small teeth

Typical body shape of large theropods

Probably three-fingered hands

Stood on two legs

ABELISAURUS
• Group: Theropoda
• Family: Abelisauridae
• Time: Cretaceous period (135–65 MYA)
• Size: 30 ft (9 m) long
• Diet: Meat
• Habitat: River plains

179

BIG MEAT-EATERS

OF ALL THE THEROPODS, the ferocious, large carnivores are probably the most famous. These fast runners had massive heads with enormous serrated and curved teeth. *Tyrannosaurus* was one of the largest and fiercest carnivores of the Cretaceous. *Allosaurus* was the top predator of the Jurassic.

Small first toe

Curved neck

ALLOSAURUS FOOT
Like all other big meat-eaters, *Allosaurus* walked on three large, clawed toes. The feet were strong, since they had to bear the weight of the body. The first toe was small and faced backward, off the ground.

Long, tooth-lined jaws could open wide to swallow lumps of meat

Large, three-fingered hands had hooked claws

Front limbs were small and weak compared with the rest of the body

Ischium

ALLOSAURUS SKELETON
It is rare to find a complete skeleton of any of the large meat-eaters. However, many fossilized parts have been found separately, allowing paleontologists to recreate a complete skeleton of an *Allosaurus*.

Long foot bones increased leg length

ALLOSAURUS

About 145 million years ago, *Allosaurus* was the terror of sauropods, ornithopods, and stegosaurs. At about 36 ft (11 m) long, and weighing 2 tons, *Allosaurus* was one of the most common dinosaurs during this time, well supplied with prey.

Thick tail

Powerful legs for chasing prey

Tail was powerful and balanced front of body

Wider skull of Tyrannosaurus

Long and narrow skull of Allosaurus

SNOUT SIZES

Allosaurus had a narrower snout than *Tyrannosaurus* and therefore probably bit out lumps of flesh rather than making bone-crushing attacks on prey.

BIG MEAT-EATER FACTS

• The oldest known member of this group is *Piatnitzkysaurus*, from the Jurassic.

• Most of these species existed in the last 10 million years of the Cretaceous.

• Remains of these dinosaurs have been found in the Americas, Asia, Africa, Europe, and Australia.

• *Allosaurus* has been known by more than nine different names since the first fossil remains were found.

CARNOTAURUS

THE MOST DISTINCTIVE features of *Carnotaurus* ("meat-eating bull") were the triangular horns over its eyes. Otherwise, it looked much like other large theropods. It had long legs and a lightly built body covered in scales and studs. Its forearms were incredibly small. Its three fingers were short and stubby, and the thumbs bore a small spike. Its tail was long, thick, and flexible.

Tail held out for balance

Very short forearms

Spiked thumb

Slim, powerful legs

Large weight-bearing toes

CARNOTAURUS
- Group: Theropoda
- Family: Abelisauridae
- Time: Cretaceous period (135–65 MYA)
- Size: 25 ft (7.5 m) long
- Diet: Meat
- Habitat: Dry plains, perhaps deserts

MYSTERY HORNS
Scientists are unsure why *Carnotaurus* had horns on its head. They were too short to kill, and in all likelihood this dinosaur hunted its prey by butting it head-first, or scavenged on dead dinosaurs. The horns may have been used by males to attract a mate and ward off rivals.

PIATNITZKYSAURUS

THIS DINOSAUR seems to have been a
tetanuran ("stiff-tailed") theropod. It
had a body to very similar *Allosaurus*, but its arms
were longer. A pair of bony crests ran from between
the eyes to the end of the snout. The arms were
relatively small, with three clawed fingers on each
hand. The body was bulky, and the tail was long
and stiff. "Piatnitzky's lizard" was named in honor
of discoverer José Bonaparte's best friend.

IDENTITY CRISIS
To date, two partial skeletons of
Piatnitzkysaurus have been excavated in
Argentina, and its exact classification is
still being debated by paleontologists.

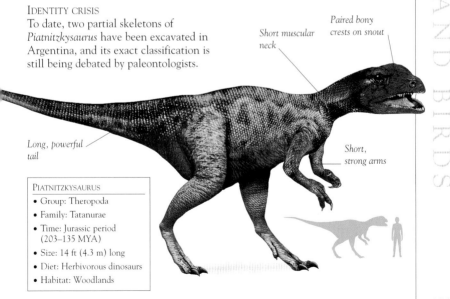

Short muscular
neck

Paired bony
crests on snout

Long, powerful
tail

Short,
strong arms

PIATNITZKYSAURUS
- Group: Theropoda
- Family: Tatanurae
- Time: Jurassic period
  (203–135 MYA)
- Size: 14 ft (4.3 m) long
- Diet: Herbivorous dinosaurs
- Habitat: Woodlands

MEGALOSAURUS

THE FIRST DINOSAUR to be scientifically named and identified, *Megalosaurus* ("great lizard") was a large, bulky, carnivorous theropod. It had a massive head carried on a short, muscular neck. *Megalosaurus* walked with its toes pointing inward and its tail swaying.

Long, thick tail

Short but strong arms

MEGALOSAURUS
- Group: Theropoda
- Family: Megalosauridae
- Time: Jurassic period (203–135 MYA)
- Size: 30 ft (9 m) long
- Diet: Large herbivorous dinosaurs
- Habitat: Forests

Sharp, serrated teeth

Cracks due to fossilization

FOSSIL TOOTH
This jawbone belonged to *Megalosaurus*. Many fossils have been wrongly identified as *Megalosaurus* remains, but very few real *Megalosaurus* fossils have been found.

LOWER JAW

XUANHANOSAURUS

THIS LITTLE-KNOWN theropod ("Xuan lizard") was named after Xuanhan in Sichuan Province, China, where its fossils were found. At present, it is known only from vertebrae and bones from the shoulder, arm, and hand. Its arms were well developed and strong, despite their short length, and the hands were small with strong claws. This *Megalosaurus*-like dinosaur may have had a large head, long and powerful hind legs, clawed feet with three forward-facing toes, and a long, stiff tail.

Tail stretched for balance

Three clawed fingers on each hand

STEADY WALKER

Xuanhanosaurus's fossils were discovered by Chinese paleontologist Dong Zhiming in 1984. He suggested that, although *Xuanhanosaurus* was bipedal (two-legged), it walked on all fours for at least some of the time. It kept its long, stiff tail outstretched for balance.

XUANHANOSAURUS

- Group: Theropoda
- Family: Uncertain
- Time: Jurassic period (203–135 MYA)
- Size: 20 ft (6 m) long
- Diet: Meat
- Habitat: Forests

185

GASOSAURUS

THIS THEROPOD was named "gas lizard" in honor of the Dashanpu gas company, which was working in the quarry in Sichuan, China, where the remains were excavated. Little is known about *Gasosaurus*, and its classification is uncertain—it may be a primitive big meat-eater. *Gasosaurus* had a typical theropod body shape of a large head, powerful legs with three claws, and a long, stiff tail.

GASOSAURUS
- Group: Theropoda
- Family: Tetanurae
- Time: Jurassic period (203–135 MYA)
- Size: 13 ft (4 m)
- Diet: Large herbivorous dinosaurs
- Habitat: Woodlands

Bulky body

Stiffened tail

Large jaws with sharp teeth

LITTLE-KNOWN
Only parts of the arm, thigh, and hip bones of this dinosaur have been found.

Relatively long arms

Three forward-facing clawed toes

Heavily built hind legs

ALLOSAURUS

ALLOSAURUS ("different lizard") was the most abundant, and probably the largest, predator in the Late Jurassic. It had a massive head, short neck, and bulky body, and its three-fingered forelimbs were strong, with large claws. *Allosaurus* had distinctive bony bumps over the eyes.

Teeth 2½–5 in (5–10 cm) long

FOSSIL SKULL
The massive skull was lightened by large gaps known as fenestrae.

OTHNIEL C. MARSH
The greatest dinosaur paleontologist of the 19th century, Othniel C. Marsh, named this dinosaur *Allosaurus*.

Tail held outstretched for balance

Sawlike teeth

ALLOSAURUS
- Group: Theropoda
- Family: Allosauridae
- Time: Jurassic period (203–135 MYA)
- Size: 40 ft (12 m) long
- Diet: Herbivorous dinosaurs, rotting flesh
- Habitat: Plains

GIGANOTOSAURUS

GIGANOTOSAURUS ("giant southern lizard") is the largest flesh-eating dinosaur yet discovered. Its skull was longer than an average man, and held long, serrated teeth. Its hands had three fingers, and it had a slim, pointed tail. Although larger than *Tyrannosaurus*, it was a lighter dinosaur. It also seems to have hunted in a different way—by slashing at its prey rather than charging and biting it head on. Despite its huge size, some scientists think that, like other large theropods, it may have been capable of running fast.

LAND OF GIANTS
This gigantic hunter from Argentina may have preyed on one of the largest-ever sauropods, *Argentinosaurus*, or eaten the flesh of dead ones. It had a relative in *Carcharodontosaurus*—another giant meat-eater that lived in Africa.

GIGANOTOSAURUS
- Group: Theropoda
- Family: Carcharodontosauridae
- Time: Cretaceous period (135–65 MYA)
- Size: 40 ft (12.5 m)
- Diet: Meat
- Habitat: Warm swamps

Three clawed fingers

Large eyes

Head twice
the size of
Allosaurus

Tail probably
swayed from
side to side

Small
shoulder

189

HOLLOW-TAIL LIZARDS

THE JURASSIC LANDSCAPE teemed with small predators, but very few left fossil remains. Among the best-known of these are *Compsognathus* and *Ornitholestes*—both fast runners, preying on smaller animals. They formed a new group—the coelurosaurs or "hollow-tail lizards"—which later gave rise to tyrannosaurs, ornithopods, and the ancestors of birds.

COMPSOGNATHUS LIFESTYLE
Compsognathus was a slender dinosaur with a long tail and bird-like legs. It lived on small desert islands in what is now southern Germany and France, and was probably the largest predator there (islands lack enough food to support large meat-eaters).

Very long, slender tail

Hip

Skin covered with scales or perhaps primitive feathers

High ankle

Three-toed, birdlike foot

Fine-grained limestone slab preserving fossil

Curved neck, pulled back by shrinkage after death

Finger bones, some scattered

THE LIZARD EATER
The fossil *Compsognathus* shown below is one of only two so far discovered. This well-preserved German specimen had swallowed a small lizard.

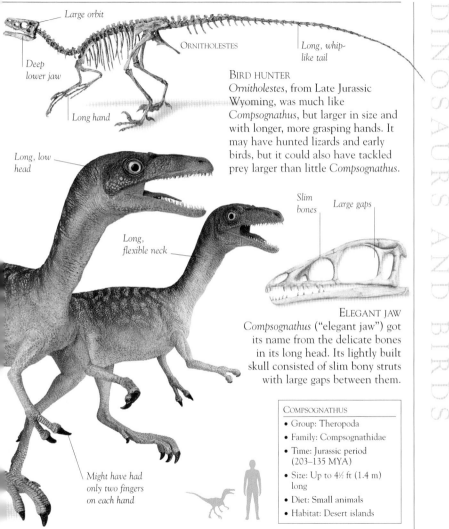

Large orbit

Deep
lower jaw

Long hand

ORNITHOLESTES

Long, whip-
like tail

Long, low
head

Long,
flexible neck

Slim
bones

Large gaps

BIRD HUNTER
Ornitholestes, from Late Jurassic
Wyoming, was much like
Compsognathus, but larger in size and
with longer, more grasping hands. It
may have hunted lizards and early
birds, but it could also have tackled
prey larger than little *Compsognathus*.

ELEGANT JAW
Compsognathus ("elegant jaw") got
its name from the delicate bones
in its long head. Its lightly built
skull consisted of slim bony struts
with large gaps between them.

Might have had
only two fingers
on each hand

COMPSOGNATHUS

- Group: Theropoda
- Family: Compsognathidae
- Time: Jurassic period
  (203–135 MYA)
- Size: Up to 4½ ft (1.4 m)
  long
- Diet: Small animals
- Habitat: Desert islands

CAUDIPTERYX

THE DISCOVERY OF this small, feathered dinosaur added further proof to the theory that theropods were the ancestors of birds. *Caudipteryx* ("tail feather") was a theropod with feathers covering its arms, most of its body, and its short tail. Some feathers were downy, while others were like quills.

Pointed beak

Small, short skull

Fan of feathers on tail

DOWN FEATHER

FEATHER FUNCTION
Caudipteryx's short down feathers gave it warmth. Its wing feathers were symmetrical, meaning that it could not fly.

WING FEATHER

Three clawed fingers

Short arms with symmetrical feathers

Birdlike feet with three forward-facing clawed toes

Long, slim legs best suited to running

CAUDIPTERYX
- Group: Theropoda
- Family: Uncertain
- Time: Cretaceous period (135–65 MYA)
- Size: 3 ft (90 cm) long
- Diet: Plants
- Habitat: Wooded lakesides

Oviraptor

THIS DINOSAUR seems to have been closely related to birds, and was probably feathered. Its most distinctive feature was its short, deep head with a stumpy beak. It had no teeth, but there were two bony projections on the upper palate. Its powerful jaws could have crushed bones.

> OVIRAPTOR
> - Group: Theropoda
> - Family: Oviraptoridae
> - Time: Cretaceous period (135–65 MYA)
> - Size: 8 ft (2.5 m) long
> - Diet: Uncertain
> - Habitat: Semidesert

UNJUSTLY NAMED
The first specimen of *Oviraptor* was found with eggs, which it was thought to have been stealing, and this led to its name, "egg thief." Later research proved that the *Oviraptor* was actually sitting on its own nest.

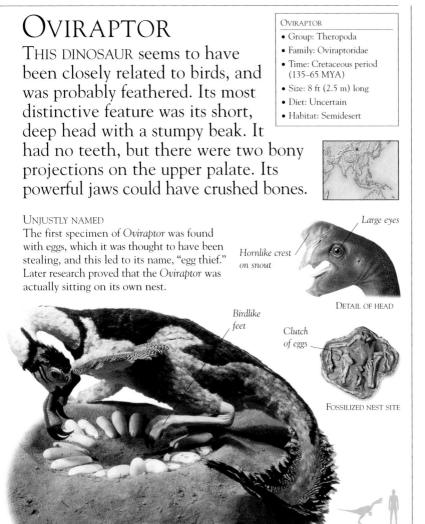

Large eyes

Hornlike crest on snout

DETAIL OF HEAD

Birdlike feet

Clutch of eggs

FOSSILIZED NEST SITE

OVIRAPTOSAURS

OVIRAPTOR WAS given the name "egg stealer" because the first fossil seemed to be lying on a nest of *Protoceratops* eggs. It was thought that it had been killed while trying to steal eggs. We now know, however, that the eggs and nest belonged to the *Oviraptor* itself and it probably died trying to protect them.

FOSSILIZED NEST OF
OVIRAPTOR EGGS

TRUE IDENTITY
Proof of the real nature of the "*Protoceratops*" eggs came when one of them was found to contain an *Oviraptor* embryo.

NEST DISCOVERY
Oviraptosaurs resembled large, flightless birds. In 1995, a fossilized *Oviraptor* was found sitting on its nest, as if brooding the eggs like a modern bird. The 18 eggs were laid in a circle in a hollow scooped out of a mound of sand.

MODEL OF
OVIRAPTOR
ON NEST

Feathers

Toothless
beak

Sharp
claws

OVIRAPTOSAUR FACTS

• Oviraptosaurs lived near the end of the Cretaceous period.

• Their large brain cavity suggests that they were intelligent.

• Most oviraptosaur skeletons were found in Mongolia, but recent discoveries have also been made in England and North America.

Brightly colored skin

HEAD DECORATIONS

Many oviraptosaurs had tall, bony head crests. *Ingenia* lacked a head crest, but it might have had brightly colored skin instead.

INGENIA HEAD

Slender skeleton OVIRAPTOR SKELETON *Muscle on tail*

Large hands

SLIM AND AGILE

Oviraptosaurs were small and lightly built, with hollow bones. They had slim but muscular back legs and could run quite fast. Their large hands had curved fingers ending in large, grasping claws.

OVIRAPTOR
MONGOLIENSIS
HEAD

Bony head crest

HEAD CRESTS

Different oviraptosaurs had different crests. A modern bird, the cassowary, uses its crest to butt its way through the forest undergrowth. Perhaps oviraptosaurs used their crest for a similar purpose.

A cassowary uses its crest to butt its way out of vegetation when escaping from enemies

CASSOWARY
HEAD

ARCHAEOPTERYX

ARCHAEOPTERYX ("ancient wing") was the size of a modern pigeon. It was not a strong flier, but its long, slim lower leg bones suggest that it could move well on land. Archaeopteryx is believed to have been warm-blooded.

Feathered wings for effective flight

Three clawed digits on elongated hand

Small head with large eyes

ARCHAEOPTERYX
- Group: Theropoda
- Family: Archaeopteridae
- Time: Jurassic period (203–135 MYA)
- Size: 1 ft (30 cm)
- Diet: Insects
- Habitat: Lakeshores or open forests

Impressions of
feathers preserved
in limestone

Feathers
attached to
sides of
bony tail

FOSSIL REMAINS
EMBEDDED IN ROCK

NEAR-BIRD
Archaeopteryx
had feathers and
wings in common with
modern birds. However,
it had a flat breastbone, a long
bony tail, and three grasping claws
on its wingtip, unlike birds of today.

Lightly
built body

197

VELOCIRAPTOR

MANY WELL-PRESERVED skeletons of *Velociraptor* ("fast thief") have been found, making it the best-known member of its family. This predator probably hunted in packs. Its hands bore three clawed fingers, and the second toe of its foot ended in a sickle-shaped slashing claw.

Stiff tail held outstretched for balance

Slim legs with long shins for speed

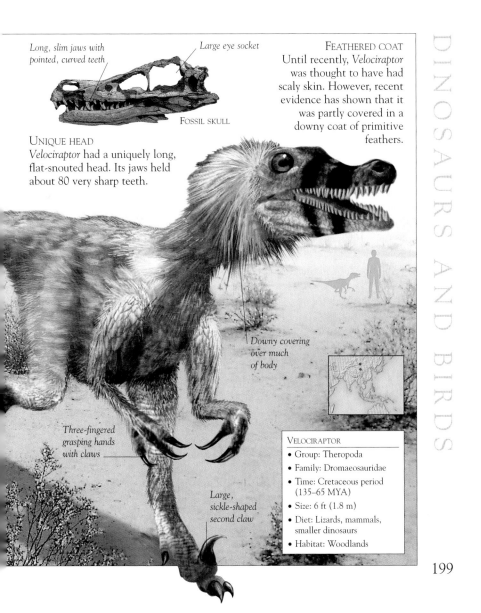

Long, slim jaws with pointed, curved teeth

Large eye socket

FOSSIL SKULL

UNIQUE HEAD
Velociraptor had a uniquely long, flat-snouted head. Its jaws held about 80 very sharp teeth.

FEATHERED COAT
Until recently, *Velociraptor* was thought to have had scaly skin. However, recent evidence has shown that it was partly covered in a downy coat of primitive feathers.

Downy covering over much of body

Three-fingered grasping hands with claws

Large, sickle-shaped second claw

VELOCIRAPTOR

- Group: Theropoda
- Family: Dromaeosauridae
- Time: Cretaceous period (135–65 MYA)
- Size: 6 ft (1.8 m)
- Diet: Lizards, mammals, smaller dinosaurs
- Habitat: Woodlands

199

DROMAEOSAURUS

DROMAEOSAURUS ("running lizard") was the first sickle-clawed dinosaur to be discovered. It was difficult to reconstruct because very few bones were found, and its true classification was only possible after another sickle-clawed dinosaur, *Deinonychus*, was described. *Dromaeosaurus* was smaller than *Deinonychus*, but otherwise very similar. Its body was slender, with long limbs and a large head. Its sharp claws would have been used for slashing prey.

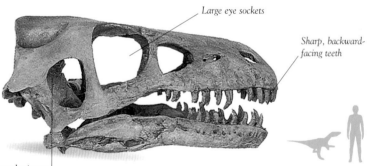

Large eye sockets

Sharp, backward-facing teeth

Large braincase indicating high intelligence

FEROCIOUS HUNTER
Dromaeosaurus belonged to the group of "running lizards" or dromaeosaurids, which were small and aggressive hunting dinosaurs. They had curved claws on their hands and feet, and their jaws bristled with huge, bladelike teeth.

DROMAEOSAURUS
- Group: Theropoda
- Family: Dromaeosauridae
- Time: Cretaceous period (135–65 MYA)
- Size: 5 ft 6 in (1.8 m) long
- Diet: Herbivorous dinosaurs
- Habitat: Forests, plains

DEINONYCHUS

ONE OF THE MOST fearsome predators of the
Cretaceous, *Deinonychus* ("terrible claw") was named
after the sickle-shaped claws on the second toe of
each foot. These were used alternately to slash at
prey as the dinosaur stood on one leg. A group of
Deinonychus skeletons preserved with that of a
large *Tenontosaurus* suggests that
Deinonychus hunted in packs.

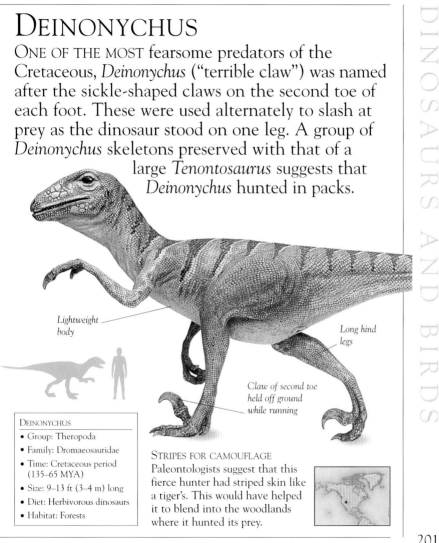

Lightweight
body

Long hind
legs

Claw of second toe
held off ground
while running

DEINONYCHUS
- Group: Theropoda
- Family: Dromaeosauridae
- Time: Cretaceous period
  (135–65 MYA)
- Size: 9–13 ft (3–4 m) long
- Diet: Herbivorous dinosaurs
- Habitat: Forests

STRIPES FOR CAMOUFLAGE
Paleontologists suggest that this
fierce hunter had striped skin like
a tiger's. This would have helped
it to blend into the woodlands
where it hunted its prey.

SAURORNITHOIDES

ONLY THE SKULL, a few arm bones, and teeth of *Saurornithoides* ("lizard bird form") have been found to date, and its classification as a dromaeosaur is therefore uncertain. Its long, narrow skull had a relatively large brain case. Its long, powerful arms ended in three-fingered hands capable of grasping prey.

Relatively large brain case

FAST RUNNER
Saurornithoides was very similar to *Troodon* and, also like *Troodon*, was a fast runner. Its remains have been found only in Mongolia.

Jaw containing many sharp teeth

Long, narrow snout

SAURORNITHOIDES
- Group: Theropoda
- Family: Dromaeosauridae
- Time: Cretaceous period (135–65 MYA)
- Size: 6½–11 ft (2–3.5 m) long
- Diet: Meat
- Habitat: Plains

TROODON

TROODON ("wounding tooth") was
named after its sharp, sawlike teeth.
Its remains are very rare and no
complete skeleton has been found
to date. *Troodon* was probably very
intelligent and an efficient hunter. It
had a large curved claw on both second
toes, and three long,
clawed fingers that
could grasp prey.

TROODON

BUSHBABY

Large, sharp eyes

NIGHT SIGHT
Troodon had large,
forward-facing eyes
like today's bushbaby.
This may have helped
it to see at night.

*Slim, lightly
built body*

FAST RUNNER
Troodon could run very
fast on its long back legs.
It probably preyed on
insects, small mammals,
lizards, and baby dinosaurs.

TROODON

- Group: Theropoda
- Family: Troodontidae
- Time: Cretaceous period
  (135–65 MYA)
- Size: 6½ ft (2 m) long
- Diet: Meat, carrion
- Habitat: Plains

*Three-
fingered
hands*

203

ORNITHOMIMOSAURS

WITH THEIR toothless beaks and slender feet, these dinosaurs looked like giant, featherless birds. But they also possessed the dinosaur features of clawed hands and a long tail. Ornithomimosaurs were long-necked and large—up to 16 ft (5 m) long—and among the fastest dinosaurs, racing on slim, powerful rear legs.

ORNITHOMIMOSAUR FACTS

- Ornithomimosaur means "bird-mimic reptile."

- Ornithomimosaurs may have run as fast as 43 mph (70 km/h).

- Predators: carnosaurs and dromaeosaurs

DROMICEIOMIMUS
This dinosaur had ten neck vertebrae, which made a flexible stem for its large-eyed head. It used its slender arms and three-fingered hands for grasping or holding prey.

Knee joint

Ankle joint far up leg

Fingers were thin with long, sharp claws

Only the toes touched the ground

Large eye sockets

Long foot bones

LIKE AN OSTRICH *Struthiomimus* had a running style similar to an ostrich's. But unlike an ostrich, it had long, mobile arms with clawed fingers to grasp prey. Its long tail was an important balancer at high speed.

Ostrich speed— up to 50 mph (80 km/h)

Struthiomimus *speed—less than 30 mph (50 km/h)*

Three locked foot bones

FOOT AND LEG
As in all other ornithomimosaurs, the feet and legs of *Dromiceiomimus* were built to give fast acceleration. Only the toes touched the ground—the foot bones were locked into a single, birdlike extension of the leg.

Sharp claws

Long, flexible neck

Mobile wrist

GALLIMIMUS
The largest ornithomimosaur was *Gallimimus*. It had a long and narrow, snouted head with large eyes for good sight. Its weak jaws were covered by a sharp, horny beak.

205

ORNITHOMIMUS

THE "BIRD MIMIC," or *Ornithomimus*, is typical of its family. It had slim arms and long, slim legs. Its stiff tail made up more than half of its length. Its small head had a toothless beak and was held upright by an S-shaped bend in the long, flexible neck. The brain cavity of *Ornithomimus* was relatively large.

Impression of toes

FOSSIL FOOTPRINTS
Ornithomimus had feet with three sharply clawed toes. It could deliver a terrible kick to a predator, such as tyrannosaur.

Large eyes on side of head

Long bones in feet

Three clawed fingers on each hand

FAST RUNNER
Ornithomimus ran at high speed with its body held horizontally and its tail outstretched for better balance.

ORNITHOMIMUS
- Group: Theropoda
- Family: Ornithomimidae
- Time: Cretaceous period (135–65 MYA)
- Size: 11 ft (3.5 m) long
- Diet: Omnivorous
- Habitat: Swamps, forests

STRUTHIOMIMUS

FOR MANY YEARS *Struthiomimus* ("ostrich mimic") was thought to be the same dinosaur as *Ornithomimus*. The two dinosaurs are remarkably similar— the main difference is that *Struthiomimus* had longer arms with stronger fingers. In addition, its thumbs did not oppose the fingers and it could not grasp so well.

"OSTRICH DINOSAUR"
Struthiomimus, like all the other "bird-mimics," had a small head with a toothless beak. Its legs, with long shins, feet, and toes, were adapted for sprinting across the countryside. Its long tail jutted out stiffly behind it.

STRUTHIOMIMUS
- Group: Theropoda
- Family: Ornithomimidae
- Time: Cretaceous period (135–65 MYA)
- Size: 11 ft (3.5 m) long
- Diet: Omnivorous
- Habitat: Open country, riverbanks

Small head

Long foot bones

Strong fingers

Birdlike hip bones

GALLIMIMUS

GALLIMIMUS ("chicken mimic") is one of the best-known ornithomimids or "bird-mimic" dinosaurs. It had a short body with a long, stiff tail stretched out for balance. Its slim legs were built for running at high speed. The skull ended in a long, toothless beak. *Gallimimus* was probably quite intelligent, since its brain case was relatively large.

Large eye socket

Toothless beak

FOSSIL SKULL

RUN LIKE AN OSTRICH
Gallimimus probably ran like an ostrich, taking long strides with its powerful hind legs. It had long arms in place of wings.

GALLIMIMUS
• Group: Theropoda
• Family: Ornithomimidae
• Time: Cretaceous period (135–65 MYA)
• Size: 20 ft (6 m) long
• Diet: Omnivorous
• Habitat: Desert plains

Slender, flexible neck

Slender feet with three toes

Long, grasping arms

DEINOCHEIRUS

THE ONLY REMAINS discovered of this little-known dinosaur are two arms 8 ft (2.4 m) in length, hence its name, "terrible hand." The arms of this bipedal hunter are similar to those of *Ornithomimus*, and are among the longest known in dinosaurs. Some experts think that the claws on the hands were too blunt for use in hunting.

DEINOCHEIRUS
- Group: Theropoda
- Family: Deinocheiridae
- Time: Cretaceous period (135–65 MYA)
- Size: 43–52 ft (12–15 m) long
- Diet: Unknown
- Habitat: Desert

GUESSWORK
The illustration here of *Deinocheirus* is based on what is known about other similar dinosaurs.

Body and tail probably similar to other theropods

Three fingers on each hand

10-in- (25-cm-) long claws

THERIZINOSAURUS

THE RECONSTRUCTION of *Therizinosaurus* ("scythe lizard") is based upon finds of other members of the family. It had very long arms ending in three fingers with claws that were too blunt to use for attack. This bipedal dinosaur was related to *Oviraptor*.

THERIZINOSAURUS
- Group: Theropoda
- Family: Therizinosauridae
- Time: Cretaceous period (135–65 MYA)
- Size: 36 ft (11 m) long
- Diet: Meat, plants or insects
- Habitat: Woodlands

Toothless beak

Claws up to 2 ft (60 cm) long

Fine, hairy feathers may have covered the skin

FOSSIL SCYTHE CLAW

BEIPIAOSAURUS

BEIPIAOSAURUS WAS NAMED after Beipiao, the Chinese city where its fossils were discovered. It had a big head, three-clawed hands, and long shins. Evidence shows that feathers covered its arms and legs, further strengthening the theory that some theropods were downy and not scaly.

BEIPIAOSAURUS
- Group: Theropoda
- Family: Therizinosauridae
- Time: Cretaceous period (135–65 MYA)
- Size: 7¼ ft (2.2 m)
- Diet: Plants
- Habitat: Woodlands

OLDEST SCYTHE LIZARD
The heavily built *Beipiaosaurus* lived more than 120 million years ago, making it older than other "scythe lizards."

Body covered with feathery filaments

Heavy build

211

SHUVUUIA

THE DISCOVERY OF *Shuvuuia* started a debate as to whether it was a bird, rather than a dinosaur. Named after the Mongolian word for bird ("shuvuu") its skull shows it to have been more closely related to birds than, for example, *Archaeopteryx*. Evidence shows it also had feathers.

Head similar to that of modern birds

Long, slender neck

Claw may have been used for opening termite nests

BIRDLIKE DINOSAUR
Shuvuuia's legs were long and slim, suggesting that it may have been a fast runner. Its short, stubby forelimbs ended in a single clawed digit.

Long, slim legs

SHUVUUIA
- Group: Theropoda
- Family: Alvarezsauria
- Time: Cretaceous period (135–65 MYA)
- Size: 3 ft 6 in (1 m) long
- Diet: Insects, small reptiles
- Habitat: Plains

Feet with three forward-facing, clawed toes

SUCHOMIMUS

THIS DINOSAUR, whose name means "crocodile-mimic," was adapted to hunt fish. It had a very long snout, and its jaws had sharp, interlocking teeth to grip slippery prey. It probably stood or lay in the water, waiting to snap up fish or hook them with its curved thumb claws.

SUCHOMIMUS
- Group: Theropoda
- Family: Spinosauridae
- Time: Cretaceous period (135–65 MYA)
- Size: 36 ft (11 m) long
- Diet: Fish, possibly meat
- Habitat: Lush forests

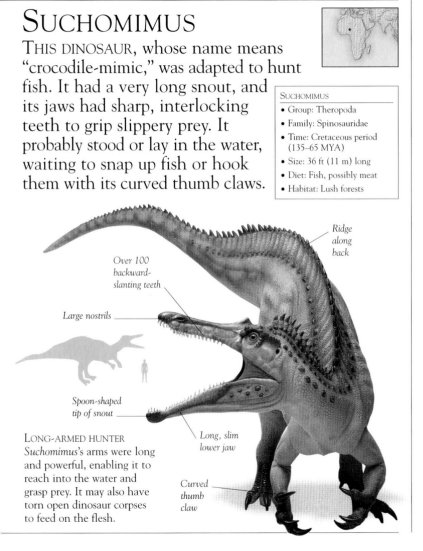

Ridge along back

Over 100 backward-slanting teeth

Large nostrils

Spoon-shaped tip of snout

Long, slim lower jaw

Curved thumb claw

LONG-ARMED HUNTER
Suchomimus's arms were long and powerful, enabling it to reach into the water and grasp prey. It may also have torn open dinosaur corpses to feed on the flesh.

BARYONYX

BARYONYX ("HEAVY CLAW") was named after its huge thumb claws. It also had an unusual crocodile-shaped skull, and its jaws were filled with 96 pointed teeth, twice as many as theropods usually possessed. These features, along with fish remains found with the skeleton, suggest that *Baryonyx* preyed on fishes.

BARYONYX CLAW

Sharp, curved thumb claw 12 in (30 cm) long

Unusually thick, powerful arm bones

Sharp claws on other fingers

It is possible that *Baryonyx* used its claws as hooks to spear fish out of the water, in the same way as a bear does.

Fenestrae reduced
weight of skull

Long, narrow
jaws

BARYONYX SKULL

Many small,
serrated teeth

Bony ridge
along spine

Relatively
stiff neck

Bony head
crest

BARYONYX
- Group: Theropoda
- Family: Spinosauridae
- Time: Cretaceous period
  (135–65 MYA)
- Size: 33 ft (10 m) long
- Diet: Fish, perhaps meat
- Habitat: Riverbanks

SPINOSAURUS

SPINOSAURUS ("spine lizard")
was an immense theropod with
an impressive sail-like structure
running down its back. The
function of the sail is not known,
but some paleontologists believe
that it served as a device to cool
the dinosaur, since it lived in a
very hot climate.

Tooth socket

FOSSIL TOOTH BATTERY
This fragment from a
Spinosaurus's jaw displays
empty tooth sockets.

*Vertical "sail"
supported by
spines*

*Large,
straight teeth*

*Stiff
tail*

*Longer-than-
usual arms for
a large theropod*

*Powerful
hind legs*

*Three long, forward-
facing, clawed toes*

SPINOSAURUS
- Group: Theropoda
- Family: Spinosauridae
- Time: Cretaceous period
  (135–65 MYA)
- Size: 50 ft (15 m) long
- Diet: Meat, perhaps fish
- Habitat: Tropical swamps

TYRANNOSAURUS

THE "TYRANT LIZARD" was one of the largest land carnivores ever. It was a heavily built theropod with a large head. It is hotly debated whether *Tyrannosaurus* was an active hunter or just a scavenger, since it had small eyes and hands and was a slow mover.

TYRANNOSAURUS
- Group: Theropoda
- Family: Tyrannosauridae
- Time: Cretaceous period (135–65 MYA)
- Size: 40 ft (12 m)
- Diet: Other dinosaurs
- Habitat: Forests, swamps

Tail held stiffly for balance

Pebbled skin texture

6-in- (15-cm-) long, serrated teeth

Extremely small hands

TYRANNOSAURUS SKELETON
The first skeletal reconstruction was prepared in 1915, showing the dinosaur standing upright.

STRONG LEGS
Tyrannosaurus had thick, long legs with powerful muscles, for walking long distances.

58 teeth

Tail made up of about 40 vertebrae

217

SAUROPODOMORPHS

THE PROSAUROPODS and sauropods belong to the sauropodomorph group. Unlike theropods, most members of this group were quadrupedal (walked on four legs) and ate plants. They had long necks and tails, and ranged in length from 6 ft 6 in (2 m) to 130 ft (40 m).

APATOSAURUS THUMB CLAW

THUMB CLAW
Many sauropodomorphs had big, curved thumb claws. They probably used these dangerous weapons for defense.

Long, flexible neck

Large front feet could hold plants when feeding

Plateosaurus may often have walked on only two legs

Prosauropods such as Plateosaurus were the first large land animals

Small skull

PLATEOSAURUS
Several complete skeletons of the prosauropod *Plateosaurus* have been found. It is one of the earliest and largest saurischian dinosaurs of the Triassic period. Although it was quadrupedal, it could probably stand on its hind legs to feed on leaves of higher branches.

Tail was held off the ground when walking

BAROSAURUS SKULL
Sauropods, such as *Barosaurus*, had no molars or grinding teeth for chewing. Their food was probably ground by pebbles in their gizzards after being swallowed whole.

Teeth raked in food

BAROSAURUS SKULL

BRACHIOSAURUS
One of the largest known land animals, *Brachiosaurus* weighed more than 70 tons. Reaching 40 ft (12 m) in height, it could eat from the tops of the tallest trees.

Long neck

STRONG SUPPORT
Brachiosaurus' dorsal (back) vertebrae had to be extremely strong to support its enormous weight.

Thick legs supported heavy weight

Front legs were longer than the back legs

SAUROPODOMORPH FACTS

• Sauropodomorph means "lizard-footed forms."

• The longest sauropod was a dinosaur called *Seismosaurus*.

• All sauropodomorphs were herbivores, although some may also have eaten meat.

PROSAUROPODS

THE PROSAUROPODS are probably ancestors of the sauropods. Both had long necks and small heads, but the prosauropods were smaller. Most were herbivores, but some ate meat.

MASSOSPONDYLUS
THUMB CLAW

THUMB CLAW
Massospondylus may have been an omnivore, since it had large, serrated front teeth. It also had sharp thumb claws, which may have been used to attack prey, as well as for defense.

Teeth

Eye socket

SMALL SKULL
Riojasaurus, at 33 ft (10 m) in length, was the largest prosauropod. As with other prosauropods, its skull was tiny compared with its massive body, and its jaws were lined with leaf-shaped teeth for shredding plant food.

Slender back leg

ANCHISAURUS
This prosauropod was designed to walk on all fours, but it may have occasionally run on two feet. *Anchisaurus* had large, sickle-shaped thumb claws that would have been dangerous weapons against attackers.

PROSAUROPOD FACTS

• The name prosauropod means "before sauropods."

• All prosauropods had small heads, long necks, and long tails.

• *Plateosaurus* was the first large dinosaur.

• Their remains have been found worldwide.

VIEW FROM ABOVE
This view from above of *Anchisaurus* shows that its body was long and slender. It would have held its tail off the ground when walking.

Slim and flexible neck

REACHING HIGH
Plateosaurus was one of the earliest and largest saurischian dinosaurs. It grew to about 26 ft (8 m) in length, and could stand on its hind legs to reach tall trees when feeding.

Lower arm

Thumb claw

Large thumb claw

PULLING CLAW
The digits on the hands of *Plateosaurus* varied greatly in length. The thumb, the largest, ended with a huge, sharp claw.

221

THECODONTOSAURUS

THIS DINOSAUR WAS the first prosauropod to be discovered, and is also one of the most primitive known. Its was named "socket-toothed lizard" because its saw-edged teeth looked like those of a monitor lizard, but were embedded in the sockets of the jaw bones. *Thecodontosaurus* had a relatively small head and neck, but a long tail.

THECODONTOSAURUS
• Group: Prosauropoda
• Family: Anchisauridae
• Time: Triassic period (250–203 MYA)
• Size: 7 ft (2 m) long
• Diet: Plants, possibly omnivorous
• Habitat: Desert plains, dry upland areas

Small head

Fairly short neck

Large thumb claw

Four-toed feet

TWO-LEGGED WALK
Although *Thecodontosaurus* was mainly bipedal (two-legged), it seems to have been capable of walking on all four limbs.

EFRAASIA

THIS EARLY PROSAUROPOD was named after its discoverer, E. Fraas. It was lightly built, with a small head, a fairly long neck, a bulky body, and a long tail. Its legs were longer than its arms, and its five-fingered hands had a large thumb claw. It may have walked on all fours, rising onto its hind legs to run.

Nostrils far forward on snout

Flexible tail

Five long digits on hands

Four-toed feet

EFRAASIA
- Group: Prosauropoda
- Family: Anchisauridae
- Time: Triassic period (250–203 MYA)
- Size: 7¼ ft (2.4 m) long
- Diet: Plants
- Habitat: Dry upland plains

ANCHISAURUS

ANCHISAURUS MEANS "near lizard" because this small, early prosauropod was very closely related to its reptilian ancestors. It had a small head with a narrow snout, a long, flexible neck, and a slim body and tail. *Anchisaurus*'s limbs were short and sturdy, although its hind limbs were larger than its forelimbs. Its feet were slender with five clawed toes. The five-fingered hand had a thumb with a large claw that may have been used for defense against attackers.

VERSATILE WALKER
Although *Anchisaurus*'s arms were a third shorter than its legs, it spent most of its time on all fours. However, it may also have run on two legs and could perhaps raise itself up on its hind legs to reach high plants.

Long hind legs

Clawed toes

Long tail

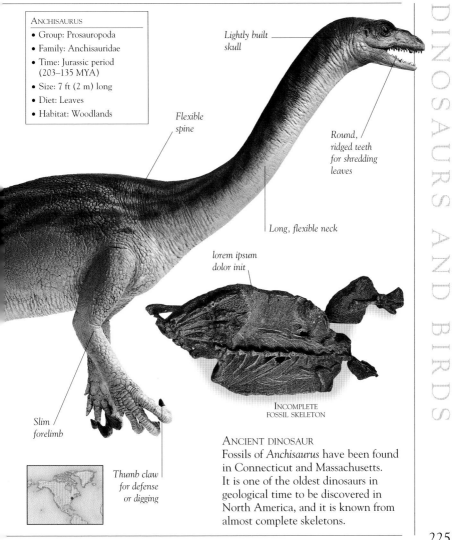

ANCHISAURUS
- Group: Prosauropoda
- Family: Anchisauridae
- Time: Jurassic period (203–135 MYA)
- Size: 7 ft (2 m) long
- Diet: Leaves
- Habitat: Woodlands

Lightly built skull

Flexible spine

Round, ridged teeth for shredding leaves

Long, flexible neck

lorem ipsum dolor init

INCOMPLETE FOSSIL SKELETON

Slim forelimb

Thumb claw for defense or digging

ANCIENT DINOSAUR
Fossils of *Anchisaurus* have been found in Connecticut and Massachusetts. It is one of the oldest dinosaurs in geological time to be discovered in North America, and it is known from almost complete skeletons.

225

MASSOSPONDYLUS

MASSOSPONDYLUS ("massive vertebrae") was so named because the first remains found of it were a few large vertebrae. More fossil finds have since been made, suggesting that this prosauropod was one of the most common in southern Africa. *Massospondylus* was four-legged, but could stand on its hind legs to feed from trees.

MASSOSPONDYLUS
- Group: Prosauropoda
- Family: Massospondylidae
- Time: Jurassic period (203–135 MYA)
- Size: 13 ft (4 m) long
- Diet: Plants
- Habitat: Scrublands and desert plains

LONG REACH
This dinosaur had a tiny head on an extremely long neck. It had massive, five-fingered hands that could be used for holding food or for walking.

Sharp end used for digging or defense

Large, curved claw

FOSSIL THUMB CLAW

Long, flexible neck

Small body ribs

Hands with massive span

LUFENGOSAURUS

LUFENGOSAURUS ("Lufeng lizard") was found in China. It was heavy and sturdy-limbed. Its small head held many widely spaced, leaf-shaped teeth, a typical feature of all prosauropods. Its lower jaw was hinged below the level of the upper teeth, making the jaw muscles more effective for feeding on tough plant food.

Large, deep head

Bulky, heavy body

Large hands to support weight when walking

LUFENGOSAURUS
- Group: Prosauropoda
- Family: Melanorosauridae
- Time: Jurassic period (203–135 MYA)
- Size: 20 ft (6 m) long
- Diet: Coniferous trees
- Habitat: Desert plains and scrublands

SPREADING HANDS AND FEET
Lufengosaurus's broad feet had four long toes, while the large hands had long, clawed fingers and thumbs with massive claws.

PLATEOSAURUS

PLATEOSAURUS WAS ONE of the most common dinosaurs of the Late Triassic Period. The large number of fossil finds suggest that *Plateosaurus* may have lived in herds and migrated in search of food and water. Its small skull was deeper than those of most other prosauropods. *Plateosaurus* had many small, leaf-shaped teeth, and the hinge of the lower jaw was low-slung to give it more flexibility. All these features indicate a diet primarily made up of plants.

Fairly short, thin, flexible neck

Plant-shredding teeth

Clawed fingers

PLATEOSAURUS

- Group: Prosauropoda
- Family: Plateosauridae
- Time: Triassic period (250–203 MYA)
- Size: 26 ft (8 m) long
- Diet: Leaves
- Habitat: Dry plains, deserts

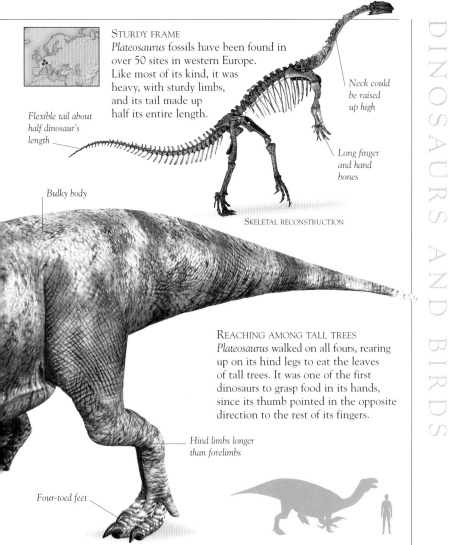

STURDY FRAME
Plateosaurus fossils have been found in over 50 sites in western Europe. Like most of its kind, it was heavy, with sturdy limbs, and its tail made up half its entire length.

Flexible tail about half dinosaur's length

Neck could be raised up high

Bulky body

Long finger and hand bones

SKELETAL RECONSTRUCTION

REACHING AMONG TALL TREES
Plateosaurus walked on all fours, rearing up on its hind legs to eat the leaves of tall trees. It was one of the first dinosaurs to grasp food in its hands, since its thumb pointed in the opposite direction to the rest of its fingers.

Hind limbs longer than forelimbs

Four-toed feet

SAUROPODS

THE LARGEST-EVER land animals belonged to the sauropod group. These plant-eating dinosaurs were quadrupedal, with long necks, elephant-like legs, and long, whiplike tails.

TAIL REINFORCEMENT
Tail bones like the one above were on the underside of *Diplodocus*'s tail. They reinforced and protected the tail when it was pressed against the ground.

FRONT TEETH
Diplodocus had a long skull with peglike teeth at the front of the jaws. The teeth would have raked in plants such as cycads, ginkgoes, and conifers. *Diplodocus* had no back teeth for chewing, so the food was probably ground in the stomach by gastroliths (stomach stones).

Back of jaw was toothless

Peglike teeth

APATOSAURUS
This dinosaur was one of the largest sauropods at 73 ft (23 m) long. This reconstruction has *Apatosaurus* dragging its tail, although it almost certainly carried it off the ground. It had a horselike head with a fist-sized brain, and powerful legs with padded feet.

Tail contained 82 bones

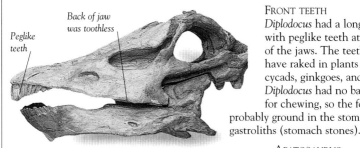

TAIL WEAPON
Barosaurus resembled *Diplodocus*, but had a slightly longer neck and a shorter tail. The narrow tail may have been a defense weapon.

Tail may have been used like a whip against enemies

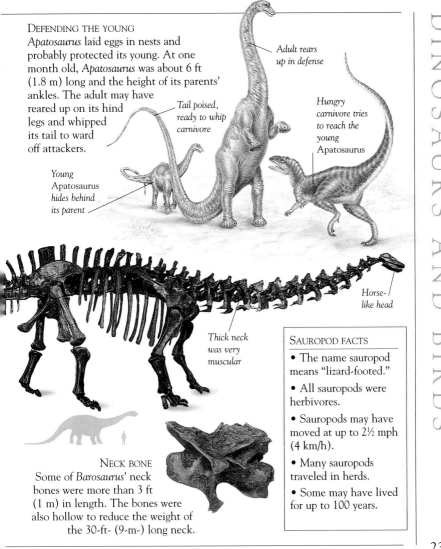

DEFENDING THE YOUNG

Apatosaurus laid eggs in nests and probably protected its young. At one month old, *Apatosaurus* was about 6 ft (1.8 m) long and the height of its parents' ankles. The adult may have reared up on its hind legs and whipped its tail to ward off attackers.

Tail poised, ready to whip carnivore

Adult rears up in defense

Hungry carnivore tries to reach the young Apatosaurus

Young Apatosaurus hides behind its parent

Horse-like head

Thick neck was very muscular

NECK BONE

Some of *Barosaurus'* neck bones were more than 3 ft (1 m) in length. The bones were also hollow to reduce the weight of the 30-ft- (9-m-) long neck.

SAUROPOD FACTS

- The name sauropod means "lizard-footed."
- All sauropods were herbivores.
- Sauropods may have moved at up to 2½ mph (4 km/h).
- Many sauropods traveled in herds.
- Some may have lived for up to 100 years.

VULCANODON

This dinosaur was named after the volcanic rock in which the first skeleton was found. With the skeleton were seven teeth, which actually came from a predator that may have eaten it. *Vulcanodon* is one of the earliest sauropods known, dating back to the Triassic. It would have been roughly the size of a large crocodile. *Vulcanodon* had blunt claws on its feet and an enlarged claw on each inner toe.

Small head

Long, slim neck

Nostrils placed high on nose

Bulky, sloping body

Shorter hind legs

VULCANODON
- Group: Sauropoda
- Family: Vulcanodontidae
- Time: Jurassic period (203–135 MYA)
- Size: 20 ft (6.5 m) long
- Diet: Plants
- Habitat: Forested plains

BARAPASAURUS

THE NAME *Barapasaurus* means "big-legged lizard." This is one of the earliest and best-known sauropods of the Early Jurassic. All parts of the skeleton, except the skull and feet, have been found. *Barapasaurus* had slim limbs, spoon-shaped, saw-edged teeth, and hollows in the vertebrae of the back. Scientists believe that its head was short and deep.

Relatively short neck

Heavy, bulky body

Long, flexible tail

BARAPASAURUS

- Group: Sauropoda
- Family: Vulcanodontidae
- Time: Jurassic period (203–135 MYA)
- Size: 60 ft (18 m) long
- Diet: Plants
- Habitat: Plains

Elephant-like legs and feet

CETIOSAURUS

THIS DINOSAUR, whose name means "whale lizard," was a large, heavy sauropod with a shorter neck and tail than other sauropods. Its head was blunt and contained spoon-shaped teeth. *Cetiosaurus* is thought to have roamed across the open countryside in large herds. It had a walking speed of about 10 mph (15 km/h).

CETIOSAURUS
- Group: Sauropoda
- Family: Cetiosauridae
- Time: Jurassic period (203–135 MYA)
- Size: 60 ft (18 m) long
- Diet: Plants
- Habitat: Plains

Solid bone

FOSSIL VERTEBRA

SOLID VERTEBRAE
Cetiosaurus was different from other sauropods in that its vertebrae were solid, without hollow spaces to lighten them.

MISTAKEN IDENTITY
This dinosaur was discovered in the early 18th century. Its huge bones were first thought to belong to a whale— hence its name.

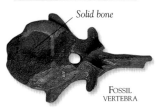

Tail held off the ground

Shoulder blade was 5 ft (1.5 m) long

SHUNOSAURUS

NEARLY COMPLETE skeletons of *Shunosaurus* ("Shuno lizard") have been discovered, meaning it is only the second sauropod to be known entirely. The skull is long and low with small teeth. A surprising feature is the small bony club at the end of its tail, formed by enlarged vertebrae (not seen in the pictured specimen).

SHUNOSAURUS
- Group: Sauropoda
- Family: Possibly Cetiosauridae
- Time: Jurassic period (203–135 MYA)
- Size: 33 ft (10 m) long
- Diet: Plants
- Habitat: Plains

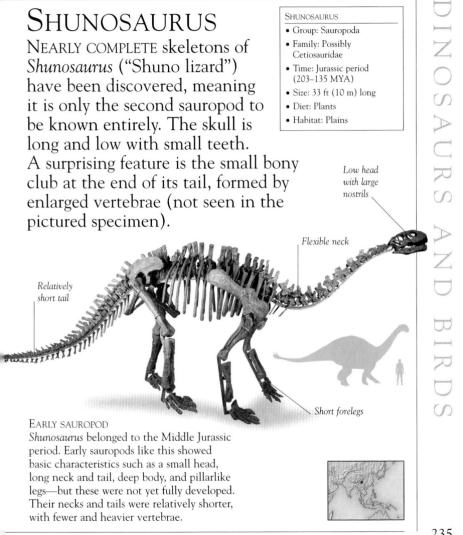

Low head with large nostrils

Flexible neck

Relatively short tail

Short forelegs

EARLY SAUROPOD

Shunosaurus belonged to the Middle Jurassic period. Early sauropods like this showed basic characteristics such as a small head, long neck and tail, deep body, and pillarlike legs—but these were not yet fully developed. Their necks and tails were relatively shorter, with fewer and heavier vertebrae.

BAROSAURUS

BAROSAURUS ("heavy lizard")
had all the typical features of its
family—a long neck and tail, a
bulky body, a tiny head, and short
legs for its huge size. *Barosaurus*
probably roamed in herds and
relied on its size for defense
against the large predators of the
time. Its tail had a thin whiplash
end and would have hit out with
great force if swung against
an attacking dinosaur.

BAROSAURUS
- Group: Sauropoda
- Family: Diplodocidae
- Time: Jurassic period
  (203–135 MYA)
- Size: 75–90 ft
  (23–27 m) long
- Diet: Plants
- Habitat: Floodplains

*Enormous,
bulky body
typical of a
sauropod*

*Powerful tail with
whiplash end*

*Elephant-like
hind limbs*

DINOSAUR HUNTING
This photograph shows the camp at Carnegie Quarry in Utah, where three *Barosaurus* skeletons were found in 1922. By the end of the year, 22 skeletons of 10 dinosaur species had been found.

Tiny head at end of incredibly long neck

GIGANTIC NECK
One-third of this dinosaur's length was made up of its long, thin neck. This creature could hold its head at a height of 50 ft (15 m). However, it would have held its neck at shoulder height most of the time.

Front legs shorter than hind legs

Single-clawed front feet

Elongated vertebra of the back

STRETCHED-OUT VERTEBRAE
The neck and back vertebrae of the *Barosaurus* were extremely stretched to create this dinosaur's enormous length.

VERTEBRA

DIPLODOCUS

DIPLODOCUS WAS ONE of the longest dinosaurs. From head to tail, it was longer than a tennis court. Its weight was finely balanced at the hips, and so it may have been able to rise on its hind legs. Its limbs were slim and it had a whiplash tail. *Diplodocus*'s name, meaning "double beam," came from twin extensions, called chevrons, under its tail bones.

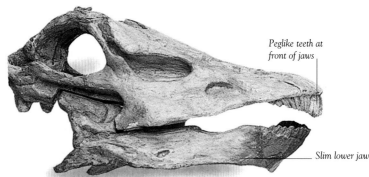

Peglike teeth at front of jaws

Slim lower jaw

VARIED EATER
The wear on the teeth of *Diplodocus* suggests that it fed both low, from ground-hugging vegetation, and high, from tree branches.

DIPLODOCUS
- Group: Sauropoda
- Family: Diplodocidae
- Time: Jurassic period (203–135 MYA)
- Size: 87 ft (27 m) long
- Diet: Leaves
- Habitat: Plains

APATOSAURUS

THIS SAUROPOD WAS shorter, yet heavier and bulkier than its close relatives. It had a tiny head at the end of a long neck made up of 15 vertebrae. Its back vertebrae were hollow, and its long tail had a whiplike end. The thick hind legs were longer than the front ones. One species of *Apatosaurus*, *A. excelsus*, was the dinosaur originally called *Brontosaurus*.

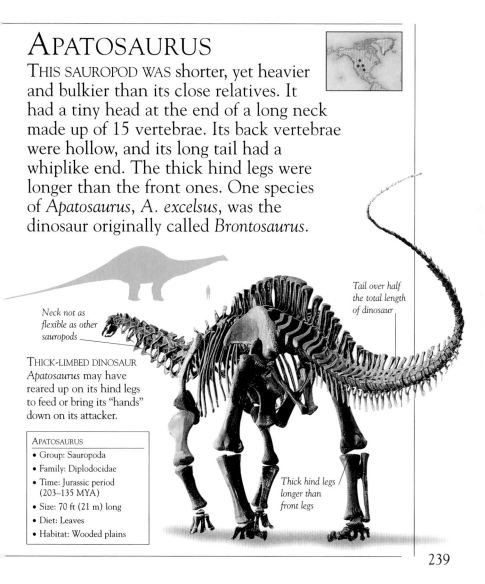

Tail over half the total length of dinosaur

Neck not as flexible as other sauropods

THICK-LIMBED DINOSAUR *Apatosaurus* may have reared up on its hind legs to feed or bring its "hands" down on its attacker.

APATOSAURUS
- Group: Sauropoda
- Family: Diplodocidae
- Time: Jurassic period (203–135 MYA)
- Size: 70 ft (21 m) long
- Diet: Leaves
- Habitat: Wooded plains

Thick hind legs longer than front legs

MAMENCHISAURUS

MAMENCHISAURUS had one of the longest necks of any known dinosaur. It was more than half of the animal's total length, and had 19 vertebrae—more than any other dinosaur. Some experts think *Mamenchisaurus* may not have been able to hold its neck much higher than shoulder height.

MAMENCHISAURUS
- Group: Sauropoda
- Family: Mamenchisauridae
- Time: Jurassic period (203–135 MYA)
- Size: 72 ft (22 m) long
- Diet: Leaves and shoots
- Habitat: Deltas and forested areas

FOSSIL REMAINS
Mamenchisaurus inhabited China, where its remains have been excavated.

Enormously elongated neck

Back sloping from shoulders

ENORMOUS NECK
Mamenchisaurus's neck alone may have measured about 45 ft (14 m) long.

CAMARASAURUS

CAMARASAURUS ("chambered lizard") was the most common sauropod of North America. It probably roamed in large herds, stripping tough leaves from shrubby trees at shoulder height. This dinosaur had a relatively large, box-shaped head, and a short neck and tail. *Camarasaurus*'s vertebrae may have contained large holes to lighten the backbone.

Nasal chambers high on snout

FOSSIL SKULL

BLUNT FACE
Camarasaurus's short, deep skull ended in a blunt muzzle similar to a bulldog's.

PILLARLIKE LIMBS
The front legs of *Camarasaurus* were relatively long. Its forefeet had one single claw and the hind feet had three.

Massive, heavy body

Short head

Three claws on hind feet

CAMARASAURUS
- Group: Sauropoda
- Family: Camarasauridae
- Time: Jurassic period (203–135 MYA)
- Size: 75 ft (23 m) long
- Diet: Tough vegetation
- Habitat: Plains

BRACHIOSAURUS

THE "ARM LIZARD,"
or *Brachiosaurus*,
was one of the
tallest and largest
sauropods, with extremely long
forelimbs compared with its hind limbs.
Its stretched-out neck, ending in a small
head, gave it enormous height. The nostrils
were large and were situated on a bulge on
the top of the head. Like other sauropods,
it probably traveled in herds, and fed on
vegetation from the tops of trees.

*Long neck made up
of vertebrae 3 ft
(1 m) long*

*Ball-like head
of femur*

MASSIVE BONES
The femur (thigh bone) of
Brachiosaurus was over 6 ft
(1.8 m) long and massively
thick to support the dinosaur's
weight. Its legs were pillarlike,
and each foot had five toes.
The first toe of the front foot
bore a claw, as did the first
three toes of the hind foot.

Nostrils on
bulge on top
of head

BRACHIOSAURUS
- Group: Sauropoda
- Family: Brachiosauridae
- Time: Jurassic period
  (203–135 MYA)
- Size: 85 ft (26 m) long
- Diet: Plants
- Habitat: Plains

Chisel-like
teeth at front
of mouth

Body sloping
downward from
shoulder to hip

Pillarlike legs

ARGENTINOSAURUS

ONLY A FEW BONES of *Argentinosaurus* ("Argentina lizard") have been found to date, including some huge vertebrae, which were over 5 ft (1.5 m) wide. Other bones found were the sacrum (the triangular bone between the hip bones), a tibia (shin bone), and a few ribs. As a result, little is known about this dinosaur. However, Argentinosaurus appears to have been the longest dinosaur ever found—the length of three big school buses parked end to end.

Huge, bulky body

GIANT DINOSAUR
Argentinosaurus is thought to have been a titanosaur with a body structure similar to that of *Diplodocus*. As in other titanosaurs, the neck and tail would have been very long and thin, and the skull is likely to have been small and triangular.

Long, whiplash tail

Elephant-like, thick limbs with clawed toes

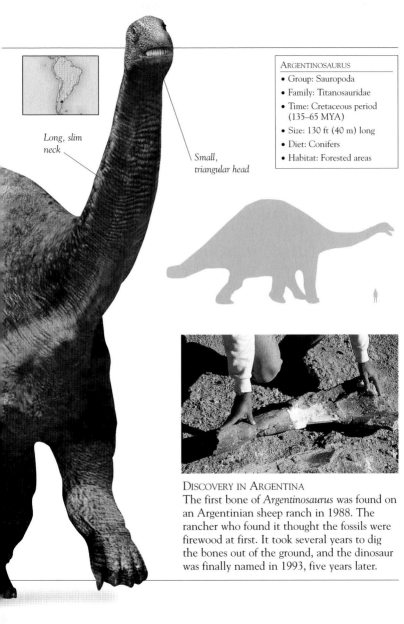

Long, slim neck

Small, triangular head

ARGENTINOSAURUS

- Group: Sauropoda
- Family: Titanosauridae
- Time: Cretaceous period (135–65 MYA)
- Size: 130 ft (40 m) long
- Diet: Conifers
- Habitat: Forested areas

DISCOVERY IN ARGENTINA
The first bone of *Argentinosaurus* was found on an Argentinian sheep ranch in 1988. The rancher who found it thought the fossils were firewood at first. It took several years to dig the bones out of the ground, and the dinosaur was finally named in 1993, five years later.

TITANOSAURUS

"TITAN LIZARD"

is known only
from some
lower-back
vertebrae and limb bones.
Its skull has never been found.
However, it probably had the
typical sauropod body shape. Its
vertebrae were not hollow for
weight-saving as they were in
most other sauropods.

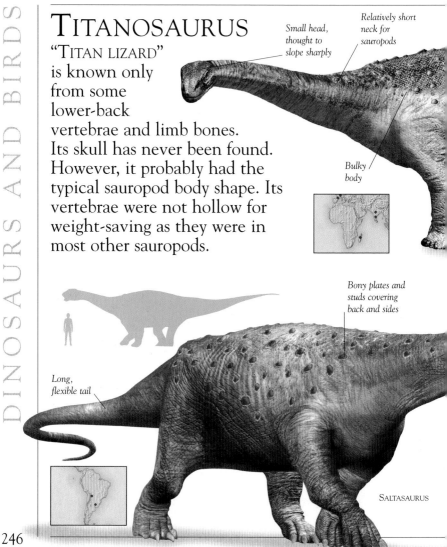

Small head, thought to slope sharply

Relatively short neck for sauropods

Bulky body

Bony plates and studs covering back and sides

Long, flexible tail

SALTASAURUS

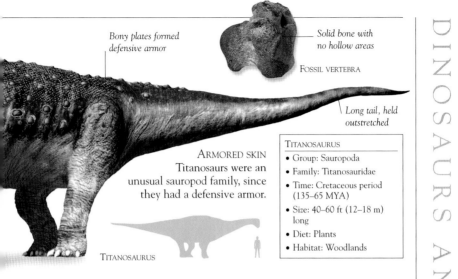

Bony plates formed defensive armor

Solid bone with no hollow areas

FOSSIL VERTEBRA

Long tail, held outstretched

ARMORED SKIN
Titanosaurs were an unusual sauropod family, since they had a defensive armor.

TITANOSAURUS

TITANOSAURUS
- Group: Sauropoda
- Family: Titanosauridae
- Time: Cretaceous period (135–65 MYA)
- Size: 40–60 ft (12–18 m) long
- Diet: Plants
- Habitat: Woodlands

Nostrils high on head

Fossilized impressions of bony plates of varying sizes

FOSSIL ARMOR

SALTASAURUS

SALTASAURUS was named after the province in Argentina where it was first found. Its fossils consisted of a group of partial skeletons surrounded by thousands of bony plates, large and small. This was the first evidence of armored skin on a sauropod. It may have used its strong tail as a prop when it reared up on its hind legs.

SALTASAURUS
- Group: Sauropoda
- Family: Titanosauridae
- Time: Cretaceous period (135–65 MYA)
- Size: 40 ft (12 m) long
- Diet: Plants
- Habitat: Woodlands

ABOUT ORNITHISCHIANS

THERE WERE FIVE main groups of ornithischians. They were all herbivores with hoofed feet and hip bones arranged like modern birds. Most of them had beaked mouths. Ornithischians were either bipedal or quadrupedal; the bipedal ones held out their tails stiffly to balance their bodies while feeding or running.

CERATOPSIANS

ANKYLOSAURS

ORNITHOPODS

PACHYCEPHALOSAURS

FIVE GROUPS
The five groups of ornithischians were: ceratopsians, with their neck frills; ankylosaurs, with their body armor; pachycephalosaurs, with their domed heads; stegosaurs, with their back plates; and the birdlike ornithopods.

STEGOSAURS

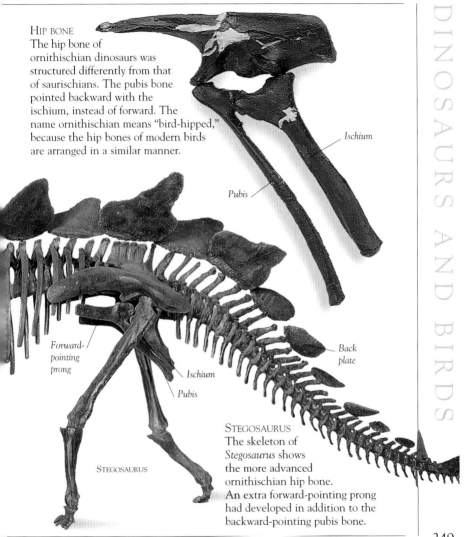

HIP BONE
The hip bone of
ornithischian dinosaurs was
structured differently from that
of saurischians. The pubis bone
pointed backward with the
ischium, instead of forward. The
name ornithischian means "bird-hipped,"
because the hip bones of modern birds
are arranged in a similar manner.

Ischium

Pubis

Forward-pointing prong

Ischium

Pubis

Back plate

STEGOSAURUS

STEGOSAURUS
The skeleton of
Stegosaurus shows
the more advanced
ornithischian hip bone.
An extra forward-pointing prong
had developed in addition to the
backward-pointing pubis bone.

ORNITHOPODS

ALL THE ORNITHOPOD dinosaurs were herbivores with horned beaks. Their jaws and leaf-shaped cheek teeth were ideal for chewing vegetation. They were bipedal, although some of them may have foraged for food on all fours. Their feet had three or four toes, and their hands had four or five fingers.

Cheek teeth

Tusklike teeth

HETERODONTOSAURUS
Heterodontosaurus had three different kinds of teeth. These were the front upper teeth, which bit against the toothless lower beak; the scissorlike cheek teeth; and a pair of upper and lower tusklike teeth.

GROUP LIVING

Hypsilophodon may have moved in herds for protection against predatory theropods. Moving as a large group, they would have been able to warn each other of danger, giving them a better chance of survival.

Group members looked from side to side for any danger

Slim, long legs for speed

Bony tendons

VERTEBRAE SUPPORT

Ornithopods such as *Iguanodon* had a crisscross of bony tendons strengthening the vertebrae above the hip and in the back. These tendons also stiffened the tail, which helped *Iguanodon* balance as it walked on its hind legs.

Toes ended in flattened hooves

ORNITHOPOD FACTS

• The name ornithopod means "bird foot."

• They ranged in length from 6½ ft (2 m) to 50 ft (15 m).

• Some ornithopods had up to 1,000 cheek teeth.

• They could run at speeds of at least 9 mph (15 km/h).

THREE-TOED FEET

The powerful three-toed feet of *Corythosaurus* were built to carry its heavy weight. *Corythosaurus* weighed approximately 4 tons and was about 24 ft (7.5 m) long. It belonged to a group of ornithopods called hadrosaurs.

HYPSILOPHODON

HETERODONTOSAURUS

AS ITS NAME ("different-toothed lizard") suggests, the most remarkable feature of this small bipedal dinosaur was its teeth. *Heterodontosaurus* had three kinds: cutting incisors at the front of the upper jaw, two pairs of large tusklike teeth, and tall chisel-like teeth used for shredding vegetation. The tusks may have been used to frighten or attack enemies, or in fights between competing males.

Relatively short neck

Tusks possibly only present in males

Bony rods stiffened back and tail

Horny beak

Hands capable of grasping

SKELETON FOSSILIZED IN CLAY

Three long, forward-facing, clawed toes

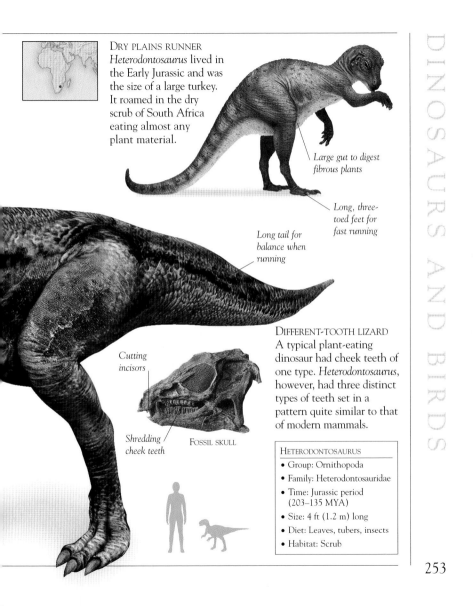

DRY PLAINS RUNNER
Heterodontosaurus lived in the Early Jurassic and was the size of a large turkey. It roamed in the dry scrub of South Africa eating almost any plant material.

Large gut to digest fibrous plants

Long, three-toed feet for fast running

Long tail for balance when running

Cutting incisors

Shredding cheek teeth

FOSSIL SKULL

DIFFERENT-TOOTH LIZARD
A typical plant-eating dinosaur had cheek teeth of one type. *Heterodontosaurus*, however, had three distinct types of teeth set in a pattern quite similar to that of modern mammals.

HETERODONTOSAURUS
• Group: Ornithopoda
• Family: Heterodontosauridae
• Time: Jurassic period (203–135 MYA)
• Size: 4 ft (1.2 m) long
• Diet: Leaves, tubers, insects
• Habitat: Scrub

DRYOSAURUS

DRYOSAURUS ("oak lizard") was a lightly built bipedal herbivore, with powerful, slender legs that were much longer than its arms. Its tail was stiffened by bony tendons for better balance. It had a short skull with large eyes. The horny beak at the front of the lower jaw met with a toothless beak on the upper jaw—perfectly suited for cropping tough vegetation.

SWIFT RUNNER
Dryosaurus lived in the woodlands of what is now North America, Africa, and Europe. Its legs and feet were meant for swift running. Although it was two-legged, hatchlings may have walked on all fours.

THIGHBONE

Short arms

Five-fingered hands

Relatively short but muscular thighs

Long, three-toed feet

DRYOSAURUS
- Group: Ornithopoda
- Family: Dryosauridae
- Time: Jurassic period (203–135 MYA)
- Size: 10–13 ft (3–4 m) long
- Diet: Leaves and shoots
- Habitat: Woodlands

CAMPTOSAURUS

CAMPTOSAURUS ("bent lizard") was a bulky plant-eater that browsed on plants and shrubs close to the ground. Its head was long and low, with a sharp, horny beak at the tip of the broad snout. Its arms were shorter than its legs, but a large wrist and hooflike claws on its fingers allowed it to walk on its hands. *Camptosaurus* probably browsed on all fours, rising onto its powerful hind legs to run.

STRONG BACKBONE
Like other ornithopods, *Camptosaurus* had crisscross tendons on the spines of its vertebrae. This strengthened the spine and made it stiff.

Tail stiffened by bony ligaments

CAMPTOSAURUS
- Group: Ornithopoda
- Family: Camptosauridae
- Time: Jurassic period (203–135 MYA)
- Size: 16–23 ft (5–7 m) long
- Diet: Low-growing herbs and shrubs
- Habitat: Open woodlands

Four-toed hind feet

Curve in neck indicates that the head was held low

HYPSILOPHODON

THIS PRIMITIVE ORNITHISCHIAN, whose name means "high-ridge tooth," was named for its grooved cheek teeth, which made it very efficient at chewing tough Cretaceous vegetation. Its jaws hinged below the level of the teeth, giving it a strong bite, and held 28 or 30 teeth that were self-sharpening. The mouth had cheek pouches that could be used for storing food. Its small head had a horny beak and large eyes.

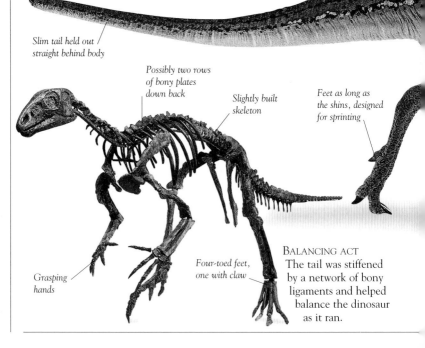

Slim tail held out straight behind body

Possibly two rows of bony plates down back

Slightly built skeleton

Feet as long as the shins, designed for sprinting

Grasping hands

Four-toed feet, one with claw

BALANCING ACT
The tail was stiffened by a network of bony ligaments and helped balance the dinosaur as it ran.

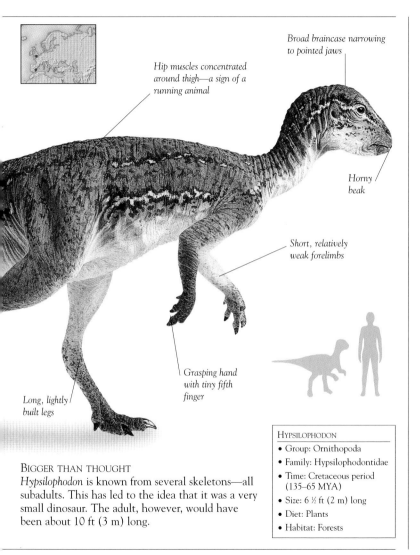

Broad braincase narrowing
to pointed jaws

Hip muscles concentrated
around thigh—a sign of a
running animal

Horny
beak

Short, relatively
weak forelimbs

Grasping hand
with tiny fifth
finger

Long, lightly
built legs

BIGGER THAN THOUGHT
Hypsilophodon is known from several skeletons—all
subadults. This has led to the idea that it was a very
small dinosaur. The adult, however, would have
been about 10 ft (3 m) long.

HYPSILOPHODON
- Group: Ornithopoda
- Family: Hypsilophodontidae
- Time: Cretaceous period
  (135–65 MYA)
- Size: 6 ½ ft (2 m) long
- Diet: Plants
- Habitat: Forests

257

IGUANODON

IGUANODON ("iguana tooth") is one of the best-known dinosaurs. Its fossils have been found in Europe, Asia, and North America. *Iguanodon* was a sturdily built herbivore that walked with its body and tail held horizontally.

IGUANODON

- Group: Ornithopoda
- Family: Iguanodontidae
- Time: Cretaceous period (135–65 MYA)
- Size: 30 ft (9 m) long
- Diet: Plants
- Habitat: Woodlands

DEXTEROUS DINOSAUR

Iguanodon was primarily quadrupedal, but also capable of bipedal walking. It had very specialized hands, which could have been used for walking, as a weapon, and to grasp food. The thumb was armed with a vicious spike. The second, third, and fourth fingers were webbed, while the fifth finger could curl and grasp.

Thumb spike
6 in (15 cm) long

FOSSIL THUMB
SPIKE

Horny beak
at front of jaw

FOSSIL SKULL

EFFICIENT JAW

Iguanodon could chew food with its batteries of cheek teeth. It had a hinged upper jaw that allowed the teeth in the upper jaw to grind over those in the lower jaw.

OURANOSAURUS

THE MOST REMARKABLE feature of this dinosaur was the row of spines growing out from its backbone—from its shoulders to halfway down its tail. Some experts think they supported a sail that acted as a heat controller; others suggest that it may have been covered by a bison-like hump.

Spines longest just behind shoulder

Height of spines less toward the tail

SKELETAL RECONSTRUCTION

Long hind limbs

Pair of bony bumps formed head crest

Tail held rigid and outstretched

Horny beak

OURANOSAURUS
- Group: Ornithopoda
- Family: Iguanodontidae
- Time: Cretaceous period (135–65 MYA)
- Size: 23 ft (7 m) long
- Diet: Leaves, fruit, and seeds
- Habitat: Tropical plains and forests

Hind legs longer than forelimbs

Hooflike nails on three-toed feet

Thumb spike

BRAVE ONE
The name *Ouranosaurus* means "brave lizard."

HADROSAURUS

HADROSAURUS ("STURDY LIZARD") was one of the first dinosaurs ever found in North America. Its skull had a toothless, horny beak used for scraping off vegetation, and hundreds of blunt cheek teeth for chewing. Although its forelimbs were much shorter than its hind legs, *Hadrosaurus* spent most of its time browsing on all fours. It walked with its stiff tail held outstretched for better balance.

Crest of solid bone

NEW TEETH
Hadrosaurus's teeth were continually replaced as they wore down from chewing on tough plant material.

Jaw would have been covered with a horny beak

Low jaw hinge for powerful chewing action

Batteries of grinding cheek teeth

HADROSAURUS
- Group: Ornithopoda
- Family: Hadrosauridae
- Time: Cretaceous period (135–65 MYA)
- Size: 30 ft (9 m) long
- Diet: Leaves and twigs
- Habitat: Swamps and forests

MAIASAURA

THIS DINOSAUR'S NAME means "good earth-mother lizard." It was so named because remains were found close to fossilized nests scooped out of mud, which contained eggs arranged in circular layers. *Maiasaura* migrated and nested each year in large herds.

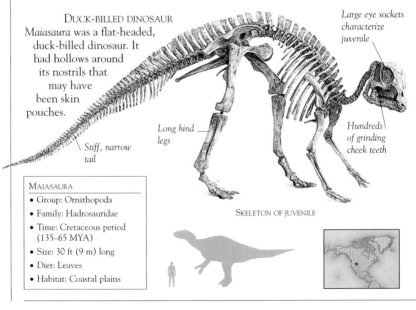

NEST-SITE RECONSTRUCTION

FEEDING THE YOUNG
Fossil evidence shows that the dinosaur parents brought food to their young at the nest site over quite a lengthy period.

DUCK-BILLED DINOSAUR
Maiasaura was a flat-headed, duck-billed dinosaur. It had hollows around its nostrils that may have been skin pouches.

Large eye sockets characterize juvenile

Stiff, narrow tail

Long hind legs

Hundreds of grinding cheek teeth

SKELETON OF JUVENILE

MAIASAURA
- Group: Ornithopoda
- Family: Hadrosauridae
- Time: Cretaceous period (135–65 MYA)
- Size: 30 ft (9 m) long
- Diet: Leaves
- Habitat: Coastal plains

CORYTHOSAURUS

CORYTHOSAURUS ("helmet lizard") was named for the distinctive hollow crest on top of its head. This seems to have been larger in males and may have produced a booming foghornlike sound used for signaling among herds. The angle of the neck, and the broad beak, suggest that *Corythosaurus* fed from low undergrowth.

CORYTHOSAURUS
- Group: Ornithopoda
- Family: Hadrosauridae
- Time: Cretaceous period (135–65 MYA)
- Size: 33 ft (10 m) long
- Diet: Leaves, seeds, pine needles
- Habitat: Forests

FOREST SWAMP DWELLER
Corythosaurus and other hadrosaurs lived among cypresses, pines and ferns in the warm forests of North America. The first flowering plants were beginning to spread during this period.

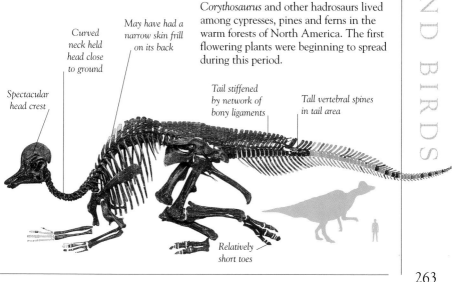

Curved neck held head close to ground

May have had a narrow skin frill on its back

Spectacular head crest

Tail stiffened by network of bony ligaments

Tall vertebral spines in tail area

Relatively short toes

LAMBEOSAURUS

LAMBEOSAURUS WAS named after Lawrence Lambe, who discovered it in 1898 in Alberta. It is closely related to *Corythosaurus*, but was unusual in having two head structures: a tall, hollow crest over the snout and a backward-pointing spike behind it. These were probably used for signaling and for recognition.

LAMBEOSAURUS
- Group: Ornithopoda
- Family: Hadrosauridae
- Time: Cretaceous period (135–65 MYA)
- Size: 30 ft (9 m) long
- Diet: Low-growing leaves, fruit, seeds
- Habitat: Woodlands

SOCIAL ANIMAL
Like other members of this family, *Lambeosaurus* had a deep, narrow tail, held stiff and immobile. It traveled in large herds, browsing on low-growing vegetation.

Tall spines on long, deep tail

Bony spike

Spine slanted downward from the hip

Hollow crest for signaling

FOSSIL SKULL

PARASAUROLOPHUS

THIS DINOSAUR is instantly recognized by its long, back-swept head crest, which was up to 6 ft (1.8 m) long. The crest was longer on males than on females. A frill of skin may have joined the crest to the neck. *Parasaurolophus* had hundreds of strong teeth for chewing tough ferns and plants.

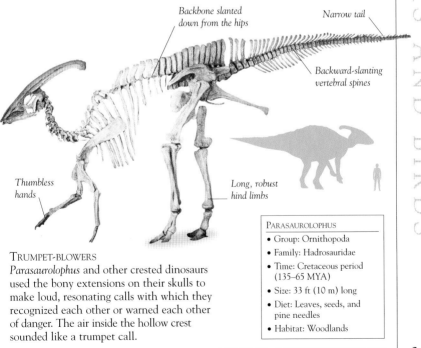

Backbone slanted down from the hips

Narrow tail

Backward-slanting vertebral spines

Thumbless hands

Long, robust hind limbs

TRUMPET-BLOWERS
Parasaurolophus and other crested dinosaurs used the bony extensions on their skulls to make loud, resonating calls with which they recognized each other or warned each other of danger. The air inside the hollow crest sounded like a trumpet call.

PARASAUROLOPHUS
- Group: Ornithopoda
- Family: Hadrosauridae
- Time: Cretaceous period (135–65 MYA)
- Size: 33 ft (10 m) long
- Diet: Leaves, seeds, and pine needles
- Habitat: Woodlands

CERATOPSIANS

HORNS, BONY FRILLS, and a parrot-like beak were the trademarks of the ceratopsians. They evolved from fleet-footed bipeds into heavy four-footed herbivores. Most ceratopsians can be divided into two groups. One group had short neck frills and the other had long neck frills. The ceratopsians were among the last surviving dinosaurs.

PSITTACOSAURUS
SKULL

Psittacosaurus
*may have moved
on all fours
when foraging*

PSITTACOSAURUS
This dinosaur was a bipedal ancestor of the ceratopsians. It had a parrotlike beak and a very small neck frill, but lacked the horns of other ceratopsians.

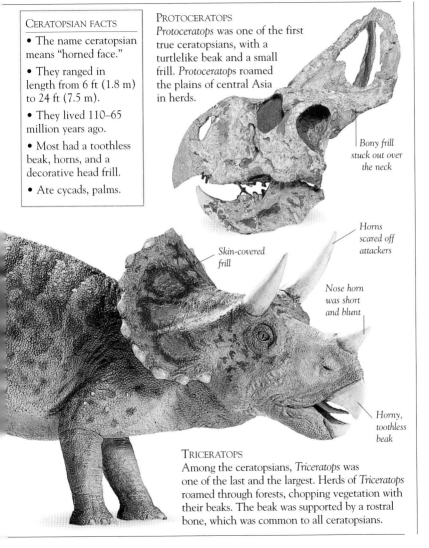

CERATOPSIAN FACTS

• The name ceratopsian means "horned face."

• They ranged in length from 6 ft (1.8 m) to 24 ft (7.5 m).

• They lived 110–65 million years ago.

• Most had a toothless beak, horns, and a decorative head frill.

• Ate cycads, palms.

PROTOCERATOPS
Protoceratops was one of the first true ceratopsians, with a turtlelike beak and a small frill. *Protoceratops* roamed the plains of central Asia in herds.

Bony frill stuck out over the neck

Horns scared off attackers

Nose horn was short and blunt

Skin-covered frill

Horny, toothless beak

TRICERATOPS
Among the ceratopsians, *Triceratops* was one of the last and the largest. Herds of *Triceratops* roamed through forests, chopping vegetation with their beaks. The beak was supported by a rostral bone, which was common to all ceratopsians.

SHORT-FRILLED CERATOPSIANS

THE GROUP OF ceratopsians with short frills had long nose horns and short brow horns. *Styracosaurus* had the most dramatic frill. *Brachyceratops* cared for its young, and when a herd was in danger, the males probably used their horned heads to protect the young and the females.

STYRACOSAURUS
SKULL

Long nose horn

STYRACOSAURUS
Six long spikes edged the frill of *Styracosaurus*. It had a lethal horn on its nose that was 2 ft (60 cm) long and 6 in (15 cm) thick. The horns above the eyes were stumps. It could run at a speed of up to 20 mph (32 km/h).

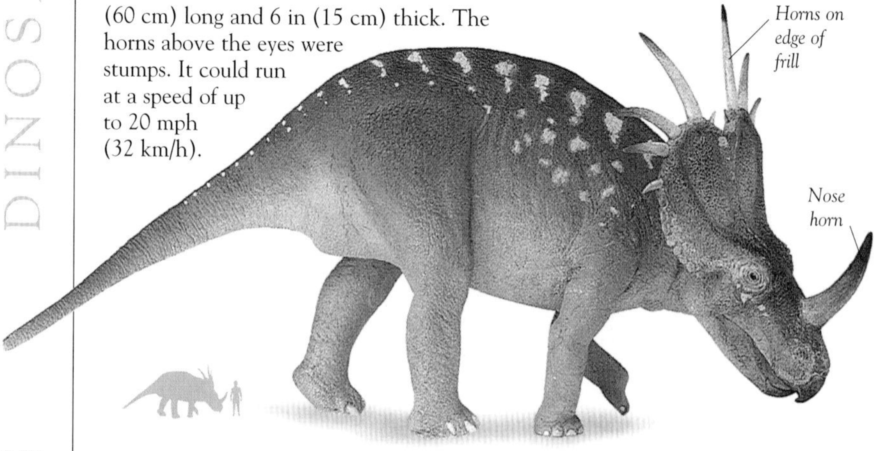

Horns on edge of frill

Nose horn

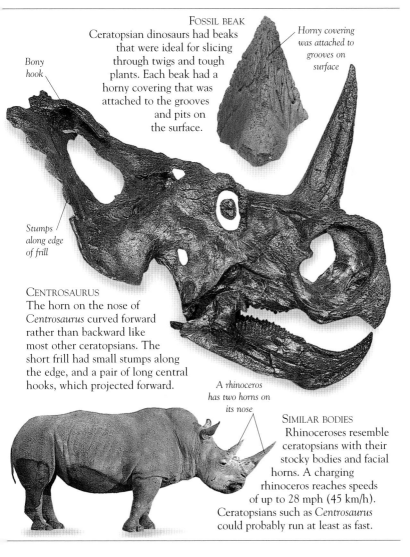

FOSSIL BEAK
Ceratopsian dinosaurs had beaks that were ideal for slicing through twigs and tough plants. Each beak had a horny covering that was attached to the grooves and pits on the surface.

Horny covering was attached to grooves on surface

Bony hook

Stumps along edge of frill

CENTROSAURUS
The horn on the nose of *Centrosaurus* curved forward rather than backward like most other ceratopsians. The short frill had small stumps along the edge, and a pair of long central hooks, which projected forward.

A rhinoceros has two horns on its nose

SIMILAR BODIES
Rhinoceroses resemble ceratopsians with their stocky bodies and facial horns. A charging rhinoceros reaches speeds of up to 28 mph (45 km/h). Ceratopsians such as *Centrosaurus* could probably run at least as fast.

269

LONG-FRILLED CERATOPSIANS

THE FRILL OF long-frilled ceratopsians extended back to, or over, the shoulders. Sometimes it had short spikes, and usually the bones had large holes to lighten the load.

Horn was made of solid bone

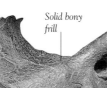

Solid bony frill

Brow horns 3 ft (1 m) long

FOSSIL HORN
This fossil is the core of the brow horn of *Triceratops*. In life it would have been sheathed in horn.

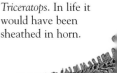

TRICERATOPS SKULL
Triceratops had a solid bony frill, a short nose horn, and two long brow horns. The parrotlike beak and sharp teeth were ideal for its vegetarian diet.

Beak was used to crop vegetation

Sharp teeth cut up leaves

TOROSAURUS
The skull of *Torosaurus* was 8½ ft (2.6 m) long, making its head bigger than that of any other known land animal.

Two large holes in the frill bone reduced its weight

CHASMOSAURUS

The earliest long-frilled ceratopsian was *Chasmosaurus*. To lighten its weight, the frill had two large holes that were probably filled with muscle. Its skeleton was solidly built to bear its 2-ton weight, and was not designed for speed. As with most ceratopsians, *Chasmosaurus* probably had few predators and used its horns mostly in territorial disputes.

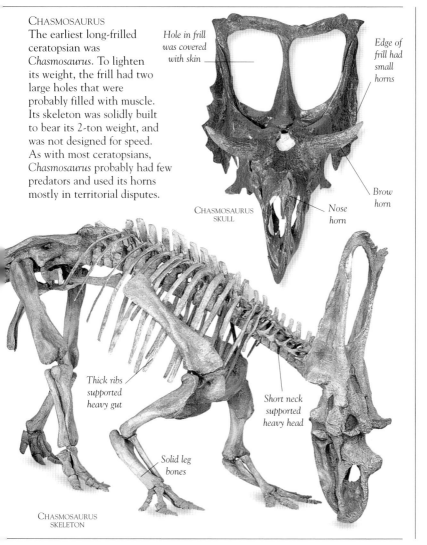

Hole in frill was covered with skin

Edge of frill had small horns

CHASMOSAURUS SKULL

Nose horn

Brow horn

Thick ribs supported heavy gut

Short neck supported heavy head

Solid leg bones

CHASMOSAURUS SKELETON

PSITTACOSAURUS

THIS DINOSAUR GOT its name, "parrot lizard," from its square skull and curved beak—similar to those of modern parrots. It had a pair of horns on its cheeks, believed to have been used for fighting or to attract mates. Members of this family are relatives of the horned dinosaurs and are the most primitive known ceratopsians, or bird-hipped dinosaurs.

TWO-FOOTED RUNNER
Psittacosaurus may have been a bipedal runner, since its hind legs were long and thin. The long toes with blunt claws were perhaps used for digging. Its long tail was stiffened by bony tendons along its length.

Tail used to maintain balance

Four clawed toes on hind feet

Bony tendons arranged along the length of the tail

PSITTACOSAURUS
- Group: Ceratopsia
- Family: Psittacosauridae
- Time: Cretaceous period (135–65 MYA)
- Size: 6 ft 3 in (2 m) long
- Diet: Plants
- Habitat: Deserts and scrublands

Cheek horn

Teeth behind toothless beak

PSITTACOSAURUS SKULL

MODERN PARROT HEAD

PARROTLIKE HEADS
The psittacosaurs'
remarkably deep skulls
superficially resemble
those of parrots.

Sharp claws suggest that Psittacosaurus *may have been a good digger*

FOSSILIZED PSITTACOSAURUS
Found in the 1920s, this
was the first psittacosaur to
be discovered. *Psittacosaurus*
skeletons are often found
in desert sandstone,
indicating its arid habitat.

273

PROTOCERATOPS

PROTOCERATOPS ("before the horned faces") was an early horned dinosaur with a relatively small horn. It had a broad neck frill at the back of its skull, which was larger and taller in males. Its small nasal horn was between the eyes, and it had two pairs of teeth in the upper jaw. Tall spines on the top of its tail made it appear humped.

SHEEP OF THE GOBI
Protoceratops is very well-known from the many specimens discovered buried under the sand in Mongolia. Its fossils are so abundant in the Gobi Desert that it has been called "sheep of the Gobi."

PROTOCERATOPS
- Group: Ceratopsia
- Family: Ceratopsidae
- Time: Cretaceous period (135–65 MYA)
- Size: 6 ft (1.8 m) long
- Diet: Plants
- Habitat: Scrublands and deserts

Nasal horn between the eyes

Protoceratops *was a four-footed animal*

Hump in tail for display or for fat storage

The Velociraptor's *arm is gripped by the* Protoceratops' *beak*

Protoceratops

Velociraptor

Large eyes

FOSSILIZED BATTLE SCENE
This famous fossil was discovered in the Gobi Desert in 1971. It preserves a *Protoceratops* locked in battle with a *Velociraptor*. Both animals died in the fight.

STAGES OF DEVELOPMENT
The frill on the *Protoceratops*'s head grew with age. Several fossils at different stages of growth have been found to prove this. The females' frills were probably smaller.

Possibly female

Possibly female

HATCHLING   BABY   JUVENILE   SUBADULT   SUBADULT   ADULT   ADULT

CHASMOSAURUS

CHASMOSAURUS ("cleft lizard") was
a typical frilled, horned dinosaur. It
had a large body with four stocky
legs. Its enormous neck frill, which
reached over the shoulders, was likely
to have been brightly colored and
used to attract females. The bony
structure below it was lightened by
two large holes covered with skin.

Blunt brow horn on either side

Small nose horn

TOP VIEW OF SKULL

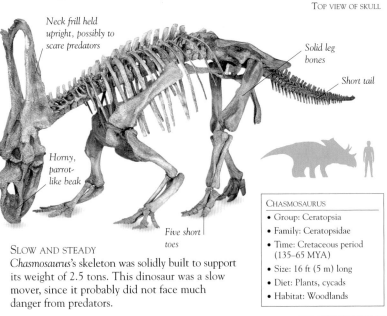

Neck frill held upright, possibly to scare predators

Solid leg bones

Short tail

Horny, parrot-like beak

Five short toes

SLOW AND STEADY
Chasmosaurus's skeleton was solidly built to support
its weight of 2.5 tons. This dinosaur was a slow
mover, since it probably did not face much
danger from predators.

CHASMOSAURUS
- Group: Ceratopsia
- Family: Ceratopsidae
- Time: Cretaceous period (135–65 MYA)
- Size: 16 ft (5 m) long
- Diet: Plants, cycads
- Habitat: Woodlands

CENTROSAURUS

CENTROSAURUS ("pointed lizard") is a commonly found horned dinosaur of the late Cretaceous. Its most distinctive feature was the long rhinolike horn on its snout. It also had two small brow horns and a neck frill standing up behind the head. This had a wavy edge and was frilled with spines. *Centrosaurus* had a massive body, quite a short tail, and sturdy legs.

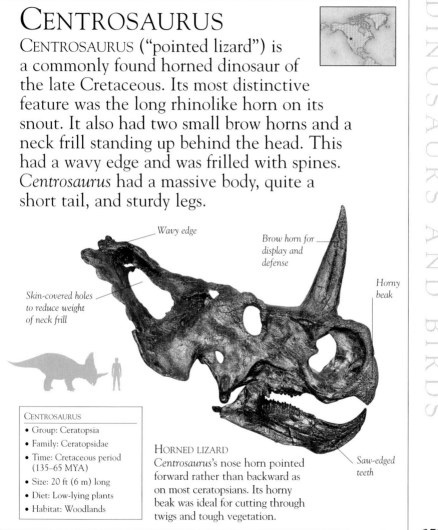

Wavy edge

Brow horn for display and defense

Horny beak

Skin-covered holes to reduce weight of neck frill

CENTROSAURUS
- Group: Ceratopsia
- Family: Ceratopsidae
- Time: Cretaceous period (135–65 MYA)
- Size: 20 ft (6 m) long
- Diet: Low-lying plants
- Habitat: Woodlands

HORNED LIZARD
Centrosaurus's nose horn pointed forward rather than backward as on most ceratopsians. Its horny beak was ideal for cutting through twigs and tough vegetation.

Saw-edged teeth

STYRACOSAURUS

ONE OF THE MOST spectacular of the horned lizards, *Styracosaurus* ("spiked lizard") had six long spikes on the back edge of its neck frill, and smaller spikes around them. There was a large horn on the snout that pointed upward. All four feet had five fingers or toes with clawlike hooves.

STYRACOSAURUS
- Group: Ceratopsia
- Family: Ceratopsidae
- Time: Cretaceous period (135–65 MYA)
- Size: 17 ft (5 m) long
- Diet: Ferns and palmlike plants
- Habitat: Open woodlands

Holes in neck frill to reduce weight

Six long spikes around frill

DECEPTIVELY LARGE *Styracosaurus*'s enormous head gear made it look bigger and more fierce than it actually was. Bright colors may have also frightened away attackers.

FOSSIL SKULL

Defensive horn on snout

PENTACERATOPS

PENTACERATOPS ("five-horn face") had a straight horn on the snout and two large, curved brow horns. Two small "horns," or rather outgrowths of the cheekbones, made up the total of five. Its most unusual feature was its huge head—over 10 ft (3 m) long—with a spectacular frill.

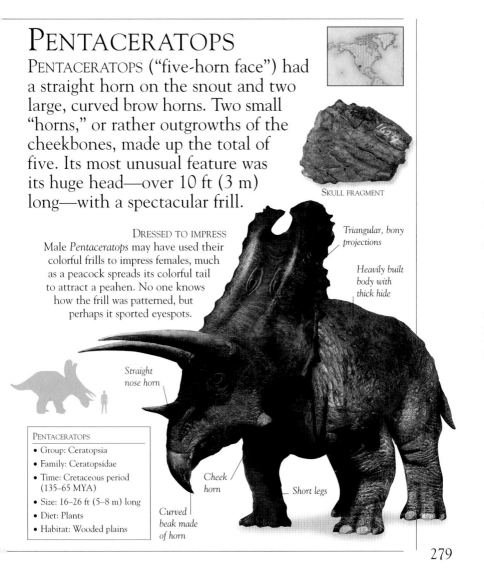

SKULL FRAGMENT

DRESSED TO IMPRESS

Male *Pentaceratops* may have used their colorful frills to impress females, much as a peacock spreads its colorful tail to attract a peahen. No one knows how the frill was patterned, but perhaps it sported eyespots.

Triangular, bony projections

Heavily built body with thick hide

Straight nose horn

PENTACERATOPS
- Group: Ceratopsia
- Family: Ceratopsidae
- Time: Cretaceous period (135–65 MYA)
- Size: 16–26 ft (5–8 m) long
- Diet: Plants
- Habitat: Wooded plains

Cheek horn

Short legs

Curved beak made of horn

279

TRICERATOPS

PROBABLY THE BEST-KNOWN of the horned dinosaurs, *Triceratops* ("three-horned face") lived in North America at the end of the Cretaceous. Many of the fossil skulls found are scarred, suggesting that *Triceratops* may have fought with rival males by locking its horns.

Bony studs around margin of frill

THREE-HORNED FACE
A short, thick nose horn and two longer brow horns adorned the face. There were studs around the neck frill.

TRICERATOPS
- Group: Ceratopsia
- Family: Ceratopsidae
- Time: Cretaceous period (135–65 MYA)
- Size: 30 ft (9 m) long
- Diet: Plants
- Habitat: Woodlands

Strong hip bone

Short nose horn

RECONSTRUCTION OF SKELETON

Head joined to neck by ball-and-socket joint

Heavy frill of solid bone

Brow horns much longer than nose horn

Solid neck frill

Horny beak

TRICERATOPS SKULL
The skulls of *Triceratops* have survived fossilization very well because they are so solid.

PACHYCEPHALOSAURS

THE THICK, DOMED skulls of pachycephalosaurs earned them the name "bone-headed dinosaurs." Rival males used to bash their heads together, their brains protected by the thick bone. Pachycephalosaurs probably had a good sense of smell, which would have allowed them to detect nearby predators and escape from them.

HORN CLUSTER
Stygimoloch had a cluster of horns behind its dome. But the horns were probably just for show, and had no practical use.

LOTS OF NODULES
Prenocephale's head had a well-developed solid dome and small nodules on the back of the skull.

PACHYCEPHALOSAUR FACTS

• The name pachycephalosaur means "thick-headed lizard."

• They ranged in length from 3 ft (90 cm) to 15 ft (4.6 m).

• Diet included fruits, leaves, and insects.

STEGOCERAS
Goat-sized *Stegoceras* was about 8 ft (2.4 m) long. Several *Stegoceras* skulls have been found with domes of various thicknesses. The domes of juveniles were not as thick or high as those of adults, especially adult males.

BATTLING
PRENOCEPHALE

HEAD-BANGERS
Male pachycephalosaurs
may have had head-
butting bouts when
fighting over territory
and females, the way
mountain goats do today.

PACHYCEPHALOSAURUS
SKULL

*Knobs
on nose*

*Skull cap thickened
into dome of bone*

THICK SKULL
The solid dome of
Pachycephalosaurus could be as
thick as 9 in (23 cm). Small
knobs and spikes fringed the
dome and decorated the nose.

STEGOCERAS
SKELETON

*Bony tendons held
the back vertebrae
stiffly together*

STRAIGHT BACK
Stegoceras, like all
pachycephalosaurs,
was bipedal, but it
was probably not
very fast on its feet.
It kept its body
horizontal, balanced
by the stiff tail.

STEGOCERAS
(HORNY ROOF)

*Short arms
and small
hands*

283

STEGOCERAS

Bony ridge over eye and around back of head

Skull thickened into dome of bone

A FAST RUNNER, *Stegoceras* (meaning "roof horn") had a body made for head-butting. When charging, it held its head in a straight line with its neck, body, and tail. The top of its skull was a thick dome of solid bone. Two types of skulls have been found—ones with flat domes, and others with rounded ones. *Stegoceras* had small, sawlike teeth for shredding plants.

FOSSIL SKULL

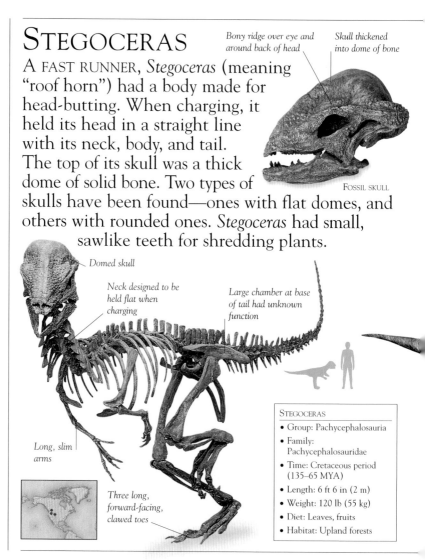

Domed skull

Neck designed to be held flat when charging

Large chamber at base of tail had unknown function

Long, slim arms

Three long, forward-facing, clawed toes

STEGOCERAS
- Group: Pachycephalosauria
- Family: Pachycephalosauridae
- Time: Cretaceous period (135–65 MYA)
- Length: 6 ft 6 in (2 m)
- Weight: 120 lb (55 kg)
- Diet: Leaves, fruits
- Habitat: Upland forests

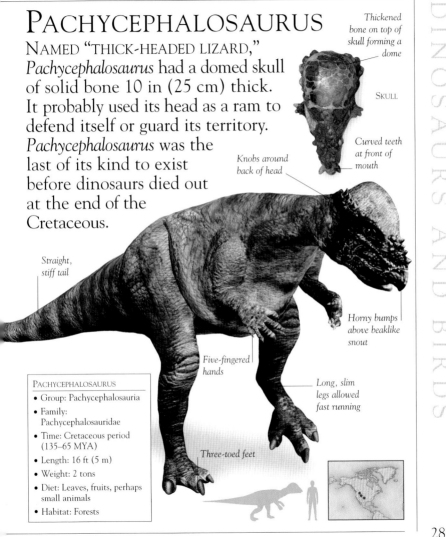

PACHYCEPHALOSAURUS

NAMED "THICK-HEADED LIZARD," *Pachycephalosaurus* had a domed skull of solid bone 10 in (25 cm) thick. It probably used its head as a ram to defend itself or guard its territory. *Pachycephalosaurus* was the last of its kind to exist before dinosaurs died out at the end of the Cretaceous.

Thickened bone on top of skull forming a dome

SKULL

Curved teeth at front of mouth

Knobs around back of head

Straight, stiff tail

Horny bumps above beaklike snout

Five-fingered hands

Long, slim legs allowed fast running

Three-toed feet

PACHYCEPHALOSAURUS
- Group: Pachycephalosauria
- Family: Pachycephalosauridae
- Time: Cretaceous period (135–65 MYA)
- Length: 16 ft (5 m)
- Weight: 2 tons
- Diet: Leaves, fruits, perhaps small animals
- Habitat: Forests

THYREOPHORANS

THYREOPHORANS or "shield barriers" is the name given to a large family of quadrupedal, low-walking dinosaurs that were covered in protective armor. This armor came in the form of spikes, plates, and protruding bones. This family includes the plated dinosaurs, such as *Stegosaurus*, and those with body armor and tail clubs, including *Ankylosaurus* and *Euoplocephalus*.

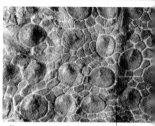

FOSSILIZED SAUROPELTA HIDE

Continuous mass of plates

Bony studs along shoulder and back

Parallel row of spikes along tail

EMAUSAURUS

SCELIDOSAURIDS

The first of the thyreophorans to evolve, scelidosaurids were also the first dinosaurs to have armor in the form of a hard leather jacket. One such dinosaur was *Emausaurus*, with cone-shaped plates in the skin of the back and sides, and flat plates on its tail.

ANKYLOSAURIDS

The most developed of the thyreophorans were the ankylosaurids, which had bands of studs, horns, and spikes on the entire back, neck, and parts of the tail. *Sauropelta* had armor (shown at left) like chain mail, with rows of bony cones set among studs.

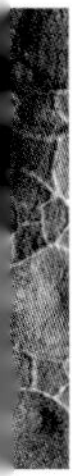

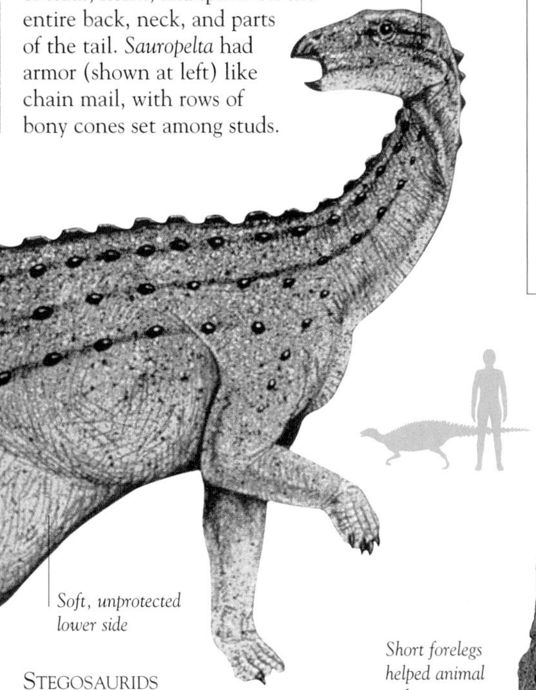

Small head ending in horny beak
Soft, unprotected lower side

THYREOPHORAN FACTS

- Thyreophorans lived from the Mid-Jurassic until the end of the Cretaceous.
- "Thyreophoran" was coined as a word in 1915 and covered the horned dinosaurs as well as the armored forms. It was not accepted as an official classification until the 1980s.

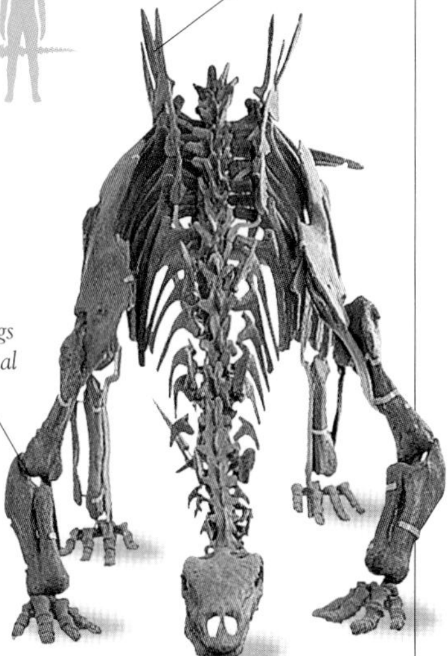

Twin spikes along back
Short forelegs helped animal to browse

TUOJIANGOSAURUS

STEGOSAURIDS

These are the most commonly found of the thyreophoran family. They are characterized as having protection in the form of rows of spikes, like that of *Stegosaurus*. Another feature characteristic of these dinosaurs is their short front legs. This reconstruction of *Tuojiangosaurus* clearly shows the difference in length of the front and back legs.

SCUTELLOSAURUS

SCUTELLOSAURUS OR "little
shield lizard" had a long body
and slim limbs. Over 300 low,
bony studs covered its back,
flanks, and the base of its tail
to form a defensive armor.
Scutellosaurus probably ran away
from predators on its hind legs,
holding its tail stiffly out behind
it to counterbalance the weight
of its armor.

SCUTELLOSAURUS
• Group: Thyreophora
• Family: Scutellosauridae
• Time: Jurassic period (203–135 MYA)
• Size: 4 ft (1.2 m) long
• Diet: Leaves
• Habitat: Woodlands

*Row of large studs
down the middle
of the back*

HEAVY FOR ITS SIZE
Scutellosaurus is the
smallest armored dinosaur
known. Its bony armor
made its body heavy from
the front, so it probably
ambled on all fours.

*Long, slim
hind legs*

*Serrated,
leaflike teeth*

*Very long tail
for bipedal balance*

SCELIDOSAURUS

THIS SMALL, HEAVY, armored dinosaur seems to be one of the earliest and most primitive ornithischians. It had impressive defensive armor: its back was covered with bony plates and a double row of bony spikes. Additional rows of studs ran along its sides, and there was a pair of triple-spiked bony plates behind the neck.

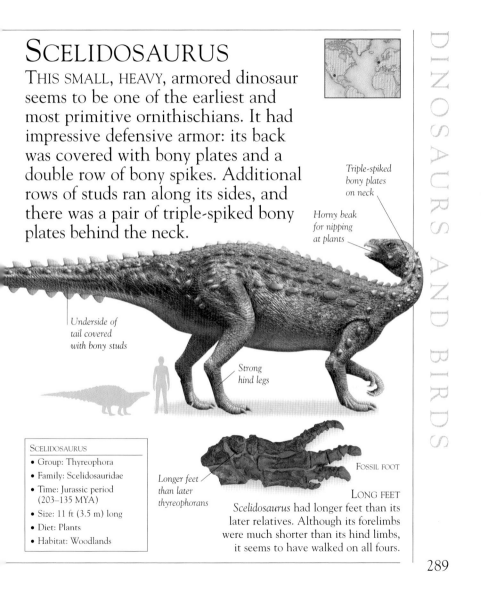

Triple-spiked bony plates on neck

Horny beak for nipping at plants

Underside of tail covered with bony studs

Strong hind legs

SCELIDOSAURUS
- Group: Thyreophora
- Family: Scelidosauridae
- Time: Jurassic period (203–135 MYA)
- Size: 11 ft (3.5 m) long
- Diet: Plants
- Habitat: Woodlands

Longer feet than later thyreophorans

FOSSIL FOOT

LONG FEET
Scelidosaurus had longer feet than its later relatives. Although its forelimbs were much shorter than its hind limbs, it seems to have walked on all fours.

STEGOSAURS

THE MOST NOTICEABLE features of the stegosaurs were the large plates, or spines, along an arched back. These plates may have regulated body temperature, and they may have also given protection,

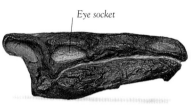

Eye socket

STEGOSAURUS SKULL
The skull of *Stegosaurus* was long and narrow. It had a toothless beak and small cheek teeth for chewing vegetation.

or even attracted a mate. Stegosaurs had small heads, and tiny brains no larger than a golf ball. The head was carried close to the ground for eating short, leafy plants and fruits.

TAIL END
Stegosaurus is the most commonly found of all stegosaurs. It had long, horny spines on the end of its tail. With a quick swing of the tail, these spines could inflict a crippling stab on a predator, such as *Allosaurus*.

Spines had a sharp end

PLATES AND SPINES
From above, you can see the staggered plates along the top of *Stegosaurus*'s body. This view also shows the tail spines pointing backward and outward—protection against attack from behind for when *Stegosaurus* was escaping.

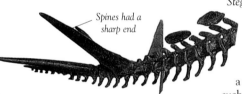

Sideways-pointing spines

Staggered plates

STEGOSAUR FACTS

• The name stegosaur means "roofed reptile."

• Stegosaurs ranged in size from 15 ft (4.5 m) to 30 ft (9 m).

• The stegosaur group survived for over 50 million years.

• They ate only certain plants, probably seed ferns and cycads.

• All stegosaurs had tail spines for defense.

STEGOSAURUS

The plates on *Stegosaurus*'s back were tallest in the region of the hips, reaching about 2½ ft (75 cm) in height. From a distance, or in silhouette, the plates may have made *Stegosaurus* look much bigger than it really was, thus acting as a deterrent to predators.

Plates were covered in skin or horn

FOSSIL PLATE

This fossil plate was one of the small plates at the front of *Stegosaurus*. The plates were thin and made of bone, and contained a network of blood vessels.

Small head

TUOJIANGOSAURUS

TUOJIANGOSAURUS ("Tuojiang lizard") had 15 pairs of pointed spines running down its neck, shoulders, and back, and two pairs of long spikes at the end of its tail. Unlike *Stegosaurus*, it did not have broad plates over its hips and lower back. It was similar to *Kentrosaurus*.

TUOJIANGOSAURUS
- Group: Stegosauria
- Family: Stegosauridae
- Time: Jurassic period (203–135 MYA)
- Size: 23 ft (7 m) long
- Diet: Low-lying vegetation
- Habitat: Forests

Paired bony spines running along back

Spines became taller and more pointed over hips

LOW BROWSER
Tuojiangosaurus probably fed on low-lying plants. Its head was long and low, with small cheek teeth and a horny beak at the front of the snout.

KENTROSAURUS

THIS EAST AFRICAN dinosaur lived
during the time of *Stegosaurus*. It
was smaller than its more famous
relative, but as well protected.
Kentrosaurus ("spiked lizard") had
paired rectangular plates running
down from the neck to half of the
back. Sharp spikes ran down in pairs
from the hips to the tip of the tail.
A pair of longer spikes also jutted
out from the shoulders.

KENTROSAURUS
- Group: Stegosauria
- Family: Stegosauridae
- Time: Jurassic period
  (203–135 MYA)
- Size: 16 ft (5 m) long
- Diet: Low-lying vegetation
- Habitat: Forests

Paired bony plates
running down neck
and upper back

Small,
sloping
head

Relatively long,
sturdily built
hind legs

Large
body
cavity

Forelegs much
shorter than hind
legs for low browsing

TINY HEAD
The skull of *Kentrosaurus*
housed a tiny brain, and is
known only from fragments of bone.
It was probably long and slender with
a toothless, horny beak.

DINOSAURS AND BIRDS

STEGOSAURUS

STEGOSAURUS ("roof lizard") was
the largest plated dinosaur. It
had a tiny head, a toothless beak, and
two rows of bony plates running
from its neck to halfway along its
tail. The hind legs were twice
as long as the forelegs.

*Plate had
pointed
tip*

*Very sharp,
bony tail
spike*

FOSSIL PLATE

FOSSIL
TAIL
SPIKE

PLATES AND SPIKES
The plates may have been in pairs,
or arranged in a zigzag. The tail
ended in long, pointed spikes.

Very small brain case

Massive body

SKELETAL RECONSTRUCTION

Long spines on tail vertebrae

STEGOSAURUS

- Group: Stegosauria
- Family: Stegosauridae
- Time: Jurassic period (203–135 MYA)
- Size: 20 ft (6 m) long
- Diet: Plants
- Habitat: Woodlands

Covering of skin or tough horn over plates

ANKYLOSAURS

PROTECTED BY SPIKES and bony plates, the stocky ankylosaurs were the armored "tanks" of the dinosaur world. Slow on their feet, they relied on their armor for defense against predators. There were two main groups of ankylosaurs—the ankylosaurids and the nodosaurids.

ANKYLOSAURUS SKULL
The triangular skull of *Ankylosaurus* was covered with bony plates. It ended with a horny beak, which it used to crop vegetation.

ANKYLOSAURIDS
Many ankylosaurids had spines on their sides as well as bony body scutes (plates). Their most notable feature was a heavy tail club, which they used as a formidable weapon.

EUOPLOCEPHALUS
Euoplocephalus's head was armored with bony slabs. Its eyelids were bony, too. The sturdy body and tail club were typical of ankylosaurids.

ANKYLOSAUR FACTS

• The name ankylosaur means "jointed reptile."

• They ranged in length from 6 ft (1.8 m) to 30 ft (9 m).

• They have been found in North America, Europe, Asia, Australia and Antarctica.

• All were covered in bony scutes on their upper side, but few were armored on their lower side.

TAIL CLUB

The bony plates were good protection, but the tail club was a very effective weapon. A fearsome tyrannosaurid could be crippled with a well-directed blow to the ankle or shin.

Tyrannosaurus receives a crippling blow

Ankylosaur lashes out at the knee

TAIL CLUB

The tail club was formed by bony plates that were fused together. Powerful tail muscles were used to swing the club. These muscles were anchored by tail vertebrae stiffened by bony tendons.

FOSSILIZED ANKYLOSAURID TAIL CLUB

EUOPLOCEPHALUS

Stiffened, muscular tail

Heavy tail club

ACANTHOPHOLIS

ACANTHOPHOLIS ("spiny scales")
is a little-known nodosaur (a type
of ankylosaur) with a low-slung,
bulky body. A typical nodosaur
had armor of rows of oval plates
(scutes) set into the skin. It also had
long, bony spikes jutting out of its neck
and shoulder area along the spine.
Further spikes ran along each side down
to the end of the tail.

ACANTHOPHOLIS
• Group: Ankylosauria
• Family: Nodosauridae
• Time: Cretaceous period (135–65 MYA)
• Size: 13 ft (4 m)
• Diet: Low-lying vegetation
• Habitat: Woodlands

Rows of oval scutes along back

Protective spikes along neck and shoulders

Short, heavy legs

Pointed beak

BULKY PLANT-EATER

This bulky dinosaur had to eat a huge
amount of vegetation to keep itself
going, so its intestines must have been
very large. Studies of its tracks show that
it could run at a moderate pace.

MINMI

THIS THICKLY ARMORED dinosaur had rows of small, bony plates on its back and triangular spikes over the hips. There were also large plates over its neck and shoulders. Unlike other ankylosaurs, *Minmi* had horizontal plates of bone running along each side of the vertebrae. Its box-shaped head had a narrow snout ending in a horny beak. Four small horns jutted out from the back of its face.

SOUTHERN HEMISPHERE DINOSAUR
Named after the Minmi Crossing in Australia, this creature was the first armored dinosaur to be found south of the equator. It was smaller than most ankylosaurs, but heavily built and well armored.

Horizontal plates of bone alongside each vertebra

Short neck

Short, sturdy legs

Wide feet

GASTONIA

GASTONIA WAS named after fossil hunter Robert Gaston. This herbivore's defensive armor was impressive: it had four horns on its head, and bony rings covering the neck; rows of spikes covered its back and flanks, and fused, bony armor plates protected the hips. The tail, which could lash from side to side, had rows of triangular blades along each side.

GASTONIA
- Group: Ankylosauria
- Family: Polacanthidae
- Time: Cretaceous period (135–65 MYA)
- Size: 16 ft (5 m) long
- Diet: Plants
- Habitat: Woodlands

Fused armor over the hips

Curved dorsal spines

Horny beak

Longer hind legs than front legs

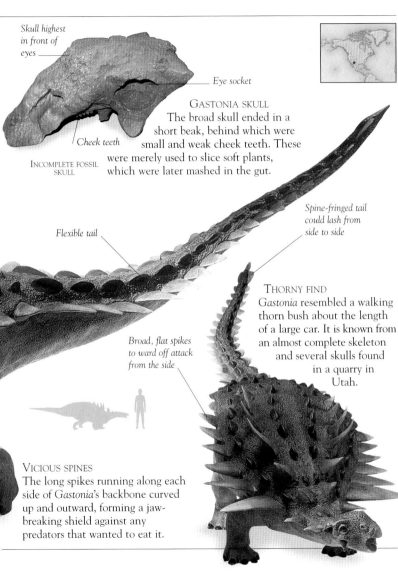

Skull highest in front of eyes

Eye socket

Cheek teeth

INCOMPLETE FOSSIL SKULL

GASTONIA SKULL
The broad skull ended in a short beak, behind which were small and weak cheek teeth. These were merely used to slice soft plants, which were later mashed in the gut.

Flexible tail

Spine-fringed tail could lash from side to side

THORNY FIND
Gastonia resembled a walking thorn bush about the length of a large car. It is known from an almost complete skeleton and several skulls found in a quarry in Utah.

Broad, flat spikes to ward off attack from the side

VICIOUS SPINES
The long spikes running along each side of *Gastonia*'s backbone curved up and outward, forming a jaw-breaking shield against any predators that wanted to eat it.

PANOPLOSAURUS

PANOPLOSAURUS WAS A typical nodosaurid ankylosaur. It did not have the bony club at the end of its tail—instead, all of its armor was concentrated around its shoulders. Huge spikes stuck out sideways and forward, and these would have been used for defense or for sparring with other nodosaurids.

PANOPLOSAURUS
- Group: Ankylosauria
- Family: Nodosauridae
- Time: Jurassic period (203–135 MYA)
- Size: 17 ft (5 m) long
- Diet: Certain low-growing plants
- Habitat: Woodlands

PICKY EATER
Panoplosaurus and the other nodosaurid ankylosaurs had narrow mouths and only ate particular plants. The ankylosaurid ankylosaurs—those with the tail clubs—had broad mouths and were less selective.

Large bony plates along back

Long, low skull covered by bony plates

Long shoulder spikes

ANKYLOSAURUS

ANKYLOSAURUS ("fused lizard") had thick bands of armor-plating on its body, neck, and head. Its skin was thick and leathery, and was studded with hundreds of oval bony plates and rows of spikes. Two long spikes emerged from its head, and its cheekbones formed another pair of spikes on its face.

ANKYLOSAURUS
- Group: Ankylosauria
- Family: Ankylosauridae
- Time: Cretaceous period (135–65 MYA)
- Size: 25–35 ft (7.5–10.5 m) long
- Diet: Large herbivorous dinosaurs
- Habitat: Woodlands

FOSSIL TAIL CLUB

LIVING TANK
Ankylosaurus has aptly been described as a living tank. Its tail was armed with a bony club, which could be swung with great force.

Horny beak

Large, bony tail club

Front legs shorter than hind legs

Unprotected underbelly

EDMONTONIA

THIS ANKYLOSAUR (whose name means "from Edmonton") had a bulky body, short, thick legs, wide feet, and a short neck. Two collars of flat, bony plates protected its neck, while a third collar lay between the shoulders, which were particularly well-armored. Its back and tail were covered with rows of bony plates (scutes) and spikes. *Edmontonia's* long, pearshaped head was covered in scales to protect the brain case. The head ended in a toothless beak, and its weak jaw had small cheek teeth.

Sloping back

Short neck protected by bony scutes

Long, flat skull

Double shoulder spike

Wide, flat feet

Horny, toothless beak

Triangular spikes
along back

EDMONTONIA
- Group: Ankylosauria
- Family: Nodosauridae
- Time: Cretaceous period (135–65 MYA)
- Size: 20 ft (6 m) long
- Diet: Low-lying vegetation
- Habitat: Woodlands

SPECIAL SHOULDER ARMOR
Some paleontologists have
suggested that *Edmontonia* may
have used its shoulder spines to
battle with other males of its
own kind, as modern deer do
with their antlers. It is also
possible that the large
spines were used by males
to display their
superiority.

Large gut for
fermenting plant
material

Relatively
rigid tail

Rows of scutes
along the length
of the tail

Hind legs longer
than forelegs

EUOPLOCEPHALUS

BUILT LIKE a military tank, *Euoplocephalus* ("well-armored head") was one of the most common Late Cretaceous ankylosaurids. Fused plates covered the back and neck, and triangular horns protected the shoulders, tail, and face. Thick legs bore the weight of its bulky body as it ambled through woodlands in search of plant food.

EUOPLOCEPHALUS
- Group: Ankylosauria
- Family: Ankylosauridae
- Time: Cretaceous period (135–65 MYA)
- Size: 20 ft (6 m) long
- Diet: Plants
- Habitat: Woodlands

CLUBBED TAIL
A large ball of fused bone at the end of the tail acted as a club that could be swung at attacking predators. This was probably the dinosaur's main weapon. The flexible, muscular tail base swung the club from side to side.

Fused bony tail plates

TAIL CLUB

Strong hips fused to backbone

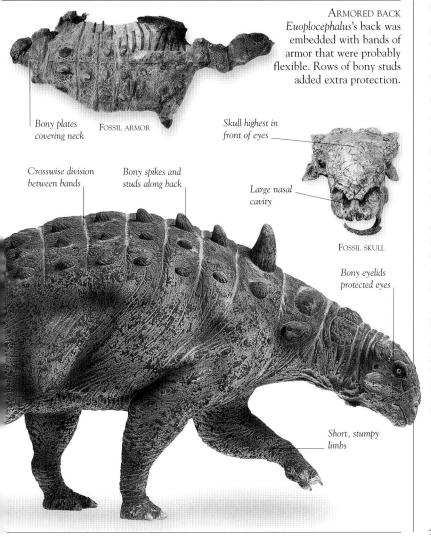

ARMORED BACK
Euoplocephalus's back was
embedded with bands of
armor that were probably
flexible. Rows of bony studs
added extra protection.

*Bony plates
covering neck*   FOSSIL ARMOR

*Skull highest in
front of eyes*

*Large nasal
cavity*

FOSSIL SKULL

*Crosswise division
between bands*

*Bony spikes and
studs along back*

*Bony eyelids
protected eyes*

*Short, stumpy
limbs*

MAMMALS AND THEIR ANCESTORS

SPRAWLING, scaly pelycosaurs with tall fins on their backs, featured below, look nothing like tigers or cows. Yet the pages in this section show that today's hairy, warm-blooded mammals, including us humans, all owe their origins to such reptilelike creatures.

EARLY SYNAPSIDS

Synapsids ("with arch") include the mammal-like "reptiles" and their descendants. They had a large hole low in the skull behind each eye, and muscles near the jaws passed through this hole. Early synapsids known as pelycosaurs died out toward the end of the Permian period.

The body was kept warm by the blood that flowed through its sail

SAIL-BACKED KILLER
Dimetrodon was one of the first big land animals to attack and kill creatures its own size. It could grow up to 11½ ft (3.5 m) in length.

Canine teeth with serrated blades

DIMETRODON
SKULL

TYPES OF TEETH
Dimetrodon's pointed upper canine teeth were used to pierce flesh. Front teeth served for biting and gripping, and back teeth aided in chewing.

DIMETRODON

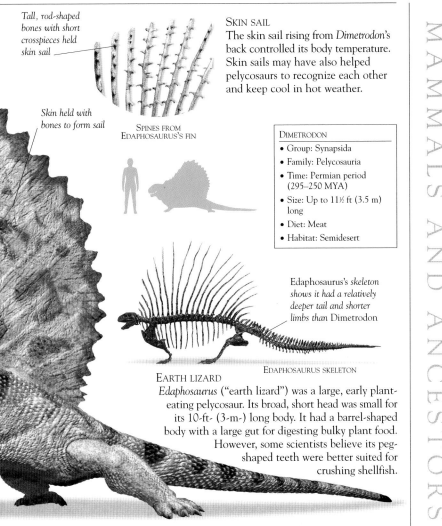

Tall, rod-shaped bones with short crosspieces held skin sail

Skin held with bones to form sail

SPINES FROM EDAPHOSAURUS'S FIN

SKIN SAIL

The skin sail rising from *Dimetrodon's* back controlled its body temperature. Skin sails may have also helped pelycosaurs to recognize each other and keep cool in hot weather.

DIMETRODON
- Group: Synapsida
- Family: Pelycosauria
- Time: Permian period (295–250 MYA)
- Size: Up to 11½ ft (3.5 m) long
- Diet: Meat
- Habitat: Semidesert

Edaphosaurus's skeleton shows it had a relatively deeper tail and shorter limbs than Dimetrodon

EDAPHOSAURUS SKELETON

EARTH LIZARD

Edaphosaurus ("earth lizard") was a large, early plant-eating pelycosaur. Its broad, short head was small for its 10-ft- (3-m-) long body. It had a barrel-shaped body with a large gut for digesting bulky plant food. However, some scientists believe its peg-shaped teeth were better suited for crushing shellfish.

TERRIBLE HEADS

DINOCEPHALIAN ("terrible head") therapsids were synapsids whose elaborately horned heads were massive compared with their bodies. They were diverse and abundant, but they did not survive beyond the Permian, and left no descendants. There were both carnivorous and herbivorous dinocephalians.

Horns of some Estemmenosuchids had many branches

Forehead bump may have been present only in males

HORNED HEADS
The herbivorous dinocephalians grew horns and bumps on their skulls. These may have been used in displays or fights between males during the breeding season.

TOP VIEW OF STRUTHIOCEPHALUS SKULL

Wide mouth with large incisors and interlocking canines

ESTEMMENOSUCHIDS
Primitive Russian dinocephalians called estemmenosuchids are famous for the massive bony protuberances that grew from their cheeks and upper skulls. These may have been covered in horn.

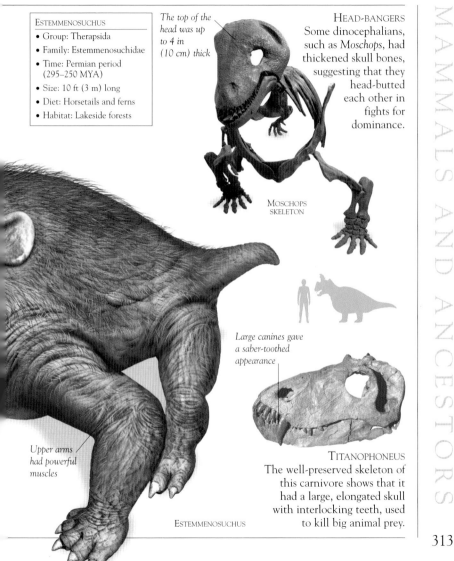

ESTEMMENOSUCHUS
- Group: Therapsida
- Family: Estemmenosuchidae
- Time: Permian period (295–250 MYA)
- Size: 10 ft (3 m) long
- Diet: Horsetails and ferns
- Habitat: Lakeside forests

The top of the head was up to 4 in (10 cm) thick

HEAD-BANGERS
Some dinocephalians, such as *Moschops*, had thickened skull bones, suggesting that they head-butted each other in fights for dominance.

MOSCHOPS SKELETON

Large canines gave a saber-toothed appearance

Upper arms had powerful muscles

ESTEMMENOSUCHUS

TITANOPHONEUS
The well-preserved skeleton of this carnivore shows that it had a large, elongated skull with interlocking teeth, used to kill big animal prey.

313

TWO DOG TEETH

DICYNODONTS ("two dog teeth") were short-tailed synapsids with beaked jaws that lived from the Early Permian to the Late Triassic. The unusual dicynodont jaw, combined with their stout, barrel-shaped bodies, suggests that they were herbivores and ate fibrous plants such as horsetails and ferns.

SINOKANNEMEYERIA
- Group: Therapsida
- Family: Kannemeyeriidae
- Time: Triassic period (250–203 MYA)
- Size: 10 ft (3 m) long
- Diet: Fibrous plants
- Habitat: Woodlands near lakes and rivers

SINOKANNEMEYERIA
This was a large, long-snouted Chinese dicynodont with downward-pointing tusks that grew from bulbous projections on its upper jaw. It did not have powerful skull muscles for cropping plants like other dicynodonts and fed by tearing plants with the front of its snout.

A broad, blunt snout allowed it to grab large mouthfuls of plant material

Skull openings housed large jaw muscles

Forelimbs sprawled sideways

LYSTROSAURUS
The small, Early Triassic dicynodont *Lystrosaurus* had a short skull with a deep snout, high nostrils, and sturdy, broad limb bones.

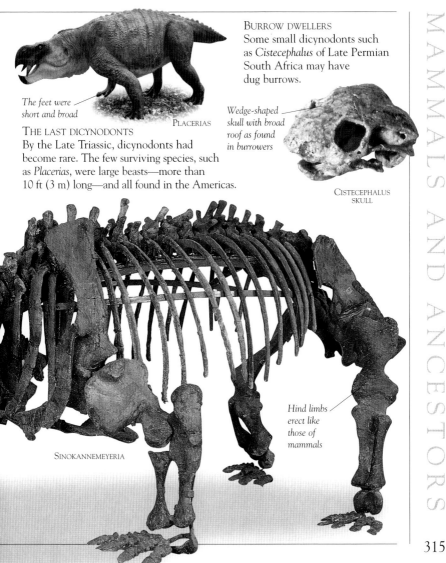

The feet were short and broad

PLACERIAS

THE LAST DICYNODONTS

By the Late Triassic, dicynodonts had become rare. The few surviving species, such as *Placerias*, were large beasts—more than 10 ft (3 m) long—and all found in the Americas.

BURROW DWELLERS

Some small dicynodonts such as *Cistecephalus* of Late Permian South Africa may have dug burrows.

Wedge-shaped skull with broad roof as found in burrowers

CISTECEPHALUS SKULL

SINOKANNEMEYERIA

Hind limbs erect like those of mammals

DOG TEETH

CYNODONTS ("dog teeth") were small to medium-sized carnivorous synapsids. A bony palate that separated the nasal passages from the mouth made this group the most likely ancestors of mammals. They lived worldwide for 80 million years, before dying out in the Mid-Jurassic—no other group of therapsids lasted as long.

Strong, upright hind limbs helped in fast running

TRIDENT TOOTH

A low-slung, sharp-toothed carnivore, *Thrinaxodon* ("trident tooth") lived in Early Triassic South Africa and Antarctica. *Thrinaxodon* lived in burrows and ate small creatures. Clues in its remains show that this creature was more mammal-like than its synapsid ancestors.

THRINAXODON
- Group: Therapsida
- Family: Galesauridae
- Time: Triassic period (250–203 MYA)
- Size: 20 in (50 cm) long
- Diet: Small animals
- Habitat: Open woodlands

DOG JAW

CYNOGNATHUS SKULL

Cynognathus ("dog jaw") was one of most dangerous of Early Triassic carnivores. It had formidable jaws capable of biting savagely.

Dentary bone

Two-part body
division into chest
and lower back

SKULL OF THE EARLY
SYNAPSID DIMETRODON

Dentary bone

SKULL OF THE
CYNODONT THRINAXODON

EVOLUTION OF THE JAW

Cynodont jaws illustrate key changes
in the evolution from synapsid to
mammal. In time, jaw bones
shrank so that the entire
lower jaw consisted of the
large dentary bone. Other
changes produced the
mammals' unique
chewing bite.

THRINAXODON

Broad back teeth
with ridged crowns
for chewing

THREE KNOB TEETH

Not all cynodonts were
carnivores. Tritylodonts
("three knob teeth") like
Bienotherium had jaws
designed for eating plants.

Incisors for gnawing
tough plants and back
teeth for chewing them

BIENOTHERIUM SKULL

THE FIRST MAMMALS

MAMMALS ARE warm-blooded, backboned animals whose females have glands that produce milk to feed their young. All mammals evolved from the therapsids. The first mammals were probably Triassic shrewlike animals that shared the same types of jawbones and middle ear bones as living mammals.

Morganucodon
stood upright

TINY MAMMAL ANCESTOR
This tiny mammal from the Jurassic, *Morganucodon* ("Morgan's tooth"), is usually grouped with the triconodonts. These extinct early mammals were named after the three cusps (points) on the surface of each tooth.

JEHOLODENS
The first complete skeleton of a triconodont to be discovered was that of *Jeholodens*, which was found in China.

Sharp claws helped subdue prey or dig holes in which to hide from enemies

JEHOLODENS

MORGANUCODON
- Group: Prototheria
- Family: Morganucodontidae
- Time: Jurassic period (203–135 MYA)
- Size: 4 in (10 cm) long
- Diet: Insects and worms
- Habitat: Forests

Reptilelike posture of early mammals

MODERN DUCK-BILLED PLATYPUS

AN ANCIENT LINE

The duck-billed platypus is one of the egg-laying monotremes—the group of living mammals with the oldest fossil record. The earliest known monotreme fossils date from 100 million years ago in Australia.

Even early mammals were covered with hair

LOWER JAWBONE OF TAENIOLABIS

RATLIKE MAMMALS

Taeniolabis is an example of the multituberculates, a major line of rodentlike, plant-eating mammals with many-cusped teeth.

Sensitive whiskers allowed Morganucodon to feel its way in the dark

MORGANUCODON

319

AUSTRALIAN POUCHED MAMMALS

MANY OF THE earliest mammals had a pouch in their skin in which they carried their developing babies. Most mammals later evolved a womb inside their body for the babies and slowly lost their pouch. Marsupials such as kangaroos and koalas kept this pouch, and have modern descendants in Australia.

SKELETON OF STHENURUS

STHENURINES
Modern grassland kangaroos evolved in the Pleistocene. The biggest was *Sthenurus*.

Thylacines had sharp teeth and powerful jaws

DIPROTODON WAS THE BIGGEST-EVER MARSUPIAL

POUCHED WOLVES
The thylacinids (marsupial wolves) were doglike hunters that survived in Tasmania until the 1930s.

THYLACINUS

DIPROTODON
- Group: Marsupialia
- Family: Diprotodontidae
- Time: Pleistocene-Holocene epochs (1.75 MYA -present)
- Size: 10 ft (3 m) long
- Diet: Shrubs and bushes
- Habitat: Scrublands, open woodlands

Worn-out teeth show that thylacoleonids were predators

THYLACOLEO SKULL

MARSUPIAL LIONS

One of the most remarkable marsupial groups are the thylacoleonids, also called "marsupial lions" because of their catlike skull and teeth.

Diprotodontids had hippopotamus-like bodies

DIPROTODON

From the Oligocene to the Pleistocene, Australia was populated by heavy-bodied herbivores called diprotodontids. The most famous is *Diprotodon*, a rhinoceros-sized herbivore. Diprotodontids died out as the tropical forests of Australia were replaced by grasslands.

Marsupials possess a pouch or skin bag in which the baby is carried

Sharp claws could have been used for digging

AMERICAN MARSUPIALS

AMERICAN POUCHED mammals evolved in the Late Cretaceous and included dog- and bear-like forms, and a species that resembled saber-toothed cats. Opossums, the most successful American marsupials, moved into other continents and survive today.

Thylacosmilus *may have had a coat like a lion's*

AMERICAN OPOSSUMS
Alphadon is one of the earliest known opossums from North America.

ALPHADON

THYLACOSMILUS
One of the most remarkable marsupials was *Thylacosmilus*, which superficially resembled saber-toothed cats. However, the details of its skeleton reveal that it was more like a giant opossum.

LYCOPSIS
SKELETON

THE DIDELPHOIDS
A major group of predatory American marsupials was known as the Didelphoids. They included *Lycopsis* and *Thylacosmilus*.

Long, powerful hind legs

Feet with five clawed toes

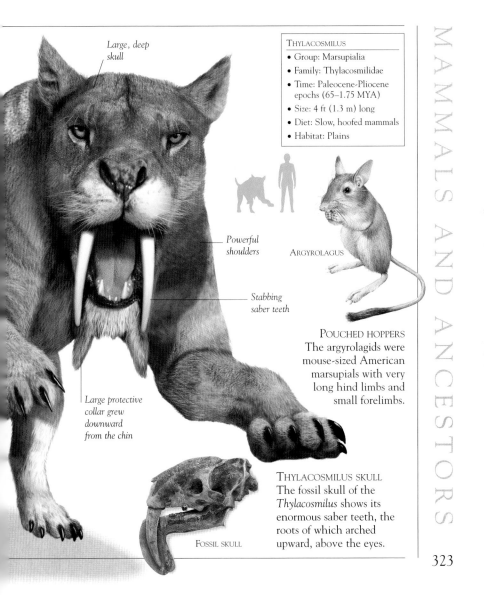

Large, deep skull

THYLACOSMILUS
- Group: Marsupialia
- Family: Thylacosmilidae
- Time: Paleocene-Pliocene epochs (65–1.75 MYA)
- Size: 4 ft (1.3 m) long
- Diet: Slow, hoofed mammals
- Habitat: Plains

ARGYROLAGUS

Powerful shoulders

Stabbing saber teeth

Large protective collar grew downward from the chin

POUCHED HOPPERS
The argyrolagids were mouse-sized American marsupials with very long hind limbs and small forelimbs.

THYLACOSMILUS SKULL
The fossil skull of the *Thylacosmilus* shows its enormous saber teeth, the roots of which arched upward, above the eyes.

FOSSIL SKULL

323

STRANGE-JOINTED MAMMALS

A GROUP of mammals called the xenarthrans are among the most primitive placental mammals (animals whose babies develop inside the womb). The name means "strange joints" and refers to the extra joints these mammals have between their vertebrae. Xenarthrans evolved in South America; some also migrated into North America. Sloths, anteaters, and armadillos are their living descendants.

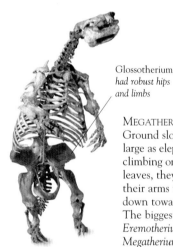

Glossotherium had robust hips and limbs

Ground sloths had a sturdy tail probably used as a prop when they stood on their back legs

MEGATHERIUM
Ground sloths grew to be as large as elephants. Rather than climbing on branches to eat leaves, they reached up with their arms to pull branches down toward their mouths. The biggest were *Eremotherium* and *Megatherium*.

GLOSSOTHERIUM
A medium-sized sloth called *Glossotherium* lived in the wooded grasslands and forests of the Americas.

Deep, short skull with massive chewing teeth

Large, curving claws were probably used as hooks to pull down branches

Fossil tracks show that ground sloths sometimes walked on two legs

MEGATHERIUM

PANOCTHUS

Glyptodonts were armored xenarthrans resembling giant armadillos, known from South America.

GLYPTODONT ARMOR

The bodies of glyptodonts were covered by a rigid shell of interlocking hexagonal scales called scutes. Rings of scutes also covered the tail and head.

PLACENTAL PIONEERS

PLACENTALS (the group of mammals whose young develop inside their bodies) arose in the Late Cretaceous, when the dinosaurs were becoming extinct. The earliest were small, nocturnal omnivores that resembled living shrews. Nearly all living mammals are classed as placentals, except for the monotremes, which lay eggs, and the marsupials, whose young are carried in a pouch.

CORYPHODON

Brain about three-fourths the size of the brain of a living shrew

ZALAMBDALESTES
One of the best-known early placentals was *Zalambdalestes* from Mongolia. It was a long-snouted mammal resembling the living elephant shrew.

ZALAMBDALESTES
- Group: Eutheria
- Family: Zalambdalestidae
- Time: Cretaceous period (135–65 MYA)
- Size: 8 in (20 cm) long
- Diet: Insects, small animals
- Habitat: Scrublands, deserts

Below its long snout, Zalambdalestes had long incisor teeth

PANTODONTS
These were bulky placental mammals that thrived 65–32 million years ago, although they left no descendants. Their feet were tipped with claws, and males had large canine teeth.

TILLODONTS
This group of placentals had clawed feet and large gnawing teeth, and probably fed on roots and tubers.

TROGOSUS SKULL

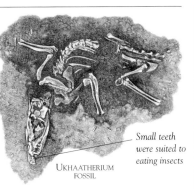

Small teeth were suited to eating insects

UKHAATHERIUM FOSSIL

UKHAATHERIUM AND RELATIVES
The asioryctitheres were Mongolian Cretaceous placentals that superficially resembled living shrews. However, features in their skulls and hip bones show that they were not actually related to shrews.

EARLY CARNIVORES

CARNIVORES—cats, hyenas, dogs, bears, and their relatives—are one of the most successful groups of mammals. Their key feature is their specialized shearing teeth, called carnassials. This group has a fossil record from the early Paleocene. The earliest carnivores—the miacoids—first appeared in North America.

Miacoids had smaller brains for their body size than modern carnivores

Flexible and powerful limbs

VULPAVUS SKELETON

LIFE IN THE TREES
The limb skeletons of miacoids, such as *Vulpavus*, show that they had highly mobile limbs like those of modern tree-dwelling carnivores.

MIACIS
One of the best-known miacoids was *Miacis* of the dog-branch group of carnivores. It was an agile climber and probably ate small animals, as well as eggs and fruit.

Large incisors for tearing flesh

CREODONTS
Hyaenodon was a wolflike animal that had slicing teeth at the back of the jaws. It is part of a group called the creodonts, which resembled modern civets, cats, or dogs.

May have used tail as a balancing aid

Early carnivores such as Miacis have five toes

Claws that can be pulled back into sheaths are unique to primitive carnivores

MIACIS
- Group: Carnivora
- Family: Canidae
- Time: Paleocene–Pliocene epochs (65–1.75 MYA)
- Size: 1 ft (30 cm) long
- Diet: Small mammals, reptiles, birds
- Habitat: Tropical forests

329

CATS AND OTHER FELIFORMS

FELIFORMS, including cats, emerged during the Eocene epoch (53–33.7 million years ago). While some feliforms became large predators in open environments, others continued as forest-dwellers. Civets and genets, properly called viverrids, are primitive feliforms that have remained largely unchanged.

HYENAS
Although hyenas resemble dogs more than cats, they belong to the cat group of carnivores.

EARLY HYENA SKULL

SKULL OF SABER-TOOTHED CAT

ENLARGED CANINES
As cats evolved, they enlarged their canines for biting, but reduced their molars. The saber-toothed cats enlarged their canines to an extreme.

TERRIBLE CAT
Dinofelis ("terrible cat"), from the Pliocene and Pleistocene, had enlarged canine teeth halfway between the conical canines of modern cats and the flattened blades of saber-tooths. *Dinofelis* had body proportions like those of modern forest-dwelling cats such as leopards and jaguars

All cats have shortened, rounded skulls and forward-facing eyes

PREHISTORIC SMILODON COMPARED WITH MODERN TIGER

MODERN CAT COMPARISONS
Most saber-toothed cats were larger than the lions and tigers of today. Because of their dependence on large prey animals, these cats were vulnerable to extinction when their prey became rare.

DINOFELIS

Large canines and protruding incisors

Dinofelis had limb proportions better suited for strength than speed

DINOFELIS
- Group: Aeluroidea
- Family: Felidae
- Time: Paleocene–Holocene epochs (65 MYA–present)
- Size: 7 ft (2.2 m) long
- Diet: Other mammals
- Habitat: Open woodlands

331

SABER-TOOTHED CATS

THE MACHAIRODONTINES, or saber-toothed cats, were prehistoric members of the cat family, known for their massive canine teeth. They diversified into American, African, European, and Asian species, ranging in size from that of a modern puma to that of a lion. The last saber-toothed cat died out as recently as 10,000 years ago. The most famous member of the family is *Smilodon*.

Smilodon *had powerful arms and shoulders, and a strong and flexible neck*

HUNTING AND SCAVENGING TOGETHER
More carnivores lived alongside one another in
the Pleistocene than today, so competition was
probably more intense. Fossils of many cats show
injuries from hunting and fighting. Perhaps
Smilodon lived in social groups, since injured
individuals would then have been able to
scavenge from kills made by other group members.

*In the largest cats, the
upper canines were more
than 1 ft (25 cm) long*

SMILODON
- Group: Carnivora
- Family: Felidae
- Time: Pleistocene–Holocene
  epochs (1.75 MYA–present)
- Size: 5–8 ft (1.7–2.5 m) long
- Diet: Large mammals
- Habitat: Grasslands

DOGS AND OTHER CANIFORMS

CANIFORMS, A GROUP THAT includes dogs, bears, and seals, evolved in the Eocene. Dogs were the earliest caniforms to appear. New types of caniforms, such as weasels, raccoons, and bears, evolved late in the Eocene. Many became omnivores, others became herbivores, and some took to life in the water.

DIRE WOLF

Canis dirus ("dire wolf") was a large wolf from Pleistocene North America. Its fossils are best known from tar pits in California, where over 1,600 wolves are preserved. Compared with modern wolves, dire wolves had larger skulls and teeth, but shorter legs.

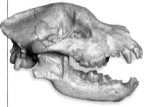

OSTEOBORUS SKULL

Canis dirus had a wider head, stronger jaws, and larger teeth than living wolves and was better at chewing bones

HYENA-LIKE DOGS

Borophagines were a group of dogs that lived from the Oligocene to the Pleistocene. They are best known for *Osteoborus*, a wolf-sized dog that had hyena-like habits. Other Borophagines may have resembled raccoons or coyotes.

THALASSOLEON
MEXICANUS SKULL

SEALS AND SEA LIONS
Seals, sea lions, and walruses evolved from bearlike ancestors. By the late Miocene, seals had spread across the world, while walruses and sea lions such as *Thalassoleon* had evolved in the Northern Hemisphere.

SKELETON OF
URSUS SPELAEUS

The tail is an important social signal in living dogs, and probably was in all prehistoric dogs also

BEARS
The eight living species of bears belong to a group called the ursines. *Ursus spelaeus*, of the Pleistocene, went on to become a cave bear.

Hands and feet were specialized for running

CANIS DIRUS
- Group: Carnivora
- Family: Canidae
- Time: Pleistocene–Holocene epochs (1.75 MYA–present)
- Size: 6½ ft (2 m) long
- Diet: Mammals, carrion
- Habitat: Grasslands, woodlands

ISLAND GIANTS AND DWARFS

AROUND 1.75 MILLION YEARS AGO, rising sea levels in the Mediterranean caused some areas to be cut off from the mainland. Unusual mammals inhabited these islands until as recently as 8,000 years ago. Hippos, deer, and elephants here were remarkable for being dwarfs, while others, such as lizards, owls, and dormice, became giants. They became extinct due to hunting and competing with farmed animals.

GIANT DORMICE

Leithia, a giant dormouse from Malta and Sicily, was closely related to living forest dormice. However, it was a giant in comparison with living dormice, reaching about 16 in (40 cm) in total length—roughly the size of a squirrel.

Dwarf elephants lived on plant food that grew close to the ground

Like its living relatives, Leithia probably had dark markings around the eyes

DWARF ELEPHANTS

Palaeoloxodon falconeri was a miniature elephant with a shoulder height of 3 ft (90 cm). The small islands provided reduced quantities of food, so smaller individuals were more likely to survive than large ones.

Like other elephants, dwarf forms had tusks that they probably used in fights and as tools

DWARF ELEPHANT

- Group: Proboscidae
- Family: Elephantidae
- Time: Pleistocene – Holocene epochs (1.75 MYA–present)
- Size: 3 ft (90 cm) tall
- Diet: Leaves, grasses, fruit
- Habitat: Forests

TERRIBLE HORNS

DINOCERATANS, the "terrible horned" mammals, were rhinoceros-like hoofed creatures famous for their paired horns and tusklike canine teeth. The earliest dinoceratan, *Prodinoceras*, first appeared in Asia during the Paleocene, but nearly all later types are from North America.

UINTAH BEAST
The largest and best-known dinoceratan, *Uintatherium*, was as big as a white rhino. It was named in 1872 after the Uintah Indians, a tribe that, like *Uintatherium*, lived in Utah.

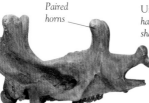

Paired horns

Uintatherium had a barrel-shaped body

CAST OF THE SKULL OF UINTATHERIUM

HORNS, BUMPS, AND TUSKS
The various shapes on the long skulls of dinoceratans such as *Uintatherium* and *Eobasileus* were probably display structures used to attract a mate.

The advanced dinoceratans had columnlike legs

UINTATHERIUM

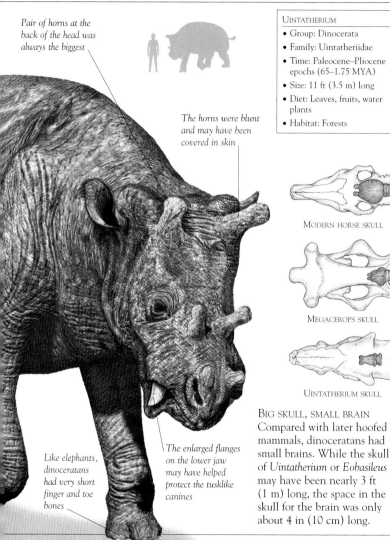

Pair of horns at the back of the head was always the biggest

The horns were blunt and may have been covered in skin

Like elephants, dinoceratans had very short finger and toe bones

The enlarged flanges on the lower jaw may have helped protect the tusklike canines

UINTATHERIUM
- Group: Dinocerata
- Family: Uintatheriidae
- Time: Paleocene–Pliocene epochs (65–1.75 MYA)
- Size: 11 ft (3.5 m) long
- Diet: Leaves, fruits, water plants
- Habitat: Forests

MODERN HORSE SKULL

MEGACEROPS SKULL

UINTATHERIUM SKULL

BIG SKULL, SMALL BRAIN
Compared with later hoofed mammals, dinoceratans had small brains. While the skull of *Uintatherium* or *Eobasileus* may have been nearly 3 ft (1 m) long, the space in the skull for the brain was only about 4 in (10 cm) long.

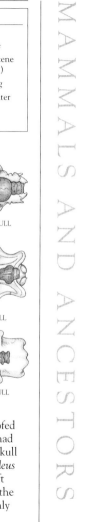

PRIMITIVE HOOFED MAMMALS

CONDYLARTHS, a recently defined group, consisted of related hoofed mammals from the early Tertiary. They ranged from the size of a rat to the size of a large sheep. Some condylarths had claws, although others had developed blunt hooves. Their teeth show that they were plant-eaters, and some had enlarged molars to pulp plant material.

PHENACODUS
The most famous condylarth is *Phenacodus*, which experts mistakenly thought was an ancestor of the horse. Like horses, it had a skeleton suited to a life of running in the open.

Long limbs were quite flexible

DIDOLODUS

DIDOLODONTIDS
These South American mammals are similar in anatomy to litopterns—horse and camel-like creatures also found there.

PHENACODUS
- Group: Condylarthra
- Family: Phenacodontidae
- Time: Paleocene–Pliocene epochs (65–1.75 MYA)
- Size: 5 ft (1.5 m) long
- Diet: Leaves
- Habitat: Grassland, open woodlands

AARDVARK PROTOTYPE
Ectoconus was from North America and perhaps Asia. Its body shape has been compared with that of the aardvark, a modern anteater.

Dappled coat for camouflage

RATLIKE HOOFED MAMMALS
Some condylarths were tiny. *Hyopsodus*, the best-known of the hyopsodontid group, was a rat-sized animal.

PHENACODUS

Phenacodus
had five toes

341

SOUTH AMERICAN HOOFED MAMMALS

IN THE TERTIARY AND EARLY Quaternary, South America was home to a range of unusual hoofed mammals—the meridiungulates. Some of these animals resembled hoofed mammals from elsewhere, such as horses and camels. These similarities probably came about due to similar lifestyles.

Macrauchenia's long neck resembled that of a camel

Macrauchenia had a small shoulder hump

It could probably kick powerfully with its hind limbs

Short trunk, like that of a modern tapir

Jaws were lined with 44 large chewing teeth

SKELETON OF MACRAUCHENIA
Macrauchenia was discovered by Charles Darwin and named and described by Sir Richard Owen, two of the most important scientists of Victorian times. Darwin wrote that the skeleton appeared to be from a large llama.

BIG LLAMA
The litopterns were a group of meridiungulates that resembled camels and horses. One of the best-known ones was *Macrauchenia* ("big llama"). It had nostrils placed high up on its head. Some experts think this shows that it had a short trunk, but others dispute this.

Chewing teeth

Incisors

SKELETON OF TOXODON

Deep, rounded body same size as a modern camel's

TOXODONTS

These plant-eaters ranged from the size of a pig to the size of a rhinoceros. *Toxodon* was a huge, hippopotamus-like animal.

FOOT OF THEOSODON

FOOT OF DIADIAPHORUS

FOOT OF THOATHERIUM

FEET FOR FAST RUNNING

Most litopterns ran on three toes. But some evolved one-toed feet, without the two side toes.

Three-toed feet, like those of rhinos

All litopterns had simple ankle joints—their name means "simple ankle"

MACRAUCHENIA

MACRAUCHENIA
- Group: Litopterna
- Family: Macraucheniidae
- Time: Pleistocene–Holocene epochs (1.75 MYA–present)
- Size: 10 ft (3 m) long
- Diet: Leaves and grasses
- Habitat: Grasslands

343

HOOFED PREDATORS

EARLY IN THEIR evolution, hoofed mammals, or Acreodi, were very different from their plant-eating descendants. Like sheep or cows, they had hoofed toes. But instead of molars shaped for munching vegetation, they had massive teeth designed for slicing meat or crushing bones. Acreodi looked and behaved very much like wolves, hyenas, and bears.

Long, narrow jaw with teeth like a bear's

GIGANTIC OMNIVORE
Andrewsarchus lived in Eocene Mongolia more than 40 million years ago, and was the biggest known carnivorous land mammal. It probably grew up to 20 ft (6 m) long. Its jaws were equipped with massive canines and molars.

Toes tipped with short hooves instead of long sharp claws

ANDREWSARCHUS

- Group: Acreodi
- Family: Mesonychidae
- Time: Paleocene – Pliocene epochs (65–1.75 MYA)
- Size: Up to 20 ft (6 m) long
- Diet: Meat, plants, insects
- Habitat: Scrub, open woodlands

Long, lean body shaped like a wolf's

Strong limbs to support its great weight

May have had a long tail

ANDREWSARCHUS

MESONYX

AGILE HUNTER

Mesonyx was a member of the mesonychids, the best-known family of the Acreodi. This wolflike predator was a fast runner, and it probably hunted hoofed plant-eaters. Its large jaw muscles gave it a powerful bite.

Long, low, narrow jaws like those of mesonychids

WHALE ANCESTORS

Although the Acreodi became extinct, a very successful and longer-lived group of mammals evolved—the whales. The skull of early whales like *Archaeocetes* resemble that of certain Acreodi.

ARCHAEOCETES
SKULL

URANOTHERES

ONE OF THE most peculiar groups of mammals is the Uranotheria, a collection of herbivorous, hoofed mammals that includes elephants, sea cows, and hyraxes. Although these animals are very different, they share features not seen in other mammals. The first elephants, for example, were dog-sized animals probably similar to hyraxes. Another group of uranotheres, the tethytheres, took to life in water and evolved into the first sea cows.

Males had larger and more pointed horns than females

ARSINOITHERIUM

- Group: Uranotheria
- Family: Arsinotheriidae
- Time: Paleocene–Pliocene epochs (65 – 1.75 MYA)
- Size: 12 ft (3.5 m) long
- Diet: Tough vegetation
- Habitat: Woodlands, wooded grasslands

Teeth had tall crowns and could have been used to chew very tough plants

Shoulders were massive and powerfully muscled

Tusklike front teeth

KVABEBIHYRAX

HYRAXES

Modern hyraxes are small African mammals that look like guinea pigs. Fossil hyraxes, however, were quite different and came in a huge range of shapes and sizes. *Kvabebihyrax*, shown here, was like a hippo and may have been amphibious.

Foot had five blunt toes, each tipped with a small hoof

ARSINOITHERES

These rhinoceros-like uranotheres lived in Asia, Europe, and Africa from the Paleocene until the Oligocene (65–23.5 million years ago). The best-known arsinoithere is *Arsinoitherium*—a large, heavy animal with two massive horns on its skull. The largest individuals of *Arsinoitherium* (probably old males) were about the size of small elephants. Unlike rhinoceros horns, arsinoithere horns were hollow.

ARSINOITHERIUM

BRONTOTHERES AND CHALICOTHERES

THESE TWO GROUPS of animals were odd-toed hoofed mammals, or perissodactyls. Brontotheres were large, rhinolike animals with horns, while Chalicotheres were horselike perissodactyls with curved claws.

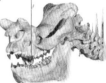

Weak teeth suggest that brontotheres mostly ate soft leaves

SKULL OF BRONTOPS

BRONTOTHERE HORNS

As brontotheres evolved, their horns became larger. Males had larger horns than females, suggesting that they were used for display and for fighting with rival males.

Injuries found on skulls suggest that brontotheres used their horns to fight

Horns were covered in skin

BRONTOPS

- Group: Perissodactyla
- Family: Brontotheriidae
- Time: Paleocene – Pliocene epochs (65–1.75 MYA)
- Size: 17 ft (5 m) long
- Diet: Leaves
- Habitat: Open woodlands

Long neck to reach up to branches

Powerful front legs were longer than the back legs

MOROPUS SKELETON

The hip bones were broad, probably to help support the weight of the body

A CLAWED "HOOFED MAMMAL"

Moropus was a chalicothere from North America. Like all chalicotheres, it had massive, powerful front legs and curving claws on its hands. Chalicotheres may have dug roots and tubers out of the ground, and also browsed on leaves.

Brontothere tails probably ended in a tuft of hairs

BRONTOPS

LAST OF THE BRONTOTHERES

Embololotherium and its relatives were related to *Brontops*, and were among the last and largest of the brontotheres. *Embololotherium* was equipped with a large, forked nose horn.

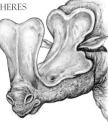

349

RHINOCEROSES

TODAY THERE ARE five surviving species of rhinoceroses—plant-eaters with horns on their snouts. Fossil rhinoceroses were diverse and evolved many different lifestyles and body shapes. Perhaps the most primitive rhinoceroses were the hornless hyracodontids, or running rhinoceroses. Another family, the amynodontids, included amphibious rhinoceroses with short mobile trunks, like the trunks of modern-day tapirs.

THE BIGGEST LAND MAMMAL
Paraceratherium was a gigantic hyracodontid rhinoceros. In contrast to the small early hyracodontids, it was 18 ft (6 m) tall at the shoulder and weighed 16 tons, making it the largest land mammal ever.

Enormous horn 6¹/2 ft (2 m) long

ELASMOTHERIUM
The surviving species of rhinos are from the rhinocerotid group. The biggest rhinocerotid was *Elasmotherium*, which reached 16 ft (5 m) in length.

Despite its great size, Paraceratherium had long, slim legs and could probably run

PARACERATHERIUM

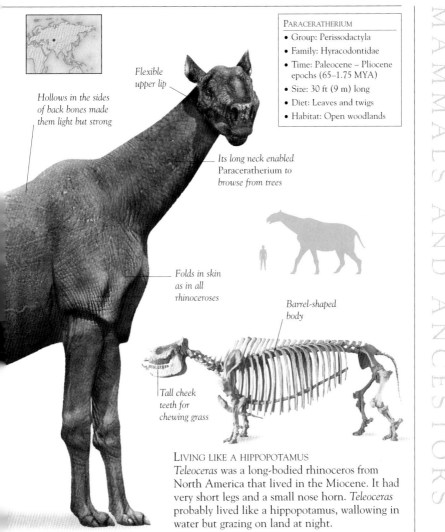

Flexible upper lip

Hollows in the sides of back bones made them light but strong

PARACERATHERIUM

• Group: Perissodactyla
• Family: Hyracodontidae
• Time: Paleocene – Pliocene epochs (65–1.75 MYA)
• Size: 30 ft (9 m) long
• Diet: Leaves and twigs
• Habitat: Open woodlands

Its long neck enabled Paraceratherium to browse from trees

Folds in skin as in all rhinoceroses

Barrel-shaped body

Tall cheek teeth for chewing grass

LIVING LIKE A HIPPOPOTAMUS
Teleoceras was a long-bodied rhinoceros from North America that lived in the Miocene. It had very short legs and a small nose horn. Teleoceras probably lived like a hippopotamus, wallowing in water but grazing on land at night.

HORSES

HORSES WERE PROBABLY the best-suited animals to life on the open grasslands. They appeared in the Eocene, and about eight species of them survive today. Successive groups of horse species evolved different features and body sizes to suit their environments. *Hipparion* lived in the Northern Hemisphere grasslands during the Miocene.

Long, squarish muzzle with large nostrils

Life in open grassland favored the evolution of large body size and long limbs in horses

HIPPARION
- Group: Perissodactyla
- Family: Equidae
- Time: Paleocene – Pliocene epochs (65–1.75 MYA)
- Size: 5 ft (1.5 m) long
- Diet: Grass, open woodlands
- Habitat: Plains

TEETH FOR GRASS-EATING

Advanced horses, such as *Hipparion*, had large, high-crowned molar teeth with complicated chewing surfaces made up of loops of enamel. Their premolars became large and squarish and came to look like the molars. These powerful teeth may have evolved when horses accidentally chewed sand, and allowed advanced horses to eat rough grasses.

THREE-TOED FEET

Like modern horses, *Hipparion* was a grassland animal. Earlier horses were probably inhabitants of forests. Unlike modern horses, which only have one toe on each foot, *Hipparion* had three-toed feet.

Moderately long tail

ELEPHANTS

THE EARLIEST KNOWN elephant was *Phosphatherium* from the Paleocene, which was just 2 ft (60 cm) tall at the shoulder. Later elephants increased in size and evolved column-like legs, and tusks in their upper jaws. Nearly all fossil elephants had a trunk.

PHIOMIA
This primitive elephant lived in northern Africa during the Oligocene. *Phiomia* was only about as big as a modern horse.

Phiomia probably had a short trunk

MOERITHERIUM
One of the most primitive known elephants is *Moeritherium*. Its skull indicates that it had an enlarged upper lip, but experts do not know whether this was a true trunk.

Moeritherium's neck was longer than that of more advanced elephants

Primitive elephants had not yet developed columnlike legs

Gomphotherium *was about as big as an Asian elephant*

GOMPHOTHERIUM
A successful group of elephants called gomphotheres spread around the world in the Miocene and Pliocene. Species such as *Gomphotherium* were the ancestors of mammoths and of modern-day elephants.

SHOVEL-TUSKERS
Like most primitive elephants, *Phiomia* had tusks in both its upper and lower jaws. Its long lower jaw had flattened tusks, which could have been used to shovel water plants or cut branches or bark from trees.

SKULL OF PHIOMIA

Deinotherium *was 13 ft (4 m) tall at the shoulder*

Trunk shorter than living elephants

DEINOTHERES
These strange elephants had no tusks in their skulls and two down-curved tusks in their lower jaws. These tusks may have been used to dig up roots.

The enlarged upper lip and nose may have formed a very short trunk

MOERITHERIUM

MOERITHERIUM
- Group: Proboscidea
- Family: Moeritheriidae
- Time: Paleocene – Pliocene epochs (65–1.75 MYA)
- Size: 10 ft (3 m) long
- Diet: Water plants
- Habitat: Lakes, rivers, riverside forests

PLATYBELODON

PLATYBELODON WAS A "shovel-tusker" from the gomphothere group. It had a long, scooplike tip to its lower jaw, formed by the tusk and jaw bone. Once thought to have lived in marshes, evidence now suggests that it lived in grasslands and forests and cropped tough vegetation from trees.

FLEXIBLE TRUNK

Old reconstructions of *Platybelodon* show it with a short, wide trunk that would not have been very flexible. This was based on evidence from the more primitive *Phiomia*, which had a short trunk. However, *Platybelodon* had the same type of nasal openings as modern elephants and it is now established that the animal had a long, flexible trunk.

PLATYBELODON
- Group: Proboscidea
- Family: Gomphotheriidae
- Time: Paleocene – Pliocene epochs (65–1.75 MYA)
- Size: 10 ft (3 m) at shoulder
- Diet: Leaves, grasses, bark
- Habitat: Grasslands, forests

Larger ears than more primitive elephants

LOWER JAW

The wear marks on *Platybelodon*'s lower jaw show that vegetation was pulled across the tips of the tusks. *Platybelodon* may have used the tusks to slice through the wood.

CAMELS

CAMELS AND THEIR relatives evolved in the Eocene and include nearly 100 fossil species. Although modern camels inhabit deserts, they were once grassland and woodland herbivores. Camels swallow their food and later regurgitate it to be chewed a second time. They also produce less urine, thus retaining more water and being better adapted to dry environments.

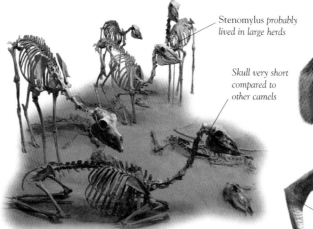

Stenomylus *probably lived in large herds*

Skull very short compared to other camels

Long, slender legs would have made Aepycamelus *a fast runner*

NARROW TOOTH

The six living camel species are native to Africa, Asia, and South America. However, most of camel history occurred in North America, and camels still lived here as recently as 11,000 years ago. The first camels, such as *Stenomylus*, were small, and perhaps resembled modern gazelles.

AEPYCAMELUS

- Group: Artiodactyla
- Family: Camelidae
- Time: Paleocene – Pliocene epochs (65–1.75 MYA)
- Size: 7 ft (2 m) at shoulder
- Diet: Tree leaves
- Habitat: Open woodlands, grasslands with trees

Teeth and skull suggest a closer link to living llamas than to modern camels

Pointed front teeth were small

GIANT GIRAFFE CAMEL
Aepycamelus ("high camel")
was a large camel with
tremendously long leg and neck
bones. It was probably a browsing
herbivore that, like modern
giraffes, fed from trees. Eight
Aepycamelus species are known.

Advanced camels such as Oxydactylus had two toes only, while more primitive species had four toes

Front and back legs of camels are more equal in size than in other hoofed mammals

Like living camels, fossil species may have had dense, woolly fur

FOSSIL OXYDACTYLUS FOOT

CAMEL FEET AND WALKING
Advanced camels have unique
feet. Unlike other artiodactyls,
they walk not on the tips of their
toes, but on the whole toe. Soft toe
pads help them walk on rocks or
sand with ease.

MAMMOTHS

THE EIGHT SPECIES of mammoths were all true elephants, closely related to present-day elephants. Mammoth genetic material, or DNA, was found in 1994, and it is almost identical to that of living elephants. The woolly mammoth is perhaps the most famous fossil animal from the Pleistocene.

Shoulder hump

Both male and female woolly mammoths had long tusks, which they used for combat and display, and for gathering food

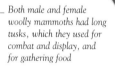

WOOLLY MAMMOTH

WOOLLY MAMMOTH
These mammoths lived in herds and fed on grasses and other small plants, which they plucked with the two "fingers" on the tips of their trunks. Several woolly mammoths have been found preserved in the frozen ground of Siberia. Their fur, skin, muscles, and even their stomach contents are still intact.

Domed skull not
yet developed

DIMA THE MAMMOTH
Dima was the name
given to a frozen
male baby woolly
mammoth, recovered in
1977 in Russia, and
preserved in a remarkably
complete condition.

WOOLLY MAMMOTH
- Group: Proboscidea
- Family: Elephantidae
- Time: Pleistocene–
  Holocene epochs
  (1.75 MYA–present)
- Size: 11 ft (3.3 m) long
- Diet: Grasses and plants
- Habitat: Woodlands,
  grasslands

Mammoth hair, found on
the frozen specimens, can
be up to 3 ft (90 cm) long

Tusks were so long
and curved that
they crossed over

Huge column-
like limbs
supported
its weight

IMPERIAL MAMMOTH
The imperial mammoth was
a giant North American
Pleistocene mammoth and one
of the biggest elephants that
ever lived. Its huge curving tusks
could be as long as 14 ft (4.3 m).

MAMMALS AND ANCESTORS

361

PIGS, HIPPOS, AND PECCARIES

THE LARGEST AND MOST successful group of hoofed mammals are the artiodactyls, or even-toed hoofed mammals. Their distinctive ankle and foot bones allow them to run fast. Most forms have two or four toes, hence the group's name. One of the groups within the artiodactyls is the suiforms, which includes pigs, hippos, and peccaries.

HIPPOPOTAMUSES

The first hippos appeared in the Late Miocene. Two kinds survive today—the large, amphibious *Hippopotamus* and the small, land-living *Hexaprotodon*. The recently extinct *Hippopotamus lemerlei* was a pygmy hippo from Madagascar.

Large cheek bones with swollen ends

Eyes located on top of the head

SKELETON OF ARCHAEOTHERIUM

Entelodonts had two toes on each foot

Amphibious hippos have elongated snouts and lower jaws

SKULL OF HIPPOPOTAMUS LEMERLEI

ANCIENT BEAST

Entelodonts were pig- to bison-sized suiforms known from Europe, Asia, and North America. They had long legs and deep bodies. Their huge skulls have bony bumps on the cheeks and lower jaws, crushing teeth, and huge, curving, canine teeth. *Archaeotherium* was a successful pig-sized entelodont.

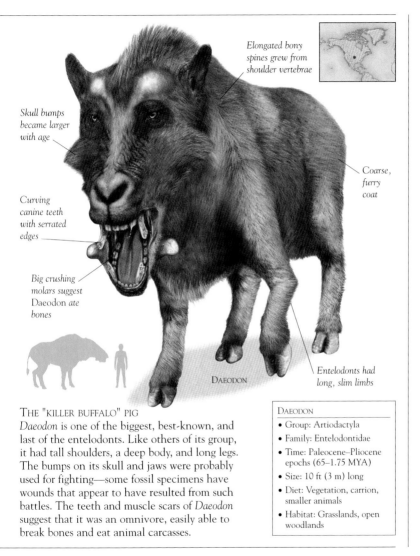

Elongated bony
spines grew from
shoulder vertebrae

Skull bumps
became larger
with age

Curving
canine teeth
with serrated
edges

Big crushing
molars suggest
Daeodon ate
bones

Coarse,
furry
coat

Entelodonts had
long, slim limbs

DAEODON

THE "KILLER BUFFALO" PIG
Daeodon is one of the biggest, best-known, and
last of the entelodonts. Like others of its group,
it had tall shoulders, a deep body, and long legs.
The bumps on its skull and jaws were probably
used for fighting—some fossil specimens have
wounds that appear to have resulted from such
battles. The teeth and muscle scars of *Daeodon*
suggest that it was an omnivore, easily able to
break bones and eat animal carcasses.

DAEODON
- Group: Artiodactyla
- Family: Entelodontidae
- Time: Paleocene–Pliocene
  epochs (65–1.75 MYA)
- Size: 10 ft (3 m) long
- Diet: Vegetation, carrion,
  smaller animals
- Habitat: Grasslands, open
  woodlands

DEER AND KIN

SEVERAL NEW GROUPS of small, forest-dwelling herbivores first appeared 24–5 million years ago. The spread of grasslands allowed some of them to move out of the forest, becoming larger and more widespread. The most successful of these were the deer family.

Antlers may have spanned 12 ft (3.7 m) in large males

GIANT ANTLERS
The largest-ever antlers belonged to *Megaloceros*, which was still living 9,000 years ago.

PROTOCERAS

SYNTHETOCERAS

Horns look impressive from front view

SYNDYOCERAS

EARLY HORNS
Male protoceratids ("early horns") that lived 55 to just 2 million years ago displayed some of the most spectacular horns ever evolved.

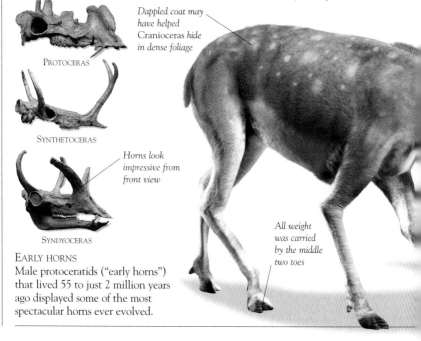

Dappled coat may have helped Cranioceras hide in dense foliage

All weight was carried by the middle two toes

THREE-HORNED DEER RELATIVE
Cranioceras was a paleomerycid—one of a
group of deerlike hoofed mammals that
lived from the Oligocene to the Pliocene
(33.7–1.75 million years ago). Many, but
not all, paleomerycids had bony horns
that grew backward, forward, or upward
from above their eyes. In the group that
includes
Cranioceras, a
third horn grew
upward and back
from the rear of
the skull.

*Long rear
ossicones*

*Third horn
at the back
of the head*

GIRAFFOKERYX

GIRAFFIDS
Giraffokeryx was a primitive giraffid
(cud-chewing hoofed animal) that
lived in Asia, Europe, and Africa,
around 5 million years ago. It had
two pairs of pointed, furry, hornlike structures called ossicones.

*Limbs were not
as long or slim as
those of grassland-
dwelling relatives*

*Horns may have
been used for
fighting rival males*

CRANIOCERAS
- Group: Artiodactyla
- Family: Dromomerycidae
- Time: Paleocene–Pliocene
  epochs (65–1.75 MYA)
- Size: 3 ft (1 m) tall at
  shoulder
- Diet: Leaves
- Habitat: Subtropical
  woodlands

CATTLE, SHEEP, AND GOATS

CATTLE AND THEIR RELATIVES are the most plentiful of the large, hoofed, grazing animals alive today. Wild and domestic cattle, sheep, goats, antelopes, and musk-oxen are grouped together as bovoids. All these animals probably evolved more than 20 million years ago from small, hornless, deerlike ancestors.

Sharp, strong horns

Cattle do not shed their horns like deer

OVIS CANADENSIS SKULL

Jaws have high-crowned teeth, which evolved for chewing

EARLY SHEEP AND GOATS

Goats and sheep, including mountain sheep like *Ovis canadensis*, shared a common ancestor with other bovoids. This animal existed over 20 million years ago. Its descendants gave rise first to antelopes, then to sheep and goats, and finally to cattle.

ANCESTRAL OX

Bos primigenius, also known as aurochs, was the ancestor of most domesticated cattle. It roamed the forests of Europe, Asia, and Africa. The last wild aurochs was killed in Poland in 1627. Prehistoric cattle are now extinct, but wild cattle such as bison, buffalo, and yaks still survive.

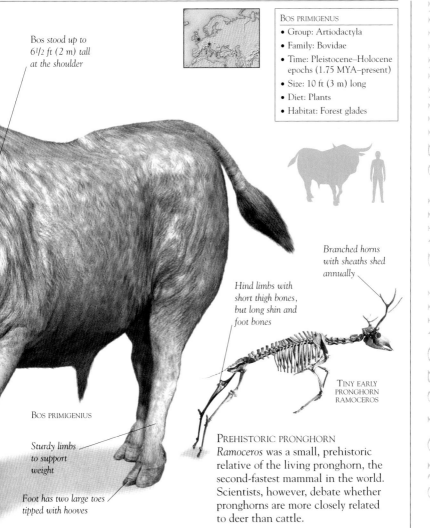

Bos stood up to
6¹/₂ ft (2 m) tall
at the shoulder

BOS PRIMIGENUS
- Group: Artiodactyla
- Family: Bovidae
- Time: Pleistocene–Holocene
  epochs (1.75 MYA–present)
- Size: 10 ft (3 m) long
- Diet: Plants
- Habitat: Forest glades

Branched horns
with sheaths shed
annually

Hind limbs with
short thigh bones,
but long shin and
foot bones

TINY EARLY
PRONGHORN
RAMOCEROS

BOS PRIMIGENIUS

Sturdy limbs
to support
weight

Foot has two large toes
tipped with hooves

PREHISTORIC PRONGHORN
Ramoceros was a small, prehistoric
relative of the living pronghorn, the
second-fastest mammal in the world.
Scientists, however, debate whether
pronghorns are more closely related
to deer than cattle.

EARLY WHALES

Long tail flukes provided the main swimming thrust

THE EARLIEST whales were very different from living whales—some had hind limbs and could probably move on land. Their skeletons show that they had started to swim with an up-and-down motion of the tail. By the end of the Eocene, fully aquatic whales like *Basilosaurus* had evolved.

Tiny, three-toed hind limbs would have projected from sides

Long skull, with nostrils close to the tip of snout

AMBULOCETUS

FIRST WHALES
Ambulocetus, an early whale, looked something like a cross between a wolf and a seal and had a long crocodile-like head. The first known whale, *Pakicetus*, comes from the Middle Eocene of Pakistan, a site rich in whale fossils.

ECHOLOCATION AT WORK
Whales gain a mental picture of their surroundings by a method called echolocation. They project noises through a structure on the forehead called the melon. Echoes of the noises are then transmitted from external objects to the whale's ears via a fatty pad in its lower jaw.

Nearby object creates an echo

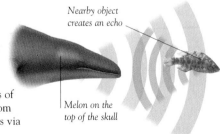

Melon on the top of the skull

DORUDON SKULL

Dorudon and other Eocene whales have two different kinds of teeth

SKULL EVOLUTION

In early whales, the nostrils were located at the tip of the snout, as in land animals. More advanced whales like *Basilosaurus* have nostrils midway along their snouts. Advanced whales, such as *Prosqualodon*, had their nostrils, or blowhole, on the top of the head.

PROSQUALODON SKULL

Teeth of advanced whales are all similar in shape

EOCENE GIANT

Basilosaurus is one of the biggest fossil whales known, measuring more than 60 ft (20 m). The vertebrae that make up *Basilosaurus*'s back and tail are unusual, elongated bones, unlike the shortened vertebrae in most whales. These could have made it more flexible than living whales.

Unique long body— other Eocene whales were much shorter

BASILOSAURUS

- Group: Cetaceae
- Family: Basilosauridae
- Time: Paleocene–Pliocene epochs (65–1.75 MYA)
- Size: 66–83 ft (20–25 m) long
- Diet: Other marine mammals, fish
- Habitat: Shallow tropical seas

Ribs were made of very thick, heavy bone

Unlike modern whales, basilosaurs had a flexible elbow

INSECTIVORES AND BATS

MOLES, HEDGEHOGS, SHREWS, and other insectivores first appeared in the Eocene and share distinctive snout muscles and skull bones. Like pterosaurs and birds, bats evolved true flapping flight and have modified forelimbs, in which the fingers support skin membranes that reach the ankles.

Icaronycteris had sharp-clawed feet

Desmans have sharp, pointed teeth for catching worms, insects, snails, and fish

LOWER JAW BONE
OF DESMANA
MOSCHATA

UNDERGROUND OR UNDERWATER
Prehistoric moles resembled shrews. Desmans are swimming moles that evolved in the Oligocene and survive today.

ICARONYCTERIS
The early bat *Icaronycteris* is known from Eocene North America. Its ear bones show that it could use sonar (detecting the presence of objects with high-pitched sounds), like modern bats.

The wing membranes of all bats are made up of skin

Bats have large ears for acute hearing

Icaronycteris had more teeth than modern insect-eating bats

LIVING
HORSESHOE BAT

VARIED DIET

Before the Eocene, the bat group split into two main groups: the insect-eating small bats and the fruit-eating large bats. Fish-eating bats evolved in the Miocene and survive today. Vampire bats feed on the blood of animals, while horseshoe bats feed on pollen.

Unlike modern bats, early forms such as Icaronycteris had claws on their second fingers as well as on their thumbs

Long, thin fingers support wing membranes

MACROCRANION FOSSIL

SPINY AND HAIRY HEDGEHOGS

Hedgehogs have a rich fossil record, and numerous types are known. Some were tiny, while others, like *Deinogalerix*, were 3 ft (1 m) long. *Macrocranion* was an Eocene hedgehog with a long tail and no spines.

ICARONYCTERIS

- Group: Chiroptera
- Family: Uncertain
- Time: Paleocene–Pliocene epochs (65–1.75 MYA)
- Size: 16-in (40-cm) wingspan
- Diet: Flying insects
- Habitat: Forests, caves, river banks

Monkeys

MONKEYS ARE PART OF a group of
primates called the anthropoidea.
There are two main types
of monkeys: the Old World
monkeys from Asia and
Africa, which are called
the catarrhines, and the
New World monkeys, which
evolved in South America
and are called the platyrrhines.

*The New World
includes North and
South America*

*The Old World includes
Africa, Europe, and Asia*

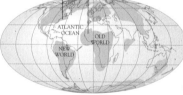

ATLANTIC
OCEAN

OLD
WORLD

NEW
WORLD

AMERICAN INVASION
In the past, experts have
wondered about the origins of
the New World monkeys.
However, new fossils show that
platyrrhines have an African
ancestor that crossed over to
South America at a time when
the Atlantic Ocean was not as
wide as it is today.

THEROPITHECUS
OSWALDI
Old World monkeys
invaded grassland habitats
to exploit new sources of
food. Various species of
Theropithecus, a seed-eating
grassland monkey, evolved in
the Pliocene and lived across
Europe, Africa, and Asia.
Theropithecus oswaldi was the
largest among them.

*Opposable thumb used
for delicate handling
of objects*

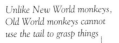

Unlike New World monkeys, Old World monkeys cannot use the tail to grasp things

PARACOLOBUS SKELETON

MONKEY EMPIRE
Old World monkeys, many of them agile tree-climbers, replaced apes during the Miocene. One group, the colobids, migrated out of Africa and evolved in Asia into the leaf-eating langurs and proboscis monkeys. *Mesopithecus* and *Paracolobus* were early colobids.

UPPER SKULL OF
TREMACEBUS

NEW WORLD FOREST-DWELLERS
New World monkeys did not take to grassland life and have remained animals of the forest. *Tremacebus*, from the late Oligocene of Patagonia, was like the living owl monkey.

THEROPITHECUS
- Group: Anthropoidea
- Family: Cercopithecidae
- Time: Paleocene – Holocene epochs (65 MYA – present)
- Size: 3–6 ft (1–2 m) long
- Diet: Grasses, seeds, fruits, insects, and worms
- Habitat: Grasslands

PRIMITIVE PRIMATES

THE PRIMATE GROUP includes
primitive forms, such as lemurs,
and advanced forms such as
apes and humans. Primatelike
mammals appeared early in the
Paleocene and evolved through
the Eocene. Lemurs, tree shrews,
and lorises are the only survivors
of the more primitive primates.

*The long skull was
unlike that of later
primates*

*Megaladapis had
a doglike head*

Huge molar teeth

LEMURS LARGE AND SMALL
Prehistoric lemurs were
more diverse than they are
today. *Megaladapis* was as
large as the living orangutan.
It died out only 600 years ago.

*Koala-like
build*

MEGALADAPIS
EDWARDSIS
SKELETON

PLESIADAPIS
The plesiadapids were an early primate group.
Best-known among them was *Plesiadapis*, which
had grasping fingers and toes, and a long tail. It
probably looked like a cross between a lemur
and a squirrel and chewed on wood, using its
large incisors to feed on grubs and sap.

Long finger

LIVING
AYE-AYE

LONG FINGER EVOLUTION
Aye-ayes are a group
of primates from
Madagascar that may
be more primitive than
lemurs. The aye-aye has
a remarkable long third
finger, which it uses to
extract grubs out of wood.

*Like squirrels,
Plesiadapis could
have used its tail
for balance*

*Long fingers
that could grip*

NOTHARCTUS
One of North America's
last native primates was
Notharctus. It was the first
North American fossil primate
to be recognized in the 1870s.

PLESIADAPIS	
• Group: Primates	
• Family: Plesiadapidae	
• Time: Paleocene–Pliocene	
epochs (65–1.75 MYA)	
• Size: 2½ ft (80 cm) long	
• Diet: Insects, fruits	
• Habitat: Subtropical forests	

375

REFERENCE

IN THIS SECTION, scan a pictorial summary of life through time. Retrace the journeys of prehistoric creatures, from their deaths millions of years ago to their stunning resurrection in museum halls. Spend time on an exotic dig with a paleontologist, then learn what goes on when fossils reach the laboratory. Read about experts who helped solve the puzzles of the past.

DINOSAUR DISCOVERERS

PEOPLE HAVE been finding dinosaur fossils for thousands of years. But it was not until 1841 that scientists first identified the dinosaur group. There have been many well-known dinosaur hunters, made famous because of the dinosaurs they have discovered.

SIR RICHARD OWEN (1804–92) was a famous British anatomist. He coined the name "dinosaur," which means "terrible lizard."

WHAT HE DISCOVERED
Owen worked at the Natural History Museum in London, where he studied fossils found in Europe. He realized that some fossils not only were reptiles, but were unknown types of giant reptiles. He concluded that they must have belonged to a group of extinct animals, and named this group dinosaurs.

DR. GIDEON MANTELL (1790–1852) was a medical doctor from Sussex, England. He was also an avid fossil-hunter. He spent much of his early life collecting fossils in the hills near where he lived. But it was one fossil find that put his name in the history books.

WHAT HE DISCOVERED
In 1820, Gideon Mantell and his wife, Mary Ann, found some large teeth and bones in some gravel near a stone quarry. They belonged to an unknown, iguana-like animal. In 1825, mantell named it *Iguanodon*, although he did not realize at the time that it was a dinosaur.

DEAN WILLIAM BUCKLAND (1784–1856) was the first professor of geology at Oxford University in England. He was fascinated by fossils from an early age.

WHAT HE DISCOVERED
In 1824, a large jawbone with a giant tooth was found near Oxford. Buckland recognized it as belonging to a previously unknown giant reptile. This reptile was named *Megalosaurus*, which means "big lizard," and was the first dinosaur to be named. Like Mantell, Buckland did not know that *Megalosaurus* was a dinosaur.

JOHN BELL HATCHER (1861–1904) was a fossil collector for Othniel Marsh. Hatcher is recognized as one of the greatest collectors of dinosaurs in the history of American paleontology.

WHAT HE DISCOVERED

In 1888, Hatcher found part of a huge horned skull beside the Judith River in Montana. It turned out to be a *Triceratops* skull, and was the first fossil of this dinosaur to be discovered. It was also the first of the horned dinosaurs to be found, which introduced a new dinosaur variety to paleontologists.

EDWARD DRINKER COPE (1840–97) was an American from Philadelphia. He was a scientific genius, and dinosaurs were just one area on which he was an expert.

WHAT HE DISCOVERED

Cope started his scientific career after the American Civil War. He traveled with fellow scientist Othniel Marsh on many of his early trips. The two men eventually became fierce rivals. Among his many finds, Cope discovered several primitive Triassic dinosaurs in New Mexico.

OTHNIEL MARSH (1831–99) was an American paleontologist born in New York. Along with E.D. Cope, Marsh was one of the great pioneers of dinosaur fossil-hunting in the United States.

WHAT HE DISCOVERED

Marsh discovered many dinosaur fossil sites in the United States. The most famous were Como Bluff in Wyoming and several sites in Colorado. His intense rivalry with Edward Drinker Cope was nicknamed the "Bone Wars."

EBERHARD FRAAS (1862–1915) was a German paleontologist. He went on long expeditions to Africa in his search for dinosaur fossils.

WHAT HE DISCOVERED

In 1907, Fraas was told of some dinosaur bones at a site in Tanzania, Africa. Fraas led an expedition to explore the site and, in 1909–12, the first fine specimens of *Kentrosaurus*, *Elaphrosaurus*, *Barosaurus*, and *Brachiosaurus* were discovered there. The *Brachiosaurus* skeleton Fraas discovered is now in a museum in Berlin, and is the largest mounted skeleton in the world.

GEORGE F. STERNBERG (1883–1969) was an American paleontologist who started collecting fossils at the age of six. He continued to work on fossils for the next 66 years.

WHAT HE DISCOVERED
Sternberg made his most important dinosaur discovery in 1908: he was the first person to find an impression of dinosaur skin, which belonged to *Anatosaurus*. Sternberg made many other amazing discoveries, including the first fossil of *Edmontosaurus*.

EDWIN COLBERT (1905–2001) was an American paleontologist and an expert in Triassic dinosaurs. He was the first to find dinosaur fossils in Antarctica. He wrote several books about the history of dinosaurs.

WHAT HE DISCOVERED
Colbert found the first complete *Coelophysis* skeletons in New Mexico in 1947. Some skeletons held the bones of young *Coelophysis* in their rib cages. This indicated that *Coelophysis* may have been a cannibal.

ANDREW CARNEGIE (1835–1919) was originally from Scotland. He emigrated with his family to the United States at the age of 11. He made his fortune in the steel industry in Pittsburgh.

WHAT HE DISCOVERED
Carnegie set up the Carnegie Museum in Pittsburgh. He sent fossil-hunters on long expeditions to find dinosaurs for his museum. They discovered two complete skeletons of *Diplodocus*. A replica of one of the skeletons stands in the Natural History Museum in London.

ROY CHAPMAN ANDREWS (1884–1960) led the first American expedition to the Gobi Desert in Mongolia in 1922. Andrews went with a team from the American Museum of Natural History (AMNH).

WHAT HE DISCOVERED
Andrews and his team discovered many new dinosaurs in the Gobi Desert. Among them were *Velociraptor* and *Oviraptor*. But the most significant find was some fossilized eggs—the first dinosaur eggs to be discovered.

EARL DOUGLASS (1862–1931) was an American from Utah. He worked at the Carnegie Museum in Pittsburgh. Andrew Carnegie, who founded the museum, wanted to exhibit skeletons of the giant dinosaurs.

WHAT HE DISCOVERED
In 1909, Douglass was sent by Andrew Carnegie to hunt for fossils in Utah. Douglass' discoveries included *Diplodocus* and *Apatosaurus*. The site where these dinosaurs were found was turned into the Dinosaur National Park, which still exists today.

BARNUM BROWN (1873–1963), an American, was hired by the American Museum of Natural History in New York because of his skill in finding dinosaur skeletons.

WHAT HE DISCOVERED
Barnum Brown's expertise in fossil-hunting earned him the nickname "Mr. Bones." He found the first *Tyrannosaurus* fossils, and named *Ankylosaurus* and *Corythosaurus*. The AMNH houses the world's greatest display of Cretaceous dinosaurs as a result of Brown's collecting.

JIM JENSEN (1910–1998) was a self-taught paleontologist. He was the curator of the Vertebrate Paleontology Research Laboratory at Brigham Young University in Utah.

WHAT HE DISCOVERED
Jensen discovered some of the largest dinosaurs. In 1972, he found a partial skeleton of a sauropod, which he named *Supersaurus*. *Supersaurus*'s height is estimated to be 54 ft (16.5 m). In 1979 he found a partial skeleton of another new sauropod. He named it *Ultrasaurus*, and it is thought to be even bigger than *Supersaurus*.

BILL WALKER (b. 1928) is a British quarry-worker who is also an amateur fossil collector. In 1982, he made an important dinosaur discovery when exploring a muddy clay pit in Surrey, England.

WHAT HE DISCOVERED
Walker found a huge claw, which broke into pieces when he held it. He took it to the British Museum in London, which organized an excavation to recover more of the creature. It turned out to be a new dinosaur, which was named *Baryonyx walkeri*, in honor of Walker.

RECORDS AND MYTHS

AS SCIENCE HAS ADVANCED, so has our understanding of dinosaurs. With almost every new discovery, we learn more about these giant reptiles. The early dinosaur experts had beliefs about dinosaurs that we now know to be incorrect. The largest, smallest, fastest, most intelligent, or the least intelligent dinosaur also changes as our knowledge increases.

DINOSAUR RECORDS

• The smallest dinosaur ever found was called *Mussaurus*. It was only 8 in (20 cm) long, but the single skeleton found may have been a hatchling. The smallest adult dinosaur we know of was *Compsognathus*, which was about the size of a chicken.

• *Dromiceiomimus* may have been the fastest of the dinosaurs, running at speeds of more than 43 mph (70 km/h).

• The sauropod *Mamenchisaurus* had the longest neck of any dinosaur. The length of the neck was around 45 ft (14 m).
• *Giganotosaurus* is the biggest meat-eating dinosaur found so far. It is even longer than the previous record-holder, *Tyrannosaurus*. It was about 50 ft (15 m) long and had teeth as long as 6 in (18 cm).
• The longest dinosaur that we know of was the sauropod *Seismosaurus*. It was about 130 ft (40 m) long and weighed about 50 tons.

• The herbivore hadrosaurs had about 960 teeth—more than any other dinosaur. That was about 480 tightly packed teeth in each jaw.

• *Troodon* had the largest brain in proportion to its size of any dinosaur.
• *Stegosaurus* had the smallest brain in proportion to its size.
• *Diplodocus* had the longest tail of all the dinosaurs, at more than 43 ft (13 m) in length.

DINOSAUR MYTHS

• In 1822, Gideon Mantell made a reconstruction of *Iguanodon*, based on the few bones he had found. He had only one thumb spike, which he thought belonged on *Iguanodon's* nose. This was similar to the nose spike of an iguana lizard, after which *Iguanodon* was named. It was not until the discovery of several skeletons in the late 1800s that scientists realized this mistake.

• In China, the word "konglong" means both "dinosaur" and "terrible dragon." The Chinese have been collecting dinosaur fossils for 2,000 years. Since the third century CE, and perhaps before then, the Chinese believed that dinosaur bones were actually the remains of dragons.

• Many movies and books portray dinosaurs and humans living at the same time. In fact, dinosaurs became extinct more than 60 million years before the first humans appeared.

• It was once thought that all dinosaurs dragged their tails on the ground, like modern lizards. Some sauropods probably did, but most dinosaurs had stiffened tails, which they held horizontally off the ground.

• *Hypsilophodon* was once thought to have lived in trees. It was believed that their long tails helped them to balance in the branches, and their sharp claws were used for clinging. We now know their fingers and toes were not designed for gripping branches.

• Many people think that dinosaurs were all huge and cumbersome. But the vast majority were only about as big as an elephant, and some were as small as a chicken. Most were very agile, too.

• *Brachiosaurus* was once believed to have lived in water because of the high position of its nostrils. But the great water pressures at depth would not have allowed it to breathe.

• *Iguanodon* was the first dinosaur to be reconstructed. At first it was shown as a slow, sprawling lizard, dragging a fat belly on the ground. We now know that *Iguanodon* was actually bipedal and much slimmer.

DIGGING UP DINOSAURS

BOTH AMATEUR and professional collectors are capable of making important dinosaur discoveries. Once discovered, fossil bones should be removed only by experienced professionals, because they are often fragile. The method of removing the bones generally follows a similar procedure.

1 SITE
Once a dinosaur site has been uncovered, the fossil bones have to be excavated (dug up). This delicate operation is carried out using special tools.

2 EXCAVATION
Hammers, chisels, and picks are used to remove most of the matrix (earth and stone material surrounding the bones).

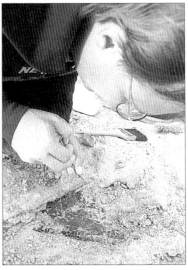

3 EXPOSING THE BONES
Whenever possible, the matrix is removed close to the bone. This is done with great care so as to not damage the bone. The bones are exposed to reveal their full size so that no fragment will be left behind when removed.

5 JACKET ON OTHER SIDE
Once the exposed part of the bone has been coated, the rest of the bone, including some of the matrix, can be dug out of the ground. It is then covered with a plaster-and-burlap jacket.

4 PLASTER JACKET
The exposed parts of the bones are coated with glue and covered with a jacket of plaster and burlap. This will protect the bones as they travel from the site to a museum, where they can be studied in more detail.

6 REMOVAL FROM SITE
The jacketed bones are sometimes so big and heavy that a crane is needed to lift them onto a truck.

PREPARING DINOSAURS

SCIENTISTS TRY TO arrange dinosaur skeletons in different poses at museums. The team at the American Museum of Natural History in New York showed a *Barosaurus* skeleton rearing up to defend its young against an *Allosaurus*. The fossil bones of *Barosaurus* were very fragile and too heavy to display, so a lightweight replica of the skeleton was made.

MAKING A MOLD
To make a mold of an original bone, liquid rubber is painted onto the surface of the bone and left to set. When the rubber has set, it is removed from the bone in sections. The rubber is then supported by cotton gauze and surrounded with a plastic jacket.

POURING THE MOLD
The inside of the rubber molds is painted with liquid plastic and strengthened by sheets of fiberglass. The mold sections are then put together to recreate the bone's shape, and filled with foam plastic.

Pouring the foam plastic into the bone cast

Filing away the rough edges of the seams

FINISHING TOUCHES
The seams in the cast bones are smoothed by filing. The plastic bones are then painted to match the colors of the original bones.

MOVING THE CAST
The skeleton is completed in sections before being mounted in its final position. Since the casts are lightweight, it is quite easy to move the skeleton in large sections, such as the entire rib cage.

Several museum workers move Barosaurus' rib cage

PLACING THE NECK
Barosaurus is mounted on a fiberglass replica of a natural landscape. The height of the *Barosaurus* skeleton rearing up is over 50 ft (15 m). The neck has to be lifted by a crane and placed carefully into its final position.

A guide rope steadies the neck as it is being raised

The welded joints must be very strong to support the skeleton

WELDING TOGETHER
A supporting steel frame runs through the skeleton sections. This frame was welded to join the sections together. The entire operation was carefully planned, since any mistake would have been very costly.

DINOSAURS ON DISPLAY

THE MOST popular feature of many natural history collections around the world is the dinosaurs on display. Scientists can use museums for storing fossils, and as laboratories for studying dinosaurs and other fossil remains.

STORING FOSSILS
The dinosaur fossils on display in museums are often just a fraction of the fossils the museum possesses. Sometimes thousands of fossils are housed in storerooms.

LIFE-SIZE SKELETON
Full-size reconstructions of dinosaurs, such as this *Tyrannosaurus* skeleton, give us an impression of how they may have looked.

When running, Tyrannosaurus would have held its tail rigid for balance

The back leg bones were thick to support Tyrannosaurus's enormous weight

DINOSAUR DRAMAS
Today, filmmakers use computer-generated effects to create very realistic impressions of what dinosaurs were like. Transferring these graphics to the large screen makes for a truly terrifying and fascinating viewing experience.

The large hips were the pivotal center of the body

Large chest cavity held the powerful heart and lungs

Leg bone is as tall as an adult human

PREPARING A SKELETON
Fossil dinosaur bones can be fragile and are often in pieces when first collected. Scientists use special tools to remove the rock surrounding a newly excavated fossil bone. This scientist is working on a *Triceratops* skull.

389

GLOSSARY

Amniotes Tetrapod vertebrates whose young develop within a special protective membrane called the amnion.

Amphibians Cold-blooded tetrapod vertebrates whose young use gills to breathe during the early stages of life.

Amphibious Inhabiting both water and land.

Ancestor An animal or plant from which others have evolved.

Arthropods Invertebrates with segmented bodies and a hard (outer) exoskeleton.

Bipedal Walking on the hind limbs rather than on all fours.

Brachiopods Marine invertebrates with a two-valved shell.

Carnivores/Carnivora A group of sharp-toothed, meat-eating mammals, including cats, dogs, bears, and their relatives and ancestors.

Clade A group of organisms (such as dinosaurs) sharing anatomical features derived from the same ancestor.

Cladogram A branching diagram showing the relationships of different clades.

Class In the Linnaean system of classification, a group of organisms containing one or more related orders.

Cold-blooded Depending upon the heat from the sun for body warmth.

Crustaceans A large class of arthropods named after the hard carapace, or "crust," that encases their bodies.

Cycads Palmlike, seed-bearing plants that are topped by a crown of fernlike leaves.

Descendant A living thing that is descended from another.

Diapsids A major group of reptiles, typically with two holes in the skull behind each eye.

Dinosaurs A large group of advanced archosaurs with erect limbs.

Echinoderms Marine invertebrates with a hard, chalky skeleton and a five-rayed symmetry.

Ectotherm A cold-blooded animal.

Eon The longest unit of geological time.

Epoch An interval of geological time that is longer than an age and shorter than a period.

Era A unit of geological time that ranks below an eon.

Erosion The wearing away of the surface of Earth by natural forces, such as wind and moving ice and water.

Evolution The process by which one species gives rise to another. It occurs when individual organisms pass on changes in genes controlling such things as body size, shape, and color. Individuals with beneficial mutations pass these on, so their kind multiplies, and new species eventually arise.

Exoskeleton An external skeleton.

Extinction The dying-out of a plant or animal species.

Fossil The remains of a prehistoric organism preserved in Earth's crust.

Gastroliths Stones that are swallowed to help grind up food in the stomach.

Geological Concerning geology, the scientific study of the composition, structure, and origins of Earth's rocks.

Gondwana The vast southern supercontinent that included South America, Africa, Antarctica, Australia, and India.

Herbivore Any animal that eats only plants.

Insectivore Any insect-eating organism, including some plants, but especially the group of mammals including moles, shrews, and hedgehogs.

Invertebrates Animals without backbones.

Juvenile A young or immature individual.

Lissamphibians Living amphibians and their closest ancestors.

Mammals Warm-blooded, hairy vertebrates that secrete milk and suckle their young.

Marsupials Mammals that give birth to small, undeveloped young that grow and mature in a skin pouch on the mother's stomach.

Metazoans Many-celled animals (this applies to the vast majority of animals).

Ornithischians—"bird hips." One of the two major dinosaur groups (see also *Saurischians*). The pelvis of ornithischians is similar to the pelvis of birds.

Ornithopods A group of large and small ornithischian dinosaurs: plant-eaters that walked on their long hind limbs.

Paleontology The scientific study of fossil plants and animals.

Parareptiles—"near/beside reptiles." Primitive reptiles, including the mesosaurs. Some people have used the term to include all the reptiles known to anapsids.

Peccary A piglike type of hoofed mammal native to the Americas.

Perissodactyls—"odd-toed." Hoofed mammals, including horses, rhinoceroses, tapirs, their ancestors, and various extinct forms.

Phalanges (singular: phalanx) Toe and finger bones.

Placoderms A class of jawed fish, protected by armorlike plates. They flourished in Devonian times.

Placodonts Aquatic reptiles of the Triassic. Some "rowed" with paddle-shaped limbs, others swam with webbed digits and by waggling their tails.

Predator Any animal or plant that preys on animals for food.

Primitive At an early stage of evolution or development.

Pubis One of the two lower hip bones of dinosaurs (the other one was the ischium). In some dinosaurs, the pubis anchored the muscle that pulled the hind legs forward.

Quadrupedal Walking on all fours.

Reptiles Lizards, snakes, turtles, crocodiles, dinosaurs, and their extinct and living relatives.

Reptiliomorphs Small, lizard-like tetrapods that gave rise to true reptiles.

Sacrum Fused vertebrae that are joined to the pelvis.

Scutes Bony plates with a horny covering set in the skin of certain reptiles to protect them from the teeth and claws of enemies.

Species In the classification of living things, the level below a genus.

Synapsids The group of tetrapod vertebrates that includes the extinct pelycosaurs and therapsids, and the therapsids' descendants—mammals.

Temnospondyls—"cut vertebrae." A group of early tetrapods.

Trilobites—"three lobed." Paleozoic marine arthropods with external skeletons divided lengthwise into three lobes.

Ungulates Hoofed mammals.

Vertebrae (singular: vertebra) The linked bones forming the backbones of vertebrate animals.

Vertebrates Animals with an internal bony or cartilaginous skeleton including a skull and a backbone made up of vertebrae.

Warm-blooded Keeping body temperature at a constant level, often above or below that of the surroundings.

INDEX

ACKNOWLEDGMENTS

Picture Credits
The publisher would like to thank the following for their kind permission to reproduce their photographs:

Abbreviations key: t-top, b-bottom, r-right, l-left, c-centre, a-above, f-far

2 DK Images: Bedrock Studios tl, tc, tr, tr, cla, cr, cr, bl, bc, br, cbr, cfr; Gary Ombler clb. 3 DK Images: Bedrock Studios c. 4 DK Images: Colin Keates br. 5 DK Images: Bedrock Studios tcl; Jonathan Hately br; Lynton Gardiner/American Museum of Natural History cfr. 6 DK Images: Tim Ridley cra. 6-7 DK Images: Bedrock Studios. 7 DK Images: Bedrock Studios tr. 10 American Museum Of Natural History: clb. 10 Jean-Loup Charmet/Bridgeman Art Library: cfl. 10 Corbis: Juan Echeverria crb. 11 DK Images: Colin Keates/Natural History Museum, London br; Harry Taylor/Hunterian Museum, University of Glasgow car. 11 Museum National d'Histoire Naturelle: Paleontologie (Paris), D. Serrette bl. 14 Corbis: Roger Garwood & Trish Ainslie clb. 14 DK Images: Colin Keates cr. 15 J & B Sibbick: cr. 16 Corbis: Bettmann tr. 16 DK Images: Christopher and Sally Gable cb; Rob Reichenfeld br. 17 DK Images: Dave King cra, cbl; Harry Taylor/Hunterian Museum University of Glasgow cfl. 21 American Museum Of Natural History: C. Chesek clb. 21 DK Images: Bedrock Studios cla, cfl; Colin Keates crb, bl, br; Colin Keates/Natural History Museum, London clb; Jon Hughes cl; M.McGregor cla; Malcolm McGregor cra. 22 DK Images: Colin Keates clb. 22-23 Corbis: Roger Ressmeyer. 23 DK Images: Colin Keates cra, br. 24 S.Conway Morris: bl. 24 DK Images: Colin Keates cl. 24-25 S.Conway Morris. 25 S.Conway Morris: tc, cra. 26 DK Images: Colin Keates cfr; Colin Keates/Natural History Museum, London tc, bc; 26-27 DK Images: Colin Keates/Natural History Museum. 27 Hunterian Museum: Dr Neil D.L.Clark tl. 28 DK Images: Natural History Museum tc, cb, cbr. 28-29 DK Images: Colin Keates; Colin Keates/Natural History Museum, London. 29 DK Images: Colin Keates tr; Natural History Museum c. 30 DK Images: Harry Taylor/Royal Museum of Scotland, Edinburgh c; Harry Taylor/University Museum of Zoology, Cambridge tr; Natural History Museum bc. 30-31 American Museum Of Natural History: C.Chesek. 31 DK Images: Colin Keates cra; Harry Taylor/University Museum of Zoology, Cambridge, on loan from the Geological Museum, University of Copenhagen, Denmark tcl. 32 American Museum Of Natural History: D.Finnin c. 32 DK Images: Harry Taylor/Royal Museum of Scotland, Edinburgh tr; Natural History Museum br. 33 DK Images: Colin Keates cfr; Natural History Museum bc. 34 DK Images: Colin Keates c; Colin Keates/Natural History Museum, London tl, tcl; Natural History Museum bcr. 35 DK Images: Natural History Museum cr; Natural History Museum bl. 36-37 Exhibit Museum of Natural History, University of Michigan. 38 DK Images: Colin Keates/Natural History Museum, London br; Natural History Museum c. 38-39 DK Images: Colin Keates/Natural History Museum, London. 39 DK Images: Harry Taylor/Natural History Museum, London tr; Natural History Museum cl, cb. 40 DK Images: Colin Keates/Natural History Museum, London bc; Gary Ombler tc; Natural History Museum cr. 40-41 DK Images: Natural History Museum. 41 DK Images: Colin Keates/Natural History Museum, London tcr; Natural History Museum cr, bl. 42 DK Images: Natural History Museum cra, bc. 42-43 DK Images: Lynton Gardiner. 43 DK Images: Natural History Museum c, cr, bl. 44-45 N.H.P.A.: Daniel Heuclin. 46 DK Images: Hunterian Museum ca; Natural History Museum bcr. 46-47 DK Images: Natural History Museum. 47 DK Images: Natural History Museum bcl. 48 DK Images: Harry Taylor/Natural History Museum, London tcr; Natural History Museum c, br. 48-49 DK Images: Colin Keates/Natural History Museum, London. 49 DK Images: American Museum Of Natural History tr; Natural History Museum cr, bl. 50 DK Images: Natural History Museum tc, cfr. 51 DK Images: Colin Keates/Natural History Museum, London bl, tcl; Natural History Museum cr. 52 DK Images: Eric Robson cr; Natural History Museum tc; Peter Chadwick br. 52-53 DK Images: Colin Keates/Natural History Museum, London. 53 DK Images: Peter Visscher cfr. 54 DK Images: Dave King c; Neil Fletcher and Matthew Ward cbr. 55 DK Images: Andrew McRobb bl; Cyril Laubscher cfr; Dave King tl. 55 Topfoto.co.uk: Press Association tcr. 58 DK Images: Colin Keates bl; 58-59 DK Images: Harry Taylor/Royal Museum of Scotland, Edinburgh. 59 DK Images: Peter Bull tr, cra. 60-61 DK Images: Bedrock Studios. 62 DK Images: Peter Bull bl. 62-63 DK Images: Colin Keates. 63 DK Images: Colin Keates b; Colin Keates/Natural History Museum, London tr; Natural History Museum tr. 64 American Museum Of Natural History: cr; Jim Coxe cr. 64-65 DK Images: Bedrock Studios. 66 DK Images: Bedrock Studios ca; Harry Taylor/Hunterian Museum, University of Glasgow car; Harry Taylor/Royal Museum of Scotland, Edinburgh cra; Peter Bull cb, crb, bc, bcr. 67 DK Images: American Museum of Natural History tl; Geoff Dann/Barleylands Farm Museum and Animal Centre, Billericay tr; Peter Bull c, car, cfl; Peter Visscher tc. 68 DK Images: Natural History Museum bl. 68-69 DK Images: Harry Taylor/Natural History Museum, London. 69 DK Images: Peter Bull ca. 69 Oxford Scientific Films: Norbert Wu tr. 70 American Museum of Natural History: D. Finnin br. 71 DK Images: Harry Taylor/Royal Museum of Scotland, Edinburgh bc. 72 American Museum Of Natural History: cl; D.Finnin br. 73 DK Images: Bedrock Studios t. 74 DK Images: Colin Keates/Natural History Museum, London cb. 74-75 DK Images: Harry Taylor/Natural History Museum, London. 75 American Museum Of Natural History: tr. 75 DK Images: Natural History Museum cr, cfr. 75 Hunterian Museum: br. 76 DK Images: American Museum Of Natural History bl. 77 DK Images: Colin Keates/Natural History Museum, London tr. 78 American Museum of Natural History: C. Chesek bl. 78 Oxford Scientific Films: Max Gibbs tr. 78-79 DK Images: Bedrock Studios. 79 American Museum Of Natural History: D.Finnin tr. 79 Bruce Coleman Ltd: Hans Reinhard br. 80 American Museum Of Natural History: C. Chesek clb. 80-81 DK Images: Harry Taylor/Hunterian Museum, University of Glasgow. 81 American Museum Of Natural History: Denis Finnin b. 81 DK Images: Natural History Museum tr. 82-83 DK Images: Luis Rey. 83 American Museum Of Natural History: crb. 83 DK Images: American Museum of Natural History tr. 86 DK Images: Peter Bull crb, bc, br, cbl; Peter Visscher cra, cfr. 87 DK Images: American Museum of Natural History cla; Jerry Young/Zoo Museum tcl; Peter Bull cra, cl, c, cfl; Peter Visscher tc. 88 DK Images: M.McGregor/University Museum Oxford cb; 88-89 DK Images: University Museum, Oxford. 89 DK Images: Harry Taylor/University Museum of Zoology, Cambridge,on loan from the Geological Museum, University of Copenhagen, Denmark br; Zoo Museum tcl. 90 American Museum Of